Unbroken

Bible

*The Incredible
History, Accuracy & Legacy
of the King James Bible*

Dr. Phil Stringer

Dr. Phil Stringer
Copyright © 2018
The Bible Nation Society
All rights reserved.

The Bible Nation Society
2680 E. M-21
Corunna, MI 48817
989-720-2267
biblenation.org

All Scripture Quotations are taken
from the King James Version
unless otherwise noted.

ISBN-13: 978-0-9984804-7-3
ISBN-10: 0-9984804-7-9

Layout and Cover Design by Josh Levesque.

Typesetting by Amber Spooner,
Maria Russell, and Morgan Levesque.

"...The Scripture Cannot Be Broken"
John 10:35

For feelings come and feelings go,
And feelings are deceiving.
My warrant is the Word of God
Naught else is worth believing.

Though all my heart should feel condemned,
For want of some sweet token,
There is One greater than my heart
Whose Word cannot be broken.

I'll trust in God's unchanging Word,
Till soul and body sever.
For though all things shall pass away,
His Word shall stand forever.

Anonymous

The Unbroken Bible

From the Publisher

"The Scriptures cannot be broken." In all of history one Bible translation best fits this description given to the true Words of God by Jesus in John 10:35. The King James Bible and its textual base are just that - Unbroken. They have stood the test of time and illustrated the power and durability of God's Words. Those who advocate for other modern, Critical text versions must cede that their Bible was at some point broken or lost, and in need of recovery or reconstruction. The King James Bible stands unique in its incredible history of transmission, accuracy of translation and legacy of unmatched cultural, linguistic, and spiritual influence on the English speaking world and beyond.

This volume is the result of the compilation of the writings of Dr. Phil Stringer on the issues related to the text of Scripture and the King James Bible. These writings represent decades of faithful scholarship and dedicated defense of the King James. May this publication be a lasting legacy to the contributions of Dr. Stringer and a help to future scholars and defenders of the Unbroken Bible.

Table of Contents

INTRODUCTION

The "King James Only" Civil War Over Inspiration 9

THE UNBROKEN BIBLE

1. The Verbal Preservation of Scripture 25
2. The Verbal Inspiration of Scripture. 55
3. The "Westcott & Hort Only" Controversy 87

THE UNBROKEN HISTORY

4. The History of the English Bible 111
5. The Real Story of King James 133

THE UNBROKEN ACCURACY

6. The Accuracy of Biblical English 161
7. In Defense of 1 John 5:7 187
8. In Defense of Mark 16:9-20 209
9. In Defense of Acts 12:4 227

THE UNBROKEN LEGACY

10. The Cultural Legacy of the King James Bible 239
11. The Linguistic Legacy of the King James Bible 255
12. The Spiritual Legacy of the King James Bible 267

APPENDICES

A. Do We Have a 1611 King James Bible Today? 283
B. The Received Text For the Whole World 293

The Unbroken Bible

Introduction

The "King James Only" Civil War Over Inspiration

Actually, I don't like the term "King James Only." It is a name given to us by our critics. I want everyone, in every language, to have the pure Word of God in their own tongue. But in this case, I use the term so that it is clear who I am talking about.

A civil war rages among independent Baptists about the "inspiration" of translations. I am not talking about the debate over which text of Scripture to use. Prominent preachers who preach the King James Bible and who defend it against its critics, are vigorously debating one another over the use of the term "inspiration" in describing the King James Bible. Sometimes the conflict is much hotter than a "vigorous debate." Good men, with deep loyalties to the King James Bible, are at odds with one another. Key terms are defined many different ways, motives are called into question and the doctrinal soundness of men is questioned.

The Unbroken Bible

I have been in many verbal conversations and email discussions over this issue. I have been asked how these discussions are going. I have answered that I feel like a man trying to stand on an ice flow, in an ocean full of sharks while juggling baby elephants. A debate over the nature of the Bible generates deep emotions.

Good men are trying to defend the King James Bible the best way that they know how. They are tired of the evangelical and fundamentalist critics of the King James Bible. They are tired of self-absorbed, pseudo-scholars. They are tired of people with slander language skills mocking the scholars who were used of God to translate the King James Bible. I completely agree!

Let me be crystal clear! I believe that the King James Bible is God's Word kept intact in English. There is not one word in the King James Bible that I would change. I would not change an italicized word.

I believe that the American republic was created by the influence of the King James Bible. I believe that the modern missions movement was created by the preaching of the King James Bible. I believe that both the fundamentalist movement and the independent Baptist movement were the product of the King James Bible.

I am not one of those preachers who believes that it is Christian liberty to attack the King James Bible but divisive to answer those attacks.

I believe that the evangelical and fundamentalist critics of the King James Bible should be answered. When I heard Elmer Fernandez say that the translators of the King James Bible were evil and wicked men, I knew that he had to be opposed. When I read Calvin George's desperate attempts to belittle the King James Bible (in order to defend the Critical Text readings of the Reina Valera 1960), I understand that he has to be answered.

The "King James Only" Civil War Over Inspiration

When I realize that the method of Bible teaching practiced by the professors of Bob Jones University and Detroit Baptist Theological Seminary is to go verse by verse and say "a better translation would be. . . ," I understand that they are pseudo-scholars. The least of the Kings James translators was a greater scholar than any of them.

When I read that the translations sponsored by Charles Keen won't be King James equivalent (his term), I understand what he is up to and that he must be answered by those loyal to the Received Text.

When I see the long-ago disproven criticisms of the King James Bible on the various Trinitarian Bible Society websites—I realize that those loyal to the King James Bible must answer the Trinitarian Bible Society's foolish attacks on the King James Bible.

I believe that the King James Bible is pure, perfect and inerrant!

However, I do not believe that the King James Bible is "inspired". That is not because I believe that there is any weakness or any inferiority in the King James Bible. There is nothing about the King James Bible that needs to be corrected or improved.

The Bible tells us what "inspiration" is! It defines itself. Many of my brethren use the term "inspiration" as a synonym for inerrant. But it means much more than that! Many of my brethren use the secular definition of the term "inspiration"—"to motivate or cause by supernatural influence" (Webster's Illustrated Contemporary Dictionary). But this definition falls far short of what the Bible says about its own "inspiration".

Many of our most famous doctrinal books offer a weak

definition of "inspiration."

One prominent advocate of the King James Bible defines "inspiration" this way. "By inspiration we mean the supernatural control by God over the production of the Old Testament and New Testaments." Another King James advocate defines "inspiration" as "divine influence." These men would consider themselves as great advocates of the King James Bible and would describe most other teachers as weak or modernist.

Yet their doctrine of "inspiration" is very weak. It was invented by modernists and spread by neo-evangelicals. Inspiration is much more than what they say it is.

If "inspiration" is really "divine influence" then many sermons, songs and books are "inspired." However, "Biblical inspiration" is much more than that.

"Inspiration" took place when God took control of a person and spoke His words through them or caused them to write down His words. "Inspiration" took place when God dictated His words to a person or even through an animal (Balaam's donkey).

You can't defend the King James Bible by weakening the doctrine of "inspiration." In their zeal to advance the King James Bible, some men have adopted a liberal position about "inspiration."

Many of the brethren are quick to quote II Timothy 3:16—"All Scripture is given by "inspiration" of God." This is, of course, true. God gave His words to men through the Greek, Aramaic and Hebrew languages. This verse means exactly what it says—and nothing more.

However, the verse does not say that the words that God gave are preserved, transmitted or translated by "inspiration".

The "King James Only" Civil War Over Inspiration

The verse means everything that it says but we have no right to add anything to it.

No matter how pure and proper our motives are—we do not help the cause of the King James Bible by defining incorrectly a Biblical term or by inventing a new Biblical doctrine. Actually we help the critics of that King James Bible by using an argument that they can easily refute.

Virtually everyone in our movement, including me, has used the term "inspiration" carelessly at one time or another. It is time to start being careful.

Recently, I was communicating by email with the head of a translation project in a foreign country. He assured me that his translation was "inspired". I told him that I didn't think so.

He was just finishing ten years of his translation effort. Men who were "moved by the Holy Spirit" (II Peter 1:21) of God wrote down the Words as God gave them. They didn't need ten years. Can you imagine John spending ten years figuring out what to write down in the book of Revelation?

The translator had a team of sixteen national helpers—men who are "inspired" don't need a "team" of helpers. Can you imagine a team of sixteen helpers helping King Saul figure out what to say when the Holy Spirit took him over?

This gentleman is getting ready to release his second edition. Men who are "inspired" of God don't need a second edition. Can you imagine Balaam's donkey issuing a second edition of his words to Balaam. The response of this translator was to call me a modernist!

The Words of God have been settled forever in heaven. God gave some of them to Moses to record on earth. He gave some to

Jeremiah, some to Paul, some to Peter and so on. They recorded the exact words that God gave them. God finished delivering His words to men as John finished the Book of Revelation. That is how "inspiration" works!

The translators of the King James Bible did not need to be "inspired". They already had God's "inspired" Words in front of them. They simply needed to faithfully and accurately translate the Words that had already been given by "inspiration". Translators today do not need to be "inspired." They already have God's "inspired" words available. They simply need to translate them correctly.

John Selden described the method of the King James translators. "The translation in King James time took an excellent way. That part of the Bible was given to him who was most excellent in such a tongue (as the Apocrypha to Andrew Downes) and then they met together and one read that translation the rest holding in their hands some Bible either of the learned tongues or French, Italian, Spanish, etc. If they found any fault they spoke, if not, they read on."

This was not the method of King Saul, Malachi, Isaiah, Matthew or Balaam's donkey when they were being "inspired" of the Lord. It is an example of men being used of God to preserve and transmit His Word.

I know that many men use the word "inspired" to describe the King James Bible because they want to defend it against its many attackers. But the King James Bible doesn't need that kind of help from us. It stands up to its attackers just fine. They always fade away and the King James Bible goes on. It doesn't need us to invent a new definition of "inspiration" or to weaken the doctrine of divine "inspiration" the way that the secular writers do.

There seem to be three prominent positions among those

The "King James Only" Civil War Over Inspiration

who use the term "inspired" to describe the King James Bible.

Some teach that God repeated the miracle of "inspiration" in 1611. They believe that the English language is the only language that currently has an "inspired Bible." Their concept of missions is to preach and teach from the English Bible to the whole world. This destroys most mission works.

This is an easy doctrine to maintain, if you are only concerned for white, Anglo-Saxon people. Of course, there is not the slightest hint of any such doctrine anywhere in the King James Bible.

The second group teaches the miracle of "inspiration" took place in 1611 in English and continues to take place in other languages today. They teach that you can recognize an "inspired" Bible if it is used by large "soul-winning" churches.

For those brethren, soul-winning is not based upon doctrine, doctrine is based upon soul winning. Since most of the Bibles in use around the world are Critical Text Versions and contradict the King James Bible, they assume that God gave one set of words in English and differing words in other languages. Their doctrine of "inspiration" justifies liberal translations.

They usually teach that only a Bible produced by a modern miracle of "inspiration" can be used to lead someone to Christ. Consequently, they would put their stamp of approval on hundreds of modernist translations.

But you can't protect the King James Bible by undermining the basis for Scriptural revelation.

Interestingly enough, both groups spend a lot of time attacking fundamental Baptists who explain "inspiration" in any way different than themselves. But you can't imagine them refuting modernists or liberal Bible societies. Their venom is reserved for the English speaking brethren who use the same Bible that they do.

There is a third group that teaches what they call "derivative inspiration." They are often very good brethren, devoted to the Bible. They understand that the miracle of "inspiration" only took place with the original earthly Scriptural penmen.

They teach that the Bible today has all the authority, influence, Holy Spirit power and purity of the original "inspired" Words of God. That is exactly what the Bible teaches about itself.

Faithful copies of the Words given by "inspiration" have all the authority and Holy Spirit power of the originals. Faithful copies of Scripture are Scripture.

Faithful translations of the Words given by "inspiration" have all the authority and Holy Spirit power of the originals. Faithful translations of Scripture are Scripture. However, the Bible calls this preservation not "derivative inspiration" (try finding that term in the King James Bible).

At least the teachers of "derivative inspiration" describe the original act of inspiration correctly, they describe the current state of the Bible correctly and it is possible for them to translate the Bible into other languages correctly. They are good brethren and I do not want to be separated from them.

However, their terminology is not Scriptural. Their teaching is easily confused with the other more dangerous teachings about "inspiration."

You do not defend the Kings James Bible by weakening the Bible's teaching about preservation. One Bible teacher called preserved words "cold, dead museum words." What an insult to a sovereign God!

Nothing could be a stronger statement about words than to say these words are "God's preserved words." God's preservation maintains all the authority and Holy Spirit power that God originally placed on and in His words.

The doctrine of preservation is not a weak doctrine. It is a doctrine filled with Holy Spirit power. It does not need to be upgraded, improved or strengthened. It is the power of God in practice.

I am for everyone that preaches, practices and defends the words of the King James Bible. If my brethren do not use the exact terminology that I think reflects the teaching of Scripture, I will be a little disappointed in them, but I will not reject them. I do not expect perfection from men. I wish to be the friend of all those that honor the words of the King James Bible.

However, I do believe that this discussion has important consequences.

Using a Biblical term in a non-Biblical way opens a new avenue of attack for the enemies of the King James Bible. There is no reason to make it easier for them to make their unholy attacks.

Secondly, this debate is creating unfortunate confusion about the matter of Bible translations. Around the world dozens of projects are taking place. Believers are concerned about getting a faithful translation of the Bible in their national language. There is a revival of understanding the issue of the Received Text.

However, too many men are producing a first edition of a translation, calling it "inspired" and stopping right there. A proper translation requires a rigorous purification process (such as the one that took place with the King James Bible). A weak or secular definition of "inspiration" is hindering the most important work of Bible translation.

Thirdly, this debate causes people to miss the genuinely important debate going on about Scripture today. Some men who are loud advocates of the "inspiration" of the King James Bible are also strong proponents of a Critical Text Bible for the Spanish people and for other language groups.

It may be expedient politics to advocate a Received Text Bible for the English speaking world and a Critical Text Bible for the Spanish speaking world, but it is horrible doctrine. Why would a "King James man" want the Hispanic world to use a Bible that conflicts with the King James Bible in hundreds of places and thousands of words?

This is hypocritical and it has a great price attached to it. If you promote the Critical Text in any language you can no longer consistently oppose Critical Text Bibles in English. Sooner or later your hypocrisy will catch up to you. There is simply no doctrinal or textual foundation to prevent such a change. No matter how loudly a man or a ministry proclaims their loyalty to the King James Bible today, if they advocate the Critical Text in other languages they will probably be using a Critical Text Bible in English in a few years.

No one can consistently claim to be a "King James preacher" and support the Reina Valera 1960 or the TBS Spanish Bible. No one can consistently claim to be a "King James preacher" and support the French Louis Segond Version (either the Bible Society version or the TBS version). The same is true for the Chinese Common Union Version (CUV) and a host of other foreign translations.

Some of the people influenced by Dr. Ruckman have called

me a modernist and a Bible corrector (even though they can't identify one word of the King James Bible that I would change). Most recently, some have called me "a King James Bible hater." Other men influenced by Dr. Ruckman have been much kinder to me.

I have been called a Ruckmanite by advocates of the Critical Text. However I have never been influenced by the writings or teachings of Dr. Ruckman (in the interest of full disclosure I met him once when I was fifteen).

Some Hispanic preachers refer to me by their pet nickname, "The Antichrist." I am sure that they mean that in Christian love. However I am grateful to have many Hispanic preacher friends who love me in spite of my faults and limitations.

I am used to being called names. Somehow, I doubt that this article will end that experience. If you preach, practice and defend the words of the King James Bible, I am for you!

I hope that we will all preach, practice and defend those blessed words wisely.

One missionary wrote, "As I understand the Scriptures, 'inspiration' is the process by which God directed and controlled the recording of His exact words for mankind. But after those words were recorded, God ceased to "inspire'. The process was completed and the message was recorded. God, from that point on, perfectly preserved exactly what He gave so that we would have every word exactly as He gave it. This is called preservation. So if you were to ask me if I believed the Bible is inspired, I would answer by saying, 'Yes, however, to be more theologically accurate, it was inspired and is now preserved.'" Amen and Amen!

Actually, it seems that much of the "civil war" today is not really about doctrine at all. It seems to be about who is going to "speak for fundamental Baptists." Again, let me be crystal clear. I am an independent Baptist. I do not recognize a pope, bishop, church councils or a Baptist Sanhedrin. I don't believe in model churches or that anyone pastors to pastors. I have no headquarters! I have a Bible and that is my sole authority.

Finally, let me appeal for grace for and from all of us. The founders of fundamentalism, for all their wonderful accomplishments, were not clear or consistent on their definition of "inspiration" or their identification of the Biblical text. We are paying for that confusion now!

Most of the leaders of the independent Baptist movement can be quoted several different ways on both the definition of "inspiration" and on textual issues.

Vigorous debate is appropriate and even beneficial. A "civil war" is not. Let us all find some grace in our hearts for those who love the Bible and strive to reach the souls of men!

Verbal, plenary inspiration, verbal, plenary preservation, verbal, plenary translation: any other doctrine of Scripture is just not enough.

The "King James Only" Civil War Over Inspiration

The Unbroken Bible

PART ONE

The Unbroken BIBLE

The Verbal Preservation of Scripture
The Verbal Inspiration of Scripture
The "Westcott & Hort Only" Theory

The Unbroken Bible

I

The Verbal Preservation of Scripture

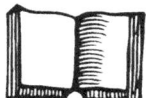

The debate about the King James Bible is essentially a debate about the verbal preservation of Scripture. This is well illustrated in the book *One Bible Only*, published in 2001 by Kregel Publications. All seven authors are or were affiliated with Central Baptist Seminary of Plymouth, Minnesota.

Central Baptist Seminary is an independent Baptist seminary. It has been considered a leading school in Baptist fundamentalism. The stated purpose of the book is to refute the "King James only movement."

The authors accurately understand that the modern debate is in reality a debate about the doctrine of verbal preservation. General Editor Kevin T. Bauder writes:

> Can a person consistently believe in the preservation of God's Word without believing in the preservation of every word of the original documents of Scripture? The

The Unbroken Bible

King James-Only advocates usually answer the question with an emphatic negative. If we do not have all of God's actual words, they insist that we do not have God's Word. We do not know what God said unless we know the exact words in which He said it. This belief commits the King James-Only people to a particular theory of preservation: the theory that all of the words, and only the words, of the original documents must be preserved somewhere. Most of these people also add two corollaries. First the words must be preserved in one place (one manuscript, edited text, family of texts or translation) rather than in the plurality of all manuscripts, texts and translations. Second, the words must be preserved in a publicly accessible fashion; the preserved words must be those that the believing community has actually used throughout the history of the people of God. The King James-Only theory of preservation, then, is a theory of verbal preservation.[1]

The authors of *One Bible Only* leave no question about their position.

> This book will dispute the King James-Only teaching by insisting that we can know what God said, even if we do not have every single word with which He said it. The authors of this book will address the very heart of the controversy.[2]

> In the following pages, we will assert that the critical Greek texts or the New American Standard Bible, for

---

[1] Roy E. Beacham and Kevin T. Bauder, One Bible Only?: Examining Exclusive Claims for the King James Bible (Grand Rapids, MI: Kregel Publications, 2001), 20.

[2] Ibid., 21.

example, are in fact the Word of God.[3]

> It is one thing to believe that God could providentially or supernaturally propagate His Word; it is another thing to believe that God did providentially or supernaturally preserve His Word in a particular edition or translation.[4]

> A proper understanding of the doctrine of preservation is a belief that God has providentially preserved His Word in and through all of the extant manuscripts, versions, and other copies of Scripture. This conviction is based upon the evidence of history. Obviously, God has preserved His Word, through His people. Has God perfectly preserved His Word so that no words have been lost? The evidence from the Old Testament text suggests that such is not the case. We might have lost a few words through negligence, but the amount that has been lost is so minimal that it has no effect on overall doctrine and little, if any, on historical or other details.[5]

> The core issue in the King James-Only controversy is whether one must have the very words of God (all of the words and only the words of the authgrapha) to have the Word of God.[6]

The authors of *One Bible Only* are to be commended for their honesty and candor. In a day when many Bible colleges try to "have it both ways" they are clear about their belief. They are also to be commended about getting to the "heart of the matter." This debate really is a debate about verbal preservation.

---

[3] Ibid, 19.

[4] Ibid., 69.

[5] Ibid., 121.

[6] Ibid., 164.

But is their doctrine of preservation the doctrine taught in the Scripture? What would a simple reading of the Scripture lead you to believe? Without "scholars" to tell you that the Scripture doesn't really teach verbal preservation, what would you believe if you just simply read the Scriptures for yourself?

THE BIBLE DOCTRINE OF THE PRESERVATION OF THE SCRIPTURES

Psalm 12:6-7, "The words of the LORD are pure words: as silver tried in a furnace of earth, purified seven times. Thou shalt keep them, O LORD, thou shalt preserve them from this generation for ever."

It is clear that this promise from God refers to the preservation of the very words of Scripture, not just doctrines, thoughts or concepts.

Psalm 119:89, 152, 160, "For ever, O LORD, thy word is settled in heaven." "Concerning thy testimonies, I have known of old that thou hast founded them for ever." "Thy word is true from the beginning: and every one of thy righteous judgments endureth for ever."

These passages make it clear that the very words of Scripture were settled in heaven before God inspired those words to be written by human authors.

Isaiah 40:8, "The grass withereth, the flower fadeth: but the word of our God shall stand for ever."

The meaning of forever is clear to anyone who doesn't have a bias against the doctrine of preservation.

Matthew 5:17-18, "Think not that I am come to destroy the law, or the prophets: I am not come to destroy, but to

The Verbal Preservation of Scripture

fulfill. For verily I say unto you, Till heaven and earth pass, one jot or one tittle shall in no wise pass from the law, till all be fulfilled."

This passage extends the doctrine of verbal preservation to the smallest details of Scripture.

Matthew 24:35, "Heaven and earth shall pass away, but my words shall not pass away."

Again, the promise of verbal preservation is made crystal clear.

John 10:35, "If he called them gods, unto whom the word of God came, and the scripture cannot be broken;"

The promise of preservation here is clearly extended to the words of Scripture.

Isaiah 59:21, "As for me, this is my covenant with them, saith the LORD; My spirit that is upon thee, and my words which I have put in thy mouth, shall not depart out of thy mouth, nor out of the mouth of thy seed, nor out of the mouth of thy seed's seed, saith the LORD, from henceforth and for ever."

Again, the promise is given that the words of God will be available forever.

Psalm 105:8, "He hath remembered his covenant for ever, the word which he commanded to a thousand generations."

If God's word was lost even for a generation, then this Scripture would be meaningless.

Psalm 111:7-8, "The works of his hands are verity and

judgment; all his commandments are sure. They stand fast for ever and ever, and are done in truth and uprightness."

God's commandments stand fast forever and ever.

The Scripture repeatedly promises that God's words, His commandments will be kept forever and ever. Where does the Scripture ever suggest that preservation is limited to the thoughts, doctrines or concepts?

> *I Peter 1:23-25, "Being born again, not of corruptible seed, but of incorruptible, by the word of God, which liveth and abideth for ever. For all flesh is as grass, and all the glory of man as the flower of grass. The grass withereth, and the flower thereof falleth away: But the word of the Lord endureth for ever. And this is the word which by the gospel is preached unto you."*

The word forever is clear!

Dr. Thomas M. Strouse comments on those evangelical teachers who try to explain away these passages:

> Some fundamentalists are following an extra-biblical authority to dictate a definition of preservation contrary to the Bible's own self-attestation to it's preservation. Fundamental Baptist scholars in Bible colleges and the seminaries are not acceptable authorities for the doctrine Biblical preservation. The Bible is its own authority and it has spoken![7]

Those who try to revamp the doctrine of preservation, to lessen it, to water it down must spend all their time quoting scholars - they have no Scriptures to quote support their doctrine.

---

[7] Strouse, Thomas M. Emmanuel Baptist Newsletter, January/February 2001. p. 7.

The Verbal Preservation of Scripture

Where is there any verse which can even faintly be said to teach concept or thought preservation? Without self-proclaimed "scholars," we could never come up with any such doctrine. It is not even vaguely suggested anywhere in the Scriptures.

Other relevant Scriptures include:

> *Proverbs 30:5-6, "Every word of God is pure: he is a shield unto them that put their trust in him. Add thou not unto his words, lest he reprove thee, and thou be found a liar."*

> *Deuteronomy 4:2, "Ye shall not add unto the word which I command you, neither shall ye diminish ought from it, that ye may keep the commandments of the LORD your God which I command you."*

David Norris writes:

> When we know what the Bible says about its own preservation, then and only then, ought we to set about looking into the history of the various manuscripts and translations. Our task will then be somewhat different to that of others; we shall be looking to see how God has preserved His Word rather than if. Then we shall be able to establish which manuscripts are genuine and which are spurious on the basis of Scripture and not from the pseudo-science of critics. Certainly those tainted with false teaching should be returned to the waste-bins. The cavalier work of men such as Westcott and Hort can then be discounted, for whatever their knowledge of the biblical languages, their unregenerate hearts and flagrant opposition to the gospel rule out their work as being of any real value. Giving such people the task of working on the sacred text is like leaving thieves in charge of your

valuables, don't expect much to be left on your return.[8]

THE DOCTRINE OF PRESERVATION PROPERLY STATED

A debate over the proper doctrine of the preservation of the Scripture rages among traditional Protestants, evangelicals and even among independent Baptists. Because of this, those who believe in the doctrine of verbal preservation of the Scriptures have been careful to clearly define their position.

Dr. Paul Fedena writes:

> By the preservation of the Scriptures is meant that God providentially protected His revelation, the entirety of God's Word, from being lost, destroyed or altered. He has seen that every age has had and will have a copy of His entire Word in the form in which they should have it, without provable error.[9]

The Institute for Biblical Textual Studies (associated with the work of David Otis Fuller) has produced this statement about verbal preservation:

- The institute for Biblical Textual Studies is committed to the immediate, verbal, plenary inspiration of the original writings of the Scripture and that they are therefore inerrant and infallible. This inspiration is unique, applicable both to the process of giving the original writings and the writings themselves which are that product;

- The verbal preservation of the Greek Received Text as published by the Trinitarian Bible Society

---

8 Norris, David. Dayspring, Autumn 1999, p. 38

9 Fedena, Paul C. We Have It In Writing, p. A.

- The verbal preservation of the Traditional Masoretic Hebrew Text of Daniel Bomberg, as edited by Jacob ben Chayim;

- The position that translation is not an inherent boundary to verbal preservation. The breath of God, product, not process, conveyed by translation from the immediately inspired language copies of the Scripture into any providentially prepared receptor language will impart to that translation infallible authority and doctrinal inerrancy inherent in the original language copies. Such a translation by the internal witness of the Holy Spirit, both with and through that translation, will evidence to the believer its own self attestation and self-authentication whereby God asserts himself as the supreme Authority to that culture. For the English speaking world this revelation of God's authority is preserved in the Authorized Version

Bible and textual scholar Edward Hills has written:

> If the doctrine of the Divine inspiration of the Old and New Testament scriptures is a true doctrine, the doctrine of the providential preservation of the scriptures must also be a true doctrine. It must be that down through the centuries God has exercised a special providential control over the copying of the scriptures and the preservation and use of the copies, so that trustworthy representatives of the original text have been available to the God's people in every age.[10]

Bruce Metzger describing Dean John Burgon wrote:

> As an ardent high-churchman he could not imagine that, if the words of the Scripture had been dictated by

---
10 KJV Defended, p. 2

the inspiration of the Holy Spirit, God would not have providentially prevented them from being seriously corrupted during the course of their transmission. Consequently it was inconceivable to Burgon that the Textus Receptus, which had been used by the church for centuries, could be in need of the drastic revision which Westcott and Hort had administered to it.[11]

INADEQUATE VIEWS OF PRESERVATION

Many evangelicals challenge the idea that God has promised to perfectly preserve His word.

Douglas Kutilek writes, "That there is no Biblical promise of perfect preservation in the process of copying."[12]

The Detroit Baptist Theological Seminary declares, "The biblical and historic fundamentalist view on the inspiration of the Scripture is that only the original manuscripts are God-breathed and therefore inerrant."

John Warwick Montgomery writes:

> Unless, therefore one wishes to maintain that a given stream of transmission or translation was kept inviolable by God (and scripture itself gives no ground for such affirmation) inerrancy must said to reside in the original manuscripts written by the biblical authors, ie., in the autographs of the Scripture.[13]

---

11 Metzger, The Text of the New Testament, pp. 135-136

12 The Preservation of the Scripture, an internet article by Doug Kutilek

13 from the book, God's Inerrant Word

The Verbal Preservation of Scripture

Dr. Steward Custer (Bob Jones University) writes:

"God's preservation is not a continuing inspiration, but a preservation so that no teaching of the Bible would be lost. Every doctrine in the originals can be found in the King James Bible..."[14]

Larry Oates (Maranatha Baptist Bible College) said, "God could have preserved His word, but history proves He did not,"[15]

W. Edward Glenny, (Central Baptist Seminary), wrote:

The doctrine of the preservation of Scripture was first included in a church creed in 1647. As we have argued above, it is not a doctrine that is explicitly taught in Scriptures, nor is it the belief that God has perfectly and miraculously preserved every word of the original autographs in one manuscript or text-type. It is a belief that God has providentially preserved His word in and through all the extant manuscripts, versions and other copies of the Scriptures...not only does no verse in Scripture explain how God will preserve His word, but there is not a statement in Scripture from which one can establish the doctrine of the preservation of the text of the Scripture...It is also obvious from the evidence of history that God has not miraculously preserve His word in any one manuscript or group of manuscripts, or in all the manuscripts.

Randolph Shaylor writes:

---

14 The Truth About the King James Controversy, p. 13

15 As quoted by Dr. Clinton Branine, Heritage Baptist University syllabus on Inspiration. This statement was made in the National Leadership Conference, Lansdale, P.A, February 1996.

The Unbroken Bible

Any claim that particular copies of these autographs are inspired in the same sense as the originals goes beyond what the Scriptures claim about themselves. That kind of transmission of inspiration would require the superintendence of the Holy Spirit over certain or all copyists. Nowhere does the Bible state or even imply this.[16]

With views about preservation like these in mind, Evangelist Don Jasmin reproduces this religious parody:

"Somewhere Out There"
A religious parody sung to the tune of "An American Tale"

Somewhere out there, the Word of God exists;
Somewhere in those manuscripts all the words consist;
Somewhere out there in parchments worn and rare,
Like a text that could be the next,
That would prove beyond compare.

Somewhere out there, the Word of God is sure;
Somewhere in those pyramids it waits for me and you.
Somewhere out there beneath the sands of time,
There's a scroll that could yet unroll
And reveal God's Word sublime!

Somewhere out there, the Word of God is sure;
Somewhere in old languages it rests so very pure.
Somewhere out there in variants so vast,
There's a reading that we're still a needing,
So we have God's Word at last!

Refrain:
Oh just imagine what a wonder it would surely be
If we could have the Word of God completely error free!

---
16 From the Mind of God to the Hand of Man, p. 22

The Verbal Preservation of Scripture

If we believe our dreams can really come right shining through
Then we shall ever have our wish - the Word of God come true!

Somewhere out there the Word of God is found;
Somewhere in those autographs all the words are sound.
Somewhere out there if only where we knew,
We could cope with a ray of light
Out there - where dreams come true![17]

These views of the preservation of the Scriptures are not based upon any Biblical statement or passage. None at all. No one could develop these positions from Biblical statements at all. Without the authority of the "scholars" no one could ever teach such a view. This raises an interesting question. Who decides who the "Scholars" are and how did they get to be the final authority. Scholar is not a title that should be given to you by yourself or your closest friends.

WISE STATEMENTS ABOUT THE PRESERVATION OF SCRIPTURES

Dr. Bruce Lackey:

The Textus Receptus, from which the King James Version was translated, is God's preserved word, because of the promises in Psalm 12:6-7, 100:5 and I Peter 1:23-25. If the Vaticanus, Sinaiticus, P. 46, P. 66, P. 75, etc., are the uncorrupted scriptures, people did not have God's pure Word for the many centuries when they were lost.

Dr. Edward Hills

But even apart from this, the hypothesis that Westcott

---
[17] Copied: The Angelus, Oct.-Dec. 1999, p. 6

and Hort and other modern critics are providentially guided is absurd and contrary to everything that the Bible teaches or implies concerning God's providential care. For why would God hide the true New Testament text for 1,500 years and allow the text used by His church to grow worse and worse and then finally, in the middle of the 19th century, guide Tischendorf and Westcott and Hort providentially to discover the true New Testament text again in a waste paper basket on Mount Sinai and in the library of the pope?[18]

As Bible-believing Christians, therefore, we take our stand upon the promise of Christ always to preserve in His church the true New Testament text. Heaven and earth shall pass away, but my words shall not pass away (Matthew 24:35; Mark 13:31; Luke 21:33). We believe that by the especial providence of God through the church, the universal priesthood of believers, this promise of Christ has been fulfilled in the traditional text found in the vast majority of the Greek New Testament manuscripts, in the Textus Receptus, and in the King James Version and other translations of the Textus Receptus. Are we unscholarly when we adopt this believing position? Certainly not. On the contrary, it is only this believing view the deals fairly with the more than 5,000 Greek New Testament manuscripts which of been discovered since the days of Erasmus and the Protestant Reformers, for approximately 90% of these manuscripts are of the Traditional or Textus Receptus type. Let us therefore proceed to enumerate the New Testament documents and then see how they appear from the believing standpoint.[19]

---

18 Believing Bible Study, p. 38

19 Believing Bible Study, p. 39

The Verbal Preservation of Scripture
John Owen

But yet we affirm, that the whole word of God in every letter and tittle as given from Him by inspiration, is preserved without corruption.[20]

Dean John Burgon
(Nineteenth Century English Theologian)

If you and I believe that the original writings of the Scriptures were verbally inspired by God then of the necessity they must have been providentially preserved through the ages.

The provision, then, which the divine author of the Scriptures is found to have made for the preservation, in its integrity, of His writing word, is of a peculiarly varied and highly complex description first- by causing that a vast multiplication of copies should be required all down the ages, -beginning at the earliest period and continuing in an ever increasing ratio until the actual invention of printing- He provided the most effectual security imaginable against fraud.[21]

Dr. Louis Gaussen
(Nineteenth Century French Theologian)

Of what use, one might have said, is the assurance that the original text was dictated by God eighteen hundred years ago, if I have no longer the certainty that the manuscript of our libraries still present it to me in its purity, and if it be true (as we are assured) that the various readings of these rolls are at least thirty thousand

---

20 Owen-Works 16-388

21 The Revision Revised, p. 8

in number?

Such is the old objection: it was specious; but nowadays it is known, by all who have studied it, to be a mere illusion. The Rationalists themselves have admitted that it can no longer be made, and must be given up.

The Lord has watched miraculously over his Word. This the facts of the case have demonstrated. [22]

The inspired word leaves us not; we need not to go in search of it to the third heaven; it is still upon the earth, just as God Himself first dictated it to us.[23]

God's phraseology is still before us, with which to confront our modern versions, as dictated by God Himself, in Hebrew or in Greek, or the day of its being revealed; and, with our dictionaries in your hand, you may, age after age, return to the examination of the infallible expression which it has been his good pleasure to give to the divine thought.[24]

Francis Turretin
(Seventeenth Century Swiss Theologian):

Although we give the Scriptures absolute integrity, we do not therefore think that the copyists and printers were inspired (Theopneustous), but only that the providence of God watched over the copying of the sacred books, so that although many errors might have crept in, it has not so happened (or they have not so crept into the manuscripts) but that they can be easily

---

[22] Theopneustia, p. 169

[23] Theopneustia, p. 160

[24] Theopneustia, p. 160-161

corrected by a collation of others (or with the Scriptures themselves). Therefore the foundation of the purity and integrity of the sources is not to be placed in the freedom from fault (anamartesia) of men, but in the providence of God which (however men employed in transcribing the sacred books might possibly mingle various errors) always diligently took care to correct them, or that they might be corrected easily either from a comparison with Scripture itself or from more approved manuscripts. It was not necessary therefore to render all the scribes infallible, but only so to direct them that the true reading may always be found out.[25]

Grant Jeffreys

I cannot imagine a God who desires to convey His instruction for life, salvation, and eternity to a lost humanity would be unwilling or unable to preserve His written revelation so that each generation would receive the genuine Word of God.[26]

Wilbur N. Pickering:

I believe that God has providentially preserved the original wording of the text down to our day ... my beliefs become presuppositions which I bring to my study of the evidence - any thoughtful person will realize that it is impossible to work without presuppositions...[27]

Jacob van Bruggen:

We can only conclude with the absolute certainty,

---

[25] Institute of Elenctic Theology, pp. 72-73

[26] The Handwriting of God, p. 19

[27] The Identity of the New Testament Text, p. 143

that the ancient text of God's inspired word both now and in the future will remain an object of God's special care. This certainty creates for us the obligation to treat the text that has been handed down to us with great care. This obligation lies in the confession of the Reformation (Westminster Confession, chapters 1, 8).[28]

David Norris

We cannot remove what the Bible teaches about preservation without immediately effecting its teaching on inspiration or revelation. There seems little point in God inspiring original autographs, in making them infallible and inerrant, if they are no longer available to us today. Of what use to us is a Bible of which we can never be sure it is in every detail the word of God? In the end the whole doctrine of Scripture will be undermined. By insisting that God preserves His words, we are saying something about the kind of God in whom we believe. We believe in an almighty God to whom the transmission of the inspired text, the translation into any language on earth, all of which He created and comprehends more fully than any native speaker, is but a small thing to accomplish. What kind of a god do they worship who scrapple about among manuscripts thinking to do the work of God among themselves, relying on finite human reason.[29]

Jerry Manley

If God could not or chose not to preserve His words, then it matters not whether the prophets received or recorded the very words of God; if the words are lost,

---

28 The Ancient Text of the New Testament, p. 40

29 Dayspring Autumn 1999, pp. 1-2

then whatever the prophets wrote "for us," never made it to us. Whether sequestered in a monastery or buried beneath middle eastern sands, the words failed to reach the destination God intended and the purpose of the eternal, omniscient, omnipotent, omnipresent God was thwarted. Inspiration without preservation is nullification.[30]

Jack Hyles

No! My Bible does not say that God has preserved the thoughts for us. My Bible does not say that God has preserved the doctrine for us. My Bible does not say that God has preserved certain truths for us. My Bible says that the words of God are perfectly pure and will be preserved forever! Since today is a part of forever, that means somewhere in this world there must be the very words of God.[31]

A NEW IDEA?

Critics of the King James position often assert that the doctrine of verbal preservation is a new idea invented by the modern King James Only crowds.

There are numerous statements about the doctrine of verbal preservation before the twentieth century.

In 1647 A.D., the Westminster Confession of Faith confidently declares about the Scripture, "being immediately inspired by God and by His singular care and providence kept pure in all ages."

---

30 Global Baptist Times, January 2004

31 The Need For An Everyword Bible, p. 13

The Unbroken Bible

In 1675 A.D., the Helveticus Consensus (Reformation Protestants) declared, "God, the Supreme Judge, not only took care to have his word, which is the power of God unto salvation to everyone that believeth, committed to writing by Moses, the prophets and the apostles, but has also watched and cherished it with paternal care ever since it was written up to the present time, so that it could not be corrupted by craft of Satan or fraud of man."

In 1742, the Baptists produced their most influential Confession of Faith ever, the Philadelphia Confession. On the subject of preservation it declares: "The Old Testament in Hebrew and the New Testament in Greek, being 'immediately' inspired by God and by his singular care an providence kept pure in all ages, are therefore authentical."

Another important Baptist Confession of Faith, the New Hampshire Confession (1833) states, "We believe that the Holy Bible was written by men divinely inspired and is a perfect treasure of heavenly instruction, that has God for its author, salvation for its end and truth, without any mixture of error, for its matter... and therefore is, and shall remain to the end of the world, the truth centre of Christian union, an the supreme standard by which all human conduct, creeds, and opinions should be tried."

THE BIBLICAL DOCTRINE OF PRESERVATION IN ACTION

God gave scripture to Jeremiah - Jeremiah 36:4, "Then Jeremiah called Baruch the son of Neriah: and Baruch wrote from the mouth of Jeremiah all the words of the LORD, which he had spoken unto him, upon a roll of book."

- The Scripture was already settled in Heaven

The Verbal Preservation of Scripture

- It was given by God to Jeremiah.
- Jeremiah had Baruch write down the first earthly copy.
- The earthly copy was taken to the scribes and princes.

Jeremiah 36:11-16, "When Michaiah the son of Gemariah, the son of Shaphan, had heard out of the book all the words of the LORD, Then he went down into the king's house, into the scribe's chamber: and, lo, all the princes sat there, even Elishama the scribe, and Delaiah the son of Shemaiach, and Elnathan the son of Achbor, and Gemariah the son of Shaphan, and Zedekiah the son of Hananiah, and all the princes. Then Michaiah declared unto them all the words that he had heard, when Baruch read the book in the ears of the people. Therefore all the princes sent Jehudi the son of Nethaniah, the son of Shelemiah, the son of Cushi, unto Baruch, saying, Take in thine hand the roll wherein thou hast read in the ears of the people, and come. So Baruch the son of Neriah took the roll in his hand, and came unto them. And they said unto him, Sit down now, and read it in our ears. So Baruch read it in their ears. Now it came to pass, when they had heard all the words, they were afraid both one and other, and said unto Baruch, We will surely tell the king of all these words."

- The Scripture is taken to the king.

Jeremiah 36:21-23, "So the king sent Jehudi to fetch the roll: and he took it out of Elishama the scribe's chamber. And Jehudi read it in the ears of the king, and in the ears of all the princes which stood beside the king. Now the king sat in the winterhouse in the ninth month: and there was a fire on the hearth burning before him. And it came to pass, that when Jehudi had read three or four leaves, he cut it with the penknife, and cast it into the fire that was on the hearth, until all the roll was consumed in the fire that was on the hearth."

- The king destroyed the original, earthly, written copy of Scriptures.

- God gave a second earthly copy. The Scripture was preserved

Jeremiah 36:27-32, "Then the word of the LORD came to Jeremiah, after that the king had burned the roll, and the words which Baruch wrote at the mouth of Jeremiah, saying, Take thee again another roll, and write in it all the former words that were in the first roll, which Jehoiakim the king of Judah hath burned. And thou shalt say to Jehoiakim king of Judah, Thus saith the LORD; Thou hast burned this roll, saying, Why hast thou written therein, saying, The king of Babylon shall certainly come and destroy this land, and shall cause to cease from thence man and beast? Therefore thus saith the LORD of Jehoiakim king of Judah; He shall have none to sit upon the throne of David: and his dead body shall be cast out in the day to the heat, and in the night to the frost. And I will punish him and his seed and his servants for their iniquity; and I will bring upon them, and upon the inhabitants of Jerusalem, and upon the men of Judah, all the evil that I have pronounced against them; but they hearkened not. Then took Jeremiah another roll, and gave it to Baruch the scribe, the son of Neriah; who wrote therein from the mouth of Jeremiah all the words of the book which Jehoiakim king Judah had burned in the fire: and they were added besides unto them many like words."

As Dr. Kulus writes:

"God gave His word, and it could not ultimately perish at the hands of a wicked king. God insures that His inspired Words continue. Inspiration demands preservation. A similar example of God insuring that His inspired Words are preserved occurs, when Moses breaks

The Verbal Preservation of Scripture

the tables of the ten commandments, and God says to him, "Hew thee two tables of stone like unto the first: and I will write upon these tables the words that were in the first tables, which thou brakest" (Exodus 34:1). The inspired Words of God cannot be permanently destroyed. God guarantees that His inspired Words are preserved.[32]

GOD PRESERVED THE OLD TESTAMENT TEXT THOUGH THE AARONIC PRIESTHOOD AND THE HEBREW SCRIBES

- The scribes had very strict rules for copying the Scripture.
- Parchments must be made from the skin of the animals only.
- Parchments must be prepared by Jews only.
- Parchments must be bound together by strings taken from clean animals only.
- Each column of writing must have between 48-and 60 lines only.
- Rolls must have the same number of columns consistently throughout, and each column was to be exactly 30 letters wide.
- Each column must be lined first, and if 3 words were written down without a line, the whole copy is made worthless and destroyed.
- The fifth Book of Moses, must terminate exactly with a line.
- Ink must be black only, and made to a recipe.
- Scribes must be clothed in full scribal dress.
- No word or letter can be written from memory. The scribe must have an authentic copy before him, and must read and pronounce each word out loud before writing it.
- Pens must be wiped reverently each time the word "God" is written.

---
[32] Those So-Called Errors, pp. 148-149

- The scribe must wash his whole body before writing the Name of God (Jehovah).
- Strict rules apply dealing with the use of the pen, shapes of the letters, and spaces between letters, words, and sections.
- Rolls must be checked and revised within 30 days, or the whole roll becomes worthless.
- One mistake condemns the sheet.
- Three mistakes on any page condemns the entire manuscript.
- Every word and letter must be counted. If one letter is missing, is added, or touches another - the whole manuscript must be destroyed.
- Between each consonant, a hair's breadth; between each section, the breadth of nine consonants; between each book, three lines.

NEW TESTAMENT PRESERVATION!

The Holy Spirit, through superintendence, used the New Testament priesthood (believers in general) and local churches to preserve His word.

- Jesus promised His word would be preserved, Matthew 24:35; Mark 13:31; Luke 21:33.
- Heretics and false teachers tried to corrupt copies of the Scriptures, II Corinthians 2:17.
- Faithful and trustworthy copies of the Scriptures were read and recopies throughout the centuries.
- Untrustworthy copies were generally rejected and as a result they were in the minority.

AUTOGRAPHA AND APOGRAPHA

When theologians before the 19th Century referred to the inspiration of the original they meant the apographa (faithful copies in the original languages) not the autographa (the first

The Verbal Preservation of Scripture

earthly copies).

> By the original texts, we do not mean the autographs written by the hand of Moses, of Moses, of the prophets and the apostles, which certainly do not now exist. We mean their apographs which are so called because they set forth to us the word of God in the very words of those who wrote under the immediate inspiration of the Holy Spirit.[33]

> By 'original' and 'authentic' text, the Protestant orthodox do not man the autographa which no one can possess but the apographa in the original tongue which are the source of all versions. The Jews throughout history and the church in the time of Christ regarded the Hebrew of the Old Testament as authentic and for nearly Six Centuries after Christ, the Greek of the New Testament was viewed as authentic without dispute. It is important to note that the reformed orthodox insistence on the identification of the Hebrew and Greek alone as authentic does not demand direct reference to autographa in those languages: the "original and authentic text" of Scriptures means, beyond the autograph copies, the legitimate tradition of Hebrew and Greek apographa. The case for Scriptures as an infallible rule of faith and practice and the separate arguments for a received text free from major (non-scribal) error rest on an examination of the apographa an does not seek the infinite regress of the lost autographa as a prop for textual infallibility."

A FAITH POSITION

Ultimately, even with all the available evidence, it is faith which leads one to trust in the verbal preservation of the Word of God. However, it is also faith which leads one to trust in the

---

[33] Francis Turretin, Calvinist Theologian

Westcott and Hort Theory or in the pronouncements of the modern critics of the King James Only position. The question is "Who do you trust?" Does God's breath evaporate with the originals?

THE ANVIL - GOD'S WORD

Last eve I passed beside a blacksmith's door,
And heard the anvil ring the vesper chime;
Then looking in, I saw upon the floor
Old hammers, worn with beating years of time.

How many anvils have you had," said I,
"To wear and batter all these hammer so?"
"Just one," said he, and then, with twinkling eye,
"The anvil wears the hammers out, you know."

And so, thought I, the anvil of God's Word,
for ages skeptic blows have beat upon;
Yet, though the noise of falling blows was heard,
The anvil is unharmed - the hammers gone.
~ ~ Author Unknown ~ ~

CONCLUSION

I am utterly disinclined to believe - so grossly improbably does it seem - that at the end of 1800 years 995 copies out of every thousand, suppose will prove untrustworthy; and that the one, two, three, four or five which remain, whose contents were till yesterday as good as unknown, will be found to have retained the secret of what the Holy Spirit originally inspired. I am utterly unable to believe, in short, that God's promise has so entirely failed, that at the end of 1800 years much of the text of the Gospel has in point of fact to be picked by a German critic out of a waste paper basket in the convent of St. Catherine; and that the entire text had to be remodeled after the pattern set by a couple of copies which had remained in neglect during Fifteen Centuries, and had probably owed their survival to that neglect; whilst hundreds of others had been thumbed to pieces, and had bequeathed their witness to copies made from them.[34]

"The question is not as to the particular corruption of some manuscripts or as to the errors which have crept into the books of particular editions through the negligence of copyist or printer. All acknowledge existence of many such small corruptions. The question is whether there are universal corruptions and errors so diffused through all the copies (both collation of various copies, or of the Scriptures itself and of parallel passages. Are there real true, and not merely apparent, contradictions? We deny the former.

The reasons are:

1). The Scriptures are inspired of God (Theopneustos, II Tim. 3:16). The word of God cannot lie (Ps. 19:8-9; Heb. 6:18); cannot pass away and be destroyed (Mt. 5:18); shall endure forever (I Pet. 1:25; and is trust itself (Jn. 17:17). For how could such things be predicated of it, if it contained dangerous contradiction, and if God suffered either the sacred writers to err and to slip in memory, or incurable blemished to creep into it?

2). Unless unimpaired integrity characterize the Scriptures, they could not be regarded as the sole rule of faith and practice, and the door would be thrown wide open to atheists, libertines, enthusiasts and other profane persons like them for destroying its authenticity

---
[34] John Burgon, The Traditional Text, pp. 11-12

(authentia) and overflowing the foundation of salvation. For since nothing false can be an object of faith, how could the Scriptures be held as authentic and reckoned divine if liable to contradictions are only in smaller things which do not affect the foundation of faith. For if once the authenticity (authentia) of the Scriptures is taken away (which would result even from the incurable corruption of one passage), And if corruption is admitted in those lesser importance, why not in others of greater? who could assure me that no error or blemish had crept into fundamental passages? Or what reply could be given to a subtle atheist or heretic who should pertinaciously assert that this or that passage less in his favor had been corrupted? It will not do to say that divine providence wished to keep it free from serious corruptions, but not from minor. For besides the fact that this is gratuitous, it cannot be held without injury, as if lacking in the necessary things which are required for the full credibility (autopistian) of Scriptures itself. Nor can we readily believe that God, Who dictated and inspired each and every words to these inspired (theoneustois) men, would not take care of their entire preservation. If men use the utmost care diligently to preserve their words (especially if they are of any importance, as for example a testament a contract) in order that it may not be corrupted, how much more must we suppose, would God take care of his word which he intended as a testament and a seal of his covenant with us, so that it might not be corrupted; especially when he could easily foresee prevent such corruptions in order to establish the faith of his church?"[35]

---

35 Francis Turretin, Institute of Elenctic Theology, p. 71

The Verbal Preservation of Scripture

The Unbroken Bible

2

The Verbal Inspiration of Scripture

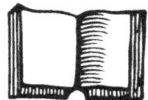

THE METHOD OF INSPIRATION

It would be irrational for us to cease to believe in the Spirit of God, who moved the mouths of the prophets like musical instruments.[1] - Athenagoras

The inspired word leaves us not; we need not go in search of it to the third heaven; it is still upon the earth, just as God himself, first dictated it to us. ...God's phraseology is still before us with which to confront our modern versions, as dictated by God himself, in Hebrew or in Greek.[2] - Dr. L. Gaussen

---

[1] Athenagoras, 177 A.D. A Place for the Christians to Emperor Marcus Aurelius

[2] Dr. L. Gaussen, Theopneusta: The Plenary Inspiration of the Holy Scriptures

"The whole scripture is dictated by God's spirit."
- King James I

One should trust God, being most properly assured that the Scriptures are indeed perfect, since they were spoken by the Word of God and His Spirit[3] - Iraneus

IS SAUL ALSO AMONG THE PROPHETS?

I Samuel 10: 9-11 - And it was so, that when he had turned his back to go from Samuel, God gave him another heart: and all those signs came to pass that day. And when they came thither to the hill, behold a company of prophets met him; and the Spirit of God came upon him, and he prophesied among them. And it came to pass, when all that knew him beforetime saw that, behold, he prophesied among the prophets, then the people said one to another, What is this that is come unto the son of Kish? Is Saul also among the prophets?

Before this incident, no one even knew that Saul was a prophet! The phrase "Is Saul also among the prophets?", became an expression of astonishment in Israel. I don't believe that even Saul knew that he was a prophet. He came to this situation and the Holy Spirit took control of him. The Holy Spirit began to speak through him and he began to prophesy.

I Samuel 19:23-24 - And he went thither to Naioth in Ramah: and the Spirit of God was upon him also, and he went on, and prophesied, until he came to Naioth in Ramah. And he stripped off his clothes also, and prophesied before Samuel in like manner, and lay down naked all that day and all that night. Wherefore they say, Is Saul also among the prophets?

---

3 Irenaeus (around 200 A.D. *Against Heresies*)

The Verbal Inspiration of Scripture

This incident took place much later in Saul's life. Saul was as backslidden and out of fellowship with God as a man can get. He is jealous of David and seeking to kill him. He has turned his back on God's instructions and gotten himself in deep trouble with God. He has run as far away from God as a man can get, and yet at this moment the Holy Spirit came over him and he began to prophesy. He was overwhelmed, he fell down and he prophesied all day long. He did not prophesy because he was a godly man but because the Holy Spirit took him over. He did not prophesy because he had planned or prepared to, but because the Holy Spirit took control of him. Earlier, the same thing had happened to three teams of his soldiers. I believe that if you understand what happened to Saul, some important things about the doctrine of the inspiration of Scripture can become clear.

In our day and age, the great battle among Christians is about the doctrine of the inspiration and preservation of Scripture. It is sad to note, but the great debate about Scripture takes place even among our independent Baptist preachers and churches. It is a dividing point among our independent Baptist colleges. There are many aspects and issues involved in this debate. I want to suggest that if we understand God's method of inspiration, some parts of this debate will just fall into place. I want to suggest that if we understand that God gave the Scriptures by mechanical dictation or verbatim reporting, many of the issues involved in the doctrine of inspiration will become clear to us.

I realize that this position is a minority position even among our fundamentalist, King James only Baptists. I don't have any fuss with anyone who has an inspired, inerrant, infallible Bible at the end of the day, even if they disagree with me about how we got such a Bible.

It is commonly taught that God inspired the Scriptures by

working in the hearts of men so that their thoughts and words came out perfect. This teaching says that God worked through men's experiences so that when they wrote, they wrote perfectly. This doctrine asserts that God superintended over the writers of Scripture so that their thoughts and their words came out perfect. An example of this approach is Dr. Edward Young: "According to the Bible, inspiration is a superintendence of God the Holy Spirit over the writers of the Scriptures, as a result of which these Scriptures possess Divine authority and trustworthiness and, possessing such Divine authority and trustworthiness, are free from error."

I want to suggest to you that there is more to the doctrine of inspiration than this. I believe that God gave the prophets and the apostles the very words that they spoke and wrote. They were not just words guaranteed by God but they were the words of God. Even when God used the personal experiences, of the Scripture writers, He dictated through them exactly His words in describing these experiences.

Many Christian teachers feel that such a doctrine is unscholarly or uneducated. They feel that the world will laugh at us when we take such a position. I hope you can get used to being laughed at by the world. In fact, I hope you can get used to being laughed at by the brethren who are so impressed with their own scholarship. Our standard cannot be the approval of the world or the current opinions of Christian "scholarship." It must be the Word of God.

Dr. Stewart Custer has said about the teaching of mechanical dictation "again and again conservatives repudiate the theory of mechanical dictation." Griffith Thomas wrote, "Verbal inspiration does not mean mechanical dictation or verbatim reporting. Dictation is not inspiration."

A.A. Hodge is just as emphatic:

The church has never held what has been stigmatized as the mechanical theory of inspiration. The sacred writers were not machines. Their .self-consciousness was not suspended nor were their intellectual powers superseded. Holy men spoke as they were moved by the Holy Ghost. It was men, not machines, not unconscious instruments; but living, thinking, willing minds whom the Spirit used as His organs. Moreover, as inspiration did not involve the suspension or the suppression of the human faculties, neither did it interfere with the free exercise of the distinctive mental characteristics of individuals.

I would like to suggest to you that the Scripture teaches just the opposite of the definitions of inspiration used by these learned, scholarly men. Inspiration is dictation. The intellectual powers of the authors of Scripture were superceded. It didn't matter whether or not their minds were willing (ask King Saul about this). Inspiration did suspend self-consciousness, suppress human faculties and interfere with the free exercise of the distinctive mental characteristics of individuals.

I believe that the Scripture teaches that the men that God used to write Scripture were not active but that they were passive. I believe that they were not just superintended, they were overwhelmed. I believe that their intellect was superceded and suppressed and that the Holy Spirit just spoke through them

THE PEN AND THE PENMAN

A. H. Strong teaches against the theory of mechanical dictation when he writes: "This theory holds that inspiration consisted in such a possession of the mind and bodies, of the Scripture writers by the Holy Spirit, that they become passive instruments or amanuenses - the pens, not the penman of God." The Scripture uses the same image that Dr. Strong does, the pen and the penman, but in quite a different way.

> *Psalm 45:1 - My heart is inditing a good matter: I speak of the things which I have made touching the king: my tongue is the pen of a ready writer.*

David is describing the process by which God is working out the Scriptures through him. He did not think of himself as the penman of God but as the pen. When someone writes with the pen is the pen active or passive? Does it make any difference what experience the pen has already had? Does it make any difference what subjects the pen has already written on? Does it make any difference whether or not the pen is willing to be used? Saul's state of mind made no difference at all in inspiration and neither did David's. The pen is just the pen. The only thing that counts is the author.

German Reformer Johannes Cocceius (1603-1669) wrote: "The men of God called prophets in general parlance, were God's assistants and amanuenses, who wrote exactly as they spoke, not by their own will but driven by the Holy Spirit."

INSPIRATION

> *II Timothy 3:16-17 - All scripture is given by inspiration of God, and is profitable for doctrine, for reproof, for correction, for instruction in righteousness: That the man of God may be perfect, throughly furnished unto all good works.*

It is important to focus on that phrase "by inspiration of God." The word inspiration did not exist before God invented it for the New Testament. God took two different Greek words, one describing God and one describing the process of breathing, and He put the two words together. Later Greek writers took this word and gave it all different kinds of meanings. Some of these definitions were deeply heretical, but when God wanted to describe the means of inspiration He chose to call it "God-breathed." When men wrote Scripture, God literally took them over and overwhelmed them. He began to control them so that it was no longer their natural breathing that was taking place. The Holy Spirit of God was literally breathing through them. Saul was not trying to prophesy. God simply took him over and for a while, the Holy Spirit simply breathed Sauls' breath for him. Human speech is formed by the interaction between man's breath, his lips, tongue, teeth, and vocal cords. Sauls' words, when he was prophesying, were not formed by his breath but by the breath of the Holy Spirit.

As Gaussen writes about II Timothy 3:16 in his classic book Theopneustia: The Plenary Inspiration of the Holy Scriptures:

> This statement admits of no exception and of no restriction . . . All Scripture is in such wise a work of God, that it is represented to us as uttered by the divine breathing, just as human speech is uttered by the breathing of a man's mouth. The prophet is the mouth of the Lord.

Over 2,200 times, (according to J. Vernon McGee) the Scripture refers to the "word of the Lord" coming to the human writers of Scripture. I would challenge anyone to find a single Scripture referring to "God's superintending of the thoughts of men."

> *I Peter:20-21 Knowing this first, that no prophecy of the scripture is of any private interpretation. For the prophecy came not in old time by the will of man: but holy men of God spake as they were moved by the Holy Ghost.*

Do you remember the definition of inspiration by Dr. Hodge? He said that it was important that men be willing instruments. But II Peter 1:20-21 says that inspiration did not come by the will of man. No one prayed and said, " Lord I'm ready! Let me prophesy today." Nobody said, "Lord I've done my preparation and my homework. I've done my research and my study. I'm ready to write scripture today." No one was qualified by their experience to write Scripture. It didn't happen that way. It didn't come by the will of man. "But holy men of God spoke as they were moved by the Holy Ghost." The Holy Spirit took over and they became simply the passive organs and instruments that the Holy Spirit used to give Scripture.

Inspiration cannot exist apart from possession.

> *Acts 1:16 Men and brethren, this scripture must needs have been fulfilled, which the Holy Ghost by the mouth of David spake before concerning Judas, which was guide to them that took Jesus.*

This passage makes reference back to Psalm 69 and Psalm 109. It is clear that the words involved came from the mouth of David. But it was the Holy words through David's mouth. The words were God-breathed. Even though David's mouth was being used these weren't David's words.

> *II Samuel 23:2 - The Spirit of the Lord spake by me, and his word was in my tongue.*

> *Mark 12:36 - For David himself said by the Holy Ghost, The Lord said to my Lord, sit thou on my right hand, till I make thine enemies thy footstool.*

This was true of all the prophets.

> *Luke 1:70 - As he spake by the mouth of his holy prophets, which have been since the world began:*

> *Acts 4:25 - Who by the mouth of thy servant David hast*

said, why did the heathen rage, and the people imagine vain things?

Acts 28:25 "And when they agreed not among themselves, they departed, after that Paul had spoken one word, Well spake the Holy Ghost by Esaias the prophet unto our fathers,"

THE STORY OF BALAAM

I think the whole process of inspiration becomes clear when you look at the story of Balaam. Balaam was a prophet. Some people have called him a false prophet, but I don't think so. The Holy Spirit of God comes over him. He wasn't a false prophet, but he was a backslidden prophet! He was out of the will of God. He wasn't putting what God wanted first.

The children of Israel began to travel through Moab. The king of Moab wanted to rally his people against the children of Israel. He summoned Balaam, a prophet of the Creator God because he wanted Balaam to curse the children of Israel. This would create the image that the Creator God was against the children of Israel. The king of Moab thought this would be good politics. He would get the message across that God was opposed to these people.

Numbers 22:18 And Balaam answered and said unto the servants of Balak, If Balak would give me his house full of silver and gold, I cannot go beyond the word of the Lord my God, to do less or more.

Balaam answered the king of Moab that he could not control what he prophesied. It wasn't that Balaam was concerned about doing right. Later he helped the king of Moab to corrupt the children of Israel, (Jude 11). Balaam was as backslidden as you can get, but he knew something about inspiration. He knew he couldn't control his words when the Lord came over him. They were not his words. They were God's.

The King of Moab put Balaam on a mountain so that he could curse Israel. The Holy Spirit of God came upon him. He opened his mouth, and out of his mouth came a prophecy of blessing. This was exactly the opposite of what Balak, the King of Moab, and Balaam wanted. They were God's words and not Balaam's. Balak was frustrated. He moved Balaam to another mountain as if that would make the difference.

Balaam really wanted to earn the gold and silver that Balak had promised. But when the Holy Ghost came over him, he was not in control of what he said. He was passive. God was not just superintending him, He was controlling him. God began to breathe through him. The Holy Spirit began to work his lungs, to breathe through his throat and nose, to position his tongue, and to make words with his breath. Again he blessed Israel. The words weren't his, they were God's. The Moabites moved him to another mountain and decided to try again. Again the Holy Spirit came over him, breathed through his lungs, and formed his words. For a third time there comes out a blessing on the children of Israel.

When God gave Scripture to Balaam, Balaam was passive. I think it would be really hard to dispute that. However, in the course of this story, one event makes the truth of mechanical dictation even clearer. At one point God takes over Balaam's donkey and begins to speak through him. Let me ask you, was the donkey active or passive? Was God using the experiences, education, training, and willing heart of the donkey? No! God just took over the donkey, breathed through his lungs, held his tongue in just the right position, and spoke His words through that donkey's lips. God could speak through that animal just as easily as He could through a human being. The issue never was the human mind. The issue was and is God. The issue was not the mind of the donkey. The issue was the mind of God.

Have you ever wondered why all the words of the prophets and apostles weren't written down as Scripture? It is simply because God was not always breathing through them. When the Holy Spirit took control of them they could tell it and so could those around them. The crowd could tell that Saul was taken over by the Holy Spirit, and they cried out, "Is Saul also among the prophets?"

Just as Balaam and Saul prophesied without wanting to, Caiaphas prophesied without even knowing it. *"And this spake he not of himself: but being high priest that year, he prophesied that Jesus should die for that nation;"* John 11:51 This will of man was simply not the issue - the will of God was.

MOSES THE MEEK

God used the man Moses to write the book of Numbers. I want you to look at what He had Moses write in Numbers 12:3.

(Now the man Moses was very meek, above all the men which were upon the face of the earth.)

Now think about that for a minute. Who, humanly speaking, is writing that. Moses is! If I wrote you a letter and said, "By the way, I am the most humble preacher on the face of the earth. I want you to know I've studied the issue and that is my opinion of myself." Tell me, would you be impressed with my humility? It reminds me of the old joke we used to tell about the famous preacher who was going to write two books, Humility and How I Obtained It, and God's Ten Most Humble Servants and How I Trained the Other Nine. You wouldn't pay any attention to someone who said things like that, but God used Moses to write about his own humility.

God wasn't using Moses' willing heart - God was controlling

him. I believe that Moses' face turned red when he wrote that. I think he was embarrassed at these words. It is the last thing he would have said if he had any choice. The Holy Spirit took over and began to move his hand and write out those words. The Holy Spirit chose to tell the people of the world that Moses was the meekest man on the face of the earth, and as embarrassed as Moses would have been, there was nothing Moses could do about it.

A lot of fundamentalists seem embarrassed about giving God recognition for exercising the kind of power involved in mechanical dictation, but it is clear that Satan and his demons exercise that kind of power. Satan spoke through a serpent. Many false religions and cults are based on materials produced by spirit writing. According, to Mohammed, the Koran was dictated to him by "angels." According to Richard Bach, the book Jonathan Livingston Seagull was dictated to him by spirits.

I once had a debate with a man who was teaching what he called the new Bible, a book called Oahsbe. Oahsbe is a strange book of several thousand pages. According to the human writer of Oahsbe, dictated to him by spirits. According to John Newborough, he set down at his typewriter and the spirits used his fingers to type the words. No doubt, someone will soon come up with a book that they claim was dictated to them by spirits through their computer. In the occult world, it is commonly believed that spirits dictate messages through human beings.

Back when I was a youth pastor, I visited a home from which two teenagers were visiting our church. One of the men of the church was with me, and we visited with the mother of the teenagers. She claimed that a spirit, which she called Felicia, lived in the home with the three of them. The teenagers confirmed that this was true. The mother claimed that the spirit would take her over and write out messages through her. She let me read some of them. They were full of blasphemy, obscenities, and attacks on the Lord Jesus. My visitation partner and I both became convinced that a spirit was really writing through her.

My point is simple, Satan and demon spirits have the power to dictate their messages. The Lord has more power than they do.

THE PROPHETS DIDN'T ALWAYS UNDERSTAND

I Corinthians 2:9-13 - But as it is written, Eye hath not seen, nor ear heard, neither have entered into the heart of man, the things which God hath prepared for them that love Him. But God hath revealed them unto us by his Spirit: for the Spirit searcheth all things, yea, the deep things of God. For what man knoweth the things of a man, save the spirit of man which is in him? even so, the things of God knoweth no man, but the Spirit of God. Now we have received, not the spirit of the world, but the spirit which is of God: that we might know the things that are freely given to us of God. Which things also we speak, not in the.e words which man's wisdom teacheth, but which the Holy Ghost teacheth: comparing spiritual things with spiritual.

This passage is very clear. The words of Scripture were not produced by man's wisdom. The words of Scripture are the very words of the Holy Ghost.

I Peter 1:10-12 - Of which salvation the prophets have enquired and searched diligently, who prophesied of the grace that should come unto you: Searching what, or what manner of time the Spirit of Christ which was in them did signify, when it testified beforehand the sufferings of Christ and the glory that should follow. Unto whom it was revealed, that not unto themselves, but unto us, they did minister the things, which are now reported unto you by them that have preached the gospel unto you with the Holy Ghost sent down from heaven: which things the angels desire to look into.

Have you ever read the Old Testament and had trouble figuring out how to put all the pieces together. Go through the books of Isaiah, Jeremiah, and Ezekiel and see how often the subject changes. Read the minor prophets and see how many different things are discussed.

When I pastored, I taught through all 66 chapters of the book of Isaiah. It took about a year and a half. Teaching Isaiah was quite an experience. It jumps from passages about the coming of the Messiah, to passages about the death of Christ, to passages about the Second Coming, to passages about the Millennium. Yet many passages are about the events of Isaiah's own time. It wasn't always easy to understand which passages were about which subjects. That is the challenge of rightly dividing the Word of Truth.

It bothered me for a while that it was so easy for me to get confused. Then I realized that even the prophets got confused about their message. The message wasn't revealed unto them. It was the message of the Spirit of Christ. The message wasn't the words of the prophets - it was the words of the Holy Spirit.

Daniel was concerned that he could not understand what the Lord was writing through him. Daniel 12:8-9 "And I heard, but I understood not: then said I,0 my Lord, what shall be the end of these things? And he said, Go thy way, Daniel: for the words are closed up and sealed till the time of the end."

God told Daniel not to be concerned that he couldn't understand. After all, Daniel was just the pen.

THE ETERNAL WORD OF GOD

There are great promises in the Scripture concerning the

eternal nature of the Word of God. Psalm 119:52 *"I remembered thy judgments of old, O Lord; and have comforted myself."* Psalm 119:89 *"For ever, O Lord, thy word is settled in heaven."*

In David's time, the word of God was already settled forever in Heaven. But all the Scriptures hadn't been given to man yet. John and Daniel and Jeremiah and Ezekiel and Matthew hadn't been born yet. But the Scripture was settled already.

Long before God ever gave man the instructions for a tabernacle on Earth there was a tabernacle in Heaven. The earthly objects were simply a copy of that which existed already in Heaven.

I want to suggest to you that before John was ever born, the book of John was written in Heaven. Before David was ever born, the Psalms were written in Heaven. When Jeremiah and Paul and Matthew were born, God brought certain experiences into their life so that God could use them to reveal His Word to us. The issue was never those men, their intelligence, their willing heart or their understanding. The wording of the Scripture was simply settled in Heaven.

God used Solomon in the book of Proverbs to write warnings about wicked women. yet, in his own personal life, Solomon collected wicked women in his harem. His personal example was not the issue in the book of Proverbs. The words of Proverbs are simply the words that the Holy Ghost wrote through Solomon.

IS THE DOCTRINE OF MECHANICAL DICTATION SCHOLARLY?

Evangelical opponents of the doctrine of inspiration by dictation are often quick to label those who teach the doctrine of inspiration by dictation as unscholarly!

As you read their writings you would think that no one has ever held the position of inspiration by dictation before this century. They are quick to assert that only a handful of half-baked radicals from the twentieth century have ever held such a view. However, their own scholarship is shallow.

Throughout history, there have been prominent teachers who taught the doctrine of inspiration by dictation. Many famous and influential figures have been very comfortable with this doctrine and with using the term dictation to apply to the Scriptures.

PROMINENT JEWISH TEACHERS

It is clear that a strong doctrine of mechanical dictation was taught among the Jews concerning the Old Testament Scriptures. Famous Jewish teacher Philo, First Century A.D., wrote, "The mind is evicted at the arrival of the divine spirit . . . the prophet, even when he seems to be speaking holds his peace, and his organs of speech, mouth, and tongue are wholly in the employ of another, to show forth what He wills.'" Philo also refers to the Old Testament Scriptures as ' 'oracles given under the agency and dictation of God."

Josephus, First Century A.D., demonstrates that he understands the dictation nature of inspiration when he comments on Balaam, "Thus did Balaam speak by inspiration, as not being in. his own power, but moved to say what he did in the Holy Spirit"[4]

EARLY CHRISTIAN APOLOGISTS AND LEADERS

It is clear that many of the early Christian apologists (those who explained and defended Christianity to a hostile world) taught the dictation of Scripture. They commonly used the illustration of the musical instrument and the musician.

---
4 Josephus, Flavius, Antiquities of the Jews IV, VI, 5.

Justin Martyr, Second Century A.D., wrote about the Scriptures: "... by the gift which then descended from above upon the holy men

> ...In order that the divine plectrum itself, descending from heaven, and using righteous men as an instrument like a harp or lyre, might reveal to the knowledge of things divine and heavenly.

Athenagoras, Second Century A.D., used similar terminology in writing about the Scriptures,

> ...while entranced and deprived of their natural powers of reason by the influence of the divine spirit, they uttered that which was wrought in them, the Spirit using them as its instrument, as a flute player might a flute." He also wrote about the writers of Scripture saying they were "lifted in ecstasy above the natural operations of their minds by the impulses of the Divine Spirit, uttered the things with which they were inspired, the Spirit making use of them as a flute-player breathes into a flute.

Other early writers (including Tatian, Militades, and Theodore of Mopsuestia). took similar positions on dictation

An early pope, Gregory the Great, Sixth Century A.D., said that it was fruitless to argue over the human authorship of the books of Scripture, "since we hold the Holy Spirit to be the author we do nothing else if we inquire the authorship than to inquire, when we read a letter, about the pen with which it was written."

Ambrose, Fourth Century A.D., wrote that "the words of Scripture were those of God and not men."

Augustine, Fourth Century AD., spoke of the apostles, "... as hands which noted down what Christ dictated."

Not all of the early Christian writers accepted the concept that the Scriptures were dictated by the Holy Spirit. Origen, Third Century AD., opposed this teaching and refuted it at length in his commentary on the gospel of John. As proof for his doctrine of inspiration, he pointed out that in his opinion the Bible contained many contradictions which would not be the case if it had been dictated by the Holy Spirit.

This is the same Origen that taught against the literal interpretation of the Scripture and who substituted a corrupt text for the common text of Scripture. This same teaching against dictation was taught by Clement of Alexandria, Second Century AD., and by Jerome, Fourth Century A.D.

THE GREAT LUTHERAN DEBATE

Not long after the death of Martin Luther, Lutheran theologians began a great debate over the doctrine of inspiration by dictation. Interestingly enough both sides realized that they were really debating about verbal inspiration. Both sides recognized that verbal inspiration could come about only by dictation from the Holy Spirit.

Some Lutheran teachers taught that God had superintended the inspiration of the Scripture in a general way and that it was the doctrines and teachings of the Scripture that were inspired. Others taught that God had dictated the Scriptures word for word and thus every word was inspired. This debate has continued throughout the history of the Lutheran movement. The Lutherans who refer to scripture as being dictated by the Holy Spirit are called Orthodox Lutherans. This debate is important to Twenty first Century Baptists because they are engaged in the same debate.

The Verbal Inspiration of Scripture

Seventeenth Century Lutheran theologian J.A. Quenstadt wrote,

> The Holy Spirit not only inspired in the prophets and apostles the content and sense contained in scripture, or the meaning of the words, so that they might of their own free will clothe and furnish these thoughts with their own style and words, but the Holy Spirit actually supplied, inspired and dictated the very words and each and every term individually.

J.K.S. Reid describes the position of Leonard Huetter, Sixteenth Century Lutheran theologian, "Huetter held the Holy Scripture is verbally dictated by the Holy Spirit, in such a way that no iota set down by the prophets and apostles in their books is not God given." Quenstadt and Huetter wrote some of the most influential doctrinal books in the Lutheran movement.

Prominent Lutheran theologian Johann Gerhard, Sixteenth Century, also wrote important Lutheran doctrinal books. He wrote " . . . The Biblical writers are mere amanuenses or secretaries." Aegidius Hunnius, Seventeenth Century Lutheran theologian, referred to the Scripture as, "Holy Scripture dictated by God".

Those who questioned the doctrine of inspiration by dictation eventually became dominant in the Lutheran denomination. The doctrine of verbal inspiration was replaced by a vague doctrine of inspiration. Many Orthodox Lutherans attribute the rise of modernism in the Lutheran movement to the door opened by this change.

Lutheran theologian Martin Chemnitz (Sixteenth Century) is said by Harold O.J. Brown, to have believed "even those things Jesus said orally in the presence of his disciples were not simply recalled, but instead, were subsequently verbally dictated to them by the Holy Spirit."

EVEN THE ROMAN CATHOLIC CHURCH TOOK A STRONG POSITION ON DICTATION AFTER THE REFORMATION.

Under pressure to clarify their doctrine of Scriptures, the Roman Catholic denomination, at the Council of Trent (1563) took a position on the heavenly dictation of Scripture. The Council of Trent stated that "the Scripture had come from the prophets and apostles the Holy Spirit dictating "

The Council of Trent also stated concerning the New Testament Scriptures, "... as having been dictated either by Christ's own word of mouth or by the Holy Ghost." This position was repeated at the Vatican Council in 1870 A.D.

JOHN CALVIN

Many Baptists who pride themselves on their scholarship are fond of quoting John Calvin as a great authority on doctrine. However, Calvin frequently used the term dictation to describe how the Scriptures were given by God. Examples include, "Whosoever then wishes to profit in the Scriptures let him first of all lay this down as a settled point, that the Law and the Prophets are not a doctrine delivered of men, but dictated by the Holy Spirit." Another representative statement is "the ancient prophecies were dictated by Christ." There are many other examples. In fact, Calvin used the illustration of an echo to explain Scripture. The Holy Spirit uttered the words. The human writers just echoed them.

Teachers who delight in calling themselves Calvinists should not so easily scoff at those who believe that the Holy Spirit dictated the Scriptures. Calvin's commentaries are full of references to the "dictation" of Scripture by the Holy Spirit.

Another example is Calvin's statement: "The prophets did not speak at their own suggestion but . . . being organs of the Holy Spirit they only uttered what they had been commissioned from heaven to declare.

PROMINENT BIBLE TEACHERS HAVE OFTEN TAUGHT THE DOCTRINE THAT SCRIPTURE WAS GIVEN BY DICTATION

Dr. Louis Gaussen, in his classic book Theopneustia: "The Plenary Inspiration of the Holy Scriptures refers to dictation over 200 times: "... and we see in it, as we shall have occasion more than once to repeat, one additional proof of the divine wisdom which has dictated the Scriptures."

He also writes: "The Bible is not a book to make under His protection, it is a book which God dictated to them." He uses the term dictation in many other places to describe inspiration.

Baptist theologian B.H. Carroll wrote:

> The second observation is that the propelling power in the speaking or writing was impulse from the Holy Spirit. They. the inspired men. became instruments by which the Holy spirit spoke or wrote. Take. for instance, that declaration in II Samuel 23:2. where David said: *"The Spirit of Jehovah spake by me. and his word was upon my tongue."* In Acts 1:16 we find that the utterances of David were being studied. We have a declaration that the Holy Spirit spake by the mouth of David concerning Judas: and in the third chapter of Acts we have another declaration of the same kind. Always the speaker or writer was an instrument of the Holy Spirit.

The Unbroken Bible

Richard Hooker, famous English theologian (Laws of Ecclesiastical Policy) wrote.

> They neither spoke nor wrote one word of their own: but uttered syllable by syllable as the Spirit put it into their mouths; no otherwise than the harp or the lute doth give a sound according to the discretion of his hands that holdeth and striketh it with skill.

The learned Dean John Burgon compared the writers of Scripture with a pipe organ. The Holy Spirit being the one who plays the organ.

Dr. John R. Rice was famous for teaching the verbal dictation of Scripture. His book, *Our God-Breathed Book the Bible*, contains several chapters on the subject. He writes:

> Is the word dictation hateful? Then liberals and infidels made it hateful. Men, too please unbelievers and too anxious to disavow the straw man of mechanical dictation, have avoided and feared the term. But that is not straight thinking, and it is not quite intellectually honest, it seems to me. Griffith Thomas' book is labeled, *God Spake All These Words*. And that quotation from Exodus 20:1, referring to the words of the Ten Commandments, is really a proper name for a book about the inspiration of the Bible. Well, if God gave all the words in the Bible, then is not that dictation?
>
> Suppose I dictate a letter to a secretary. That means I tell her word- for- word what to write. Well, did not God tell the men who wrote the Bible word- for- word what to write?

Of course, doctrine is established by the clear teaching of the Scriptures, not by men. But it is scholarship to declare that no scholarly people have ever held to the doctrine of dictation of the Scripture or that it is some kind of new doctrine.

Famed Baptist leader William Kiffin (1681) also taught inspiration by dictation.

> Now these are some of the properties of a General Rule to try controversies by... Recorded in the Scriptures, which were given for our instruction, II Timothy 3: 16 written by the immediate dictates of the Spirit preserved by the gracious providence of God in the church from the injuries of time, ignorance, and fraud through all ages...

LIBERALS AND NEO-EVANGELICALS OFTEN UNDERSTAND THE RELATIONSHIP BETWEEN DICTATION AND INSPIRATION

James Barr, who does not believe in verbal inspiration, comments on the difficulty of those who wish to claim to believe in verbal inspiration without believing in verbal dictation:

> A dictation theory would make much better sense than the sort of position that conservative apologists ask us to accept ... A dictation theory about the mode of inspiration may be wrong but it does make some kind of sense. What modern conservative apologists put before us does not make sense!

In further explaining why the dictation theory of inspiration makes sense and the superintendence theory does not he makes these telling comments:

> Thirdly, fundamentalist have probably moved quite a long distance towards the modern way of looking at historical figures like prophets and apostles. They do not, most of the time, think of them as persons who

merely received a message which was passed on to us as the Bible. They think of them to some extent as diverse consciousness and experiences, who worked out judgments and ideas out of their own experience in the life of their time. In this, they are far removed from sixteenth - or seventeenth - century orthodoxy, to which this would have been entirely strange. The modern conservative tries to allow for all this in his doctrine of scriptural inspiration. Allegations of a dictation theory infuriate him because in this respect he belongs to the modern world. But the modern world suddenly cuts off the moment any critical implications might be suggested. What if the writer of the fourth gospel, a man of lively individual consciousness, had thought up out of that consciousness some of the terms and images in which he describes Jesus? What if the story of the virgin birth is a legend worked out by the early church? What if St. John shifted the cleansing of the temple from one end of the gospel story to the other because it seemed to him to give a better literary satisfaction that way? Any suggestions of this kind and fundamentalists are back in a moment with an inspiration that excludes these ideas. They don't know how it works, but they know enough to know that it can't work in that way. The message comes from God to the biblical writers. Rigid conservative writers stress the passivity or receptivity of the biblical writers before the inspired message. Modem thought dislikes the proposition that the minds of the writers of the Bible were necessarily receptive "passive) before the divine control and it questions knowledge which is said to have been imparted solely on the divine initiative. Against this modem thinking, we must insist, along with Warfield, that 'the organs of revelation occupy a receptive attitude.' The contents of their messages are not something thought out, inferred, hoped for, or feared by them, but the irresistible might of the revealing Spirit.

The Verbal Inspiration of Scripture

Here once again, then, we find that the position of the fundamentalist is a vacillating one. He can look on the gospel of St. Mark quite happily as the product of the conscious initiative of Mark, or on Romans as the result of personal human initiative of Paul; but whenever critical questions emerge he turns to doctrine, and his doctrinal refuge is in a position quite different in character: it belongs to an older world, where the Bible is a message sent from God to men.

Fourthly, many of the views on detailed questions which fundamentalists require us to take make no sense except on the assumption of dictation, or something as near dictation as no matter. According to fundamentalist opinion, Isaiah 40-66 was spoken or written by the original Isaiah himself. Living in the later eighth century B.C., he foresaw the return of the exiles from Babylon after that city had been destroyed by the Persians about 538 B.C. Critical scholars have thought that these chapters were actually written by a later prophet, who was, in fact, a contemporary of these events. Conservatives turn deep scorn upon this critical judgment. Surely this is denying the supernatural, denying that prediction of the future can take place under the inspiration of God! Let us accept then that it was a prediction. Isaiah foretold the whole thing. It was, no doubt, the existence of these very phenomena, among others, that led older theologians, and within their terms of reference, quite reasonably, to the dictation idea.[5]

Liberal theologians frequently equate the doctrine of the verbal dictation of the Scripture with the doctrines of verbal, plenary inspiration and the doctrines "of inerrancy and infallibility." They applaud when Bible believers give up the doctrine of verbal dictation. Rod Evans and Irwin Berent write, "the doctrine of

---
5 Barr, James, Fundamentalism p. 291-292

Biblical inerrancy, as it is adopted by most fundamentalists, essentially maintains that the entire Bible was dictated word for word, directly from God to the Biblical writers, and that because it was all dictated by God, it must all be true, completely free from error (inerrant)." They commend those fundamentalists who move away from a doctrine of dictation because it makes them "increasingly flexible" in their "interpretation of inerrancy." Liberals appreciate any doctrine that opens a door for them to flee from the authority of God's Word.

PAUL AND I CORINTHIANS 7

Some would claim that Paul's statements in I Corinthians 7 would disapprove the dictation of Scripture.

v.6 - But I speak this by permission, and not of commandment.

v. 10 - And unto the married I command, yet not I, but the Lord,

v. 12 - But to rest speak I, not the Lord

However, if you acknowledge that the material in I Corinthians 7 was not dictated by the Lord it becomes the exception that proves the rule. It is marked in such a fashion as to distinguish it from all the rest of Scripture. If God did only superintend Paul's teaching in I Corinthians He clearly did something else with all the rest of Scripture.

SUPERINTENDENCE AND PRESERVATION

This is more than just a doctrinal exercise. Even when men hold to a good doctrinal position on the Scriptures, they sometimes make it sound like man had an important part in producing the Bible. The great challenge of our day is getting men to bow their hearts to the authority of Scripture. The great challenge is to get men and women to live as if they believed the Bible was really the Word of God. Maybe this problem is made worse when we repeatedly describe the Scriptures as the work of men when we make issues of their intellect or of their will.

It is important that we learn not to treat the Bible like any other book. The Scripture is binding on us. It is totally and absolutely to be obeyed. It should be interpreted literally.

People talk about the Bible as if it were any other book. They debate the preservation of the Bible as if they were debating the preservation of any other book. They debate the translation of the Bible as if they were debating the translation of any other book. But the Scripture is not just any book. The Scripture has the power of God and the promises of God upon it. It is the very Word of God.

The Bible is the only authority for faith, doctrine, and practice. Please understand that one of the Baptist distinctives is that the Bible is more than the final authority; it is the sole authority. It was given supernaturally. It is preserved supernaturally.

Because I believe that the King James Bible is the preserved Word of God in the English language, I am sometimes asked if I believe in double inspiration. I don't believe in double inspiration, but I do believe in divine preservation:

Psalm 12:6-7 - The words of the Lord are pure words: as silver tried in a furnace of earth, purified seven times. Thou shalt keep them, O Lord, thou shalt preserve them from this generation for ever.

Isaiah 59:21 - As for me, this is my covenant with them, saith the Lord; My spirit that is upon thee, and my words which I have put in thy mouth, shall not depart out of thy mouth, nor out of the mouth of thy seed, nor out of the mouth of thy seed's seed, saith the Lord, from henceforth and for ever."

Matthew 24:35 - Heaven and earth shall pass away, but my words shall not pass away.

Isaiah 40:6-8 - The voice said, Cry. And he said, What shall I cry? All flesh is grass, and all the goodliness thereof is as the flower of the field: The grass withereth, the flower fadeth: because the spirit of the Lord, bloweth upon it: surely the people is grass. The grass withereth, the flower fadeth: but the word of our God shall stand for ever.

I believe that the Scriptures were given in supernatural fashion. The writers were passive. The words of God were dictated through them. But something supernatural also has to take place for God's promise concerning preservation to be kept.

It is in the matter of translation and copying the Scripture that I believe God's superintendence takes place. The translators are active and God does superintend the work of certain translators. God uses their intellect, training, and preparation. All translations of the Scripture are not superintended but God must work in this way at times if His promises about preservation are to be kept.

I believe that God has superintended among some copyists and some translators so that the Word of God is preserved.

The Lord Jesus frequently quoted the Old Testament Scriptures from the Aramaic. He did not have the originals in front of Him, yet He referred to faithful copies as the Scripture. He had a faithful translation in front of Him and He referred to it as the Scripture. Luke 4:14-21 "And Jesus returned in the

The Verbal Inspiration of Scripture

power of the Spirit into Galilee: and there went out a fame of him through all the region round about. And he taught in their synagogues being glorified of all. And he came to Nazareth, where he had been brought up: and, as his custom was, he went into the synagogue on the sabbath day, and stood up for to read. And there was delivered unto him the book of the prophet Esaias. And when he had opened the book, he found the place where it was written, The Spirit of the Lord is upon me, because He hath anointed me To preach the gospel to the poor; he hath sent me to heal the brokenhearted, to preach deliverance to the captives, and recovering of sight to the blind, to set at liberty them that are bruised, to preach the acceptable year of the Lord. And he closed the book, and he gave it again to the minister and sat down. And the eyes of all them that were in the synagogue were fastened on him. And he began to say unto them, This day is this scripture fulfilled in your ears."

It was the goal of the King James translators to produce "one more exact translation" in the English language. I believe that God took their incredible academic accomplishments, their willing and devoted hearts, and their prayers and superintended their work. Since there are so many translations the question naturally arises, "How can I recognize a translation that has God's hand on it?" When God's Word is faithfully translated into a language, the power of God is seen through that translation in the lives of people and great works are done for God. Great works of God have been sparked by the Old Italic Bible, the Waldensian Bibles and the King James Bible for example.

When we become clear about how God's originally given, perhaps it will become easier to become clear about how it is preserved. The Scripture was supernaturally given as God breathed out His words through men. The Scripture is supernaturally preserved as God superintends the activities of faithful copyists and translators.

The Unbroken Bible

I Thessalonians 2:13 – For this cause also thank we God without ceasing, because, when ye received the word of God which ye heard of us, ye received it not as the word of men, but as it is in truth, the word of God, which effectually worketh also in you that believe.

The Verbal Inspiration of Scripture

The Unbroken Bible

3

The "Westcott & Hort Only" Controversy

You don't have to read very much in contemporary, fundamentalist, Baptist literature to come across warnings about the "King James Only Controversy"

Dr. Jerry Falwell once announced that he was hiring Dr. Harold Rawlings to "refute the 'King James Only' cultic movement that is damaging so many good churches today."

Dr. Robert Sumner warned about the "veritable fountain of misinformation and deceptive double talk on the subject of 'King James Onlyism'."

Dr. J.B. Williams referred to those who advocate the King James Only as "misinformers" and as "a cancerous sore."

Dr. Robert Joyner called King James Bible Loyalists, "Heretics"

The Unbroken Bible

Dr. James R. White warned about King James Bible proponents "undercutting the very foundations of the faith itself".

Such references to the King James Only Controversy are very common. Some refer to loyal supporters of the King James Bible as the "'King James Only Cult". Another common term is the sneering reference to the "King Jimmy Boys." However the use of the "King James Bible only'" wasn't always so controversial.

THE PRIMACY OF THE KING JAMES BIBLE

God Was doing a great work in England in the early 1600's. The preaching of the gospel of Christ out of the Matthew's Bible and the Geneva Bible was leading to multitudes of conversions. Evangelicals and Puritans were becoming a stronger force in the Church of England and in English culture.

Yet many were concerned that the final translation work into the English language had not been done. King James was persuaded to authorize a new translation. The King James Bible was printed in 1611.

At first there were questions and concerns about this new Bible translation. This was as it should be. No one should accept a Bible translation lightly. By 1640 however, the King James Bible was clearly the Bible of the English people. The Geneva and Matthew's Bible, once greatly used of God, went out of print. There was simply no demand for them anymore.

The Church of England, with its official evangelical doctrinal statement, used the King James Bible exclusively. It was the Bible of the Puritans, both inside and outside the Church of England. In fact the Puritans began to use the distinctive Biblical English of the King James Bible in their day to day speech.

The "Westcott & Hort Only" Controversy

The King James Bible was the Bible of the Presbyterians, the Congregationalists, and the Quakers. It was clearly the bible of Baptists. By 1640 it was the Bible of the Pilgrims (Some had used the Geneva Bible earlier).

The King James Bible was the Bible of evangelicals in England, Wales, Scotland and Ireland. It became the Bible of the English Colonies across the Atlantic Ocean. The only religious group of any size or importance in England that didn't use the King James Bible was Roman Catholicism. All non-Catholics could of been referred to as "King James only people." When the Methodist Revival stirred England in the 1700's, it did so with the preaching of the King James Bible. John Wesley, one of the founders of the Methodists, made his own translation of the New Testament. However, it found little acceptance, even among Methodists.

Only the King James Bible was in common use.

When English colonies flourished in Australia and New Zealand, the King James Bible was the common Bible of the settlers. When President George Washington took the first presidential oath of office in the new United States of America, he did so with his hand on a King James Bible. Every American president since, with the exception of Franklin Pierce, has done the same.

Over one hundred fifty English translations were produced between 1611 and 1880. However, they found no audience except in a few cults, Most went out of print quickly. The English speaking, Christian World was truly "King James only".

Baptist preachers produced a Baptist translation of the Bible. They replaced the word baptism with the word immersion. They replaced the word church with the word assembly. However, they found no audience, not even among Baptists. Their translation was soon out of print. The Baptists were truly "King James Only".

As hard as it maybe for the liberals and secularists to admit, the American public schools were built around the King James Bible. The Oxford Companion to the Supreme Court of the United States, (not exactly a religious right publication), describes the early public schools this way. Public schools had a distinctly protestant flavor, with teachers leading prayers and scripture reading from the King James Bible in their lessons". The Roman Catholic minority objected to the King James Bible and so they developed their own school system. With the exception of the Catholics, the United States was clearly King James Only.

Russell Kirk (a Roman Catholic historian) describes the influence of the King James Bible on the United States, " The book that was to exert a stronger influence than any other in Americans was not published until 1611, a few years after the first Virginian settlement: the 'King James translation of the Bible, the Authorized Version, was prepared by English scholars for King James I. Read from American pulpits and in the great majority of American households during colonial times, the Authorized Version shaped the style, informed the intellect, affected the laws and decreed the morals of the North American Colonies." Truly the early United States was King James only.

According to Winston Churchill, ninety million copies of the King James Bible had been printed by the mid-twentieth century.

The king James Bible was the bible of the great modern missions movement of the 1700's and 1800's. The missionaries from England and the United States were saved, called to the mission field, and trained under the preaching of the King James Bible. They traveled around the world, introducing the gospel of grace to millions. Many of these missionaries knew little or no Greek and Hebrew. They translated the Bible into 760 languages from the King James Bible. Truly the modern missions movement was a King James only movement.

THE WESTCOTT AND HORT THEORY

In the 1870's, a challenge arose in the English world to the primacy of the King James Bible. There Had always been a challenge from Roman Catholicism, but this challenge came from men who were officially Protestants: Church of England Bishop Brooke Foss Westcott and Cambridge University Professor Fenton John Anthony Hort.

The heart of the Westcott and Hort theory was that the New Testament was preserved in almost perfect condition in two Greek texts, the Vaticanus and the Sinaticus. Sinaticus was discovered in a wastebasket in St. Catherine's Monastery (near Mt. Sinai) in 1844 by Constantin von Tischendorf. The Vaticanus was found in the Vatican library in 1475 and was rediscovered in 1845.

The King James New Testament was translated from a different family of Greek texts. To Westcott and Hort, the King James Bible was clearly and inferior translation. It must be replaced by a new translation from texts that they considered to be older and better. They believed that the true work of God in English had been held back by an inferior Bible They determined to replace the King James Bible and the Greek Textus Receptus. In short,their theory suggest that for fifteen hundred years the preserved Word of God was lost until it was recovered in the nineteenth century in a trash can and in the Vatican Library. Hort clearly had a bias against the Textus Receptus, calling it "villainous" and "vile". Hort aggressively taught that the School at Antioch (associated with Lucian) had loosely translated the true text of Scripture in the second century A. D. This supposedly created an unreliable text of Scripture which became the Textus Receptus. This was called the Lucian Recension Theory.

Hort did not have a single historical reference to support the idea that such a recension took place.

He simply theorized that it must have taken place. In spite of the fact that there is not a single historical reference to the Lucian Recension, may Bible colleges teach it as a historical fact.

WESTCOTT AND HORT ONLY!

It is clear that the modern movement to revise the English Bible is based completely on the works of Westcott and Hort.

K.W. Clark writes,"...the Westcott-Hort text has become today our Textus-Receptus. We have been freed from the one only to become captivated by the other... The psychological chains so recently broken from our fathers have again been forged upon us, even more strongly."

E. C Colwell writes, " The dead hand of Fenton John Anthony Hort lies heavy upon us. In the early years of this century Kirsopp Lake described Hort's work as a failure,... But Hort did not fail to reach his major goal. He dethroned the Textus Receptus... This was a sensational achievement, and impressive success. Horts success in this task and the cogency of his tightly reasoned theory shaped- and still shapes- the thinking of those who approach the textual criticism of the New Testament through the English Language."

Zane Hodges, a long time professor at Dallas Theological Seminary, writes, "Modern textual criticism is psychologically addicted to Westcott and Hort. Westcott and Hort in turn , were rationalists in their approach to the textual problem in the New testament and employed techniques within which rationalism and every other kind of bias are free to operate."

Alfred Martin, former Vice-President at Moody Bible

Institute, wrote in 1951 "The present generation of the Bible students having been reared on Westcott and Hort have for the most part accepted this theory without independent or critical examination...if believing Bible students had the evidence of both sides put before them instead of one side only, there would not be so much blind following of Westcott and Hort." The two most popular Greek manuscripts today, Nestles-Aland and UBS (United Bible Society), differ very little from the Westcott and Hort text.

WHAT YOU HAVE TO BELIEVE TO ACCEPT THE WESTCOTT AND HORT THEORY

- You have to believe that people who believed in the Deity of Christ often corrupt Bible manuscripts.

- You have to believe that people who deny the Deity of Christ never corrupt Bible manuscripts.

- You have to believe that people who died to get the gospel to the world couldn't be trusted with the Bible.

- You have to believe that their killers could be trusted.

- You have to believe that the Celtic Christians, Waldenses, Albigenses, Henricians, Petrobrusians, Paulicians, the Greek Orthodox Church, the Protestant churches, the Anabaptists and the Baptists all did not have the pure word of God.

- You have to believe that the Roman Catholics and the nineteenth Century rationalists did have the pure word of God.

ARE WESTCOTT AND HORT INFALLIBLE?

Even though many evangelicals treat the Westcott and Hort Theory as proven fact, there have always been serious textual scholars that challenged it.

The brilliant textual scholar, Dean John Burgon, referred to Westcott and Hort's "violent recoil from Traditional Text". He refers to their theory as "superstitious veneration for a few ancient documents." Another famed textual scholar and contemporary of Westcott and Hort, F.H.P Scrivner wrote, "Dr. Hort's system therefore is entirely destitute of historical foundation. He does not so much as make a show of pretending to it; but then he would persuade us, as he persuaded himself…'.

It is a phony claim to scholarship to simply parrot the ideas of Westcott and Hort and pretend that you are superior to those who don't accept their ideas. Those who wish to change the King James Bible, so long greatly used of God and cherished by the English speaking people , need to give clear reasons why!

How do you know that the "older' Vaticanus and Sinaticus manuscripts aren't corrupt manuscripts? How do you know that the Lucian Recension ever took place? Why do you believe that the evangelicals throughout the centuries were using a corrupt text? Why would you trust Westcott and Hort Only?

WHO WERE WESTCOTT AND HORT?

B.F Westcott was born in 1825. F.J.A Hort was born in 1828. They were members of the Broad Church (or High Church) Party of the Church of England. They became friends during their student days at Cambridge University. They worked for over thirty years together on the subject of the Greek text of the New Testament.

Westcott went on to become the Bishop of Durham (England) and served for a while as chaplain to Queen Victoria. Hort is best remembered as a Professor of Divinity at Cambridge University.

Both men wrote several books. They are best remembered for their edition of the Greek New Testament entitled, 'The New testament in the Original Greek". They are also remembered for being the two most influential members of the English Revised Version committee which produced a new English translation. Scrivener thought that they exercised too much influence on this committee.

Westcott died in 1901 . Hort passed away in 1892 Both men had sons who collected their personal correspondence and who wrote biographies about them.

THE DOCTRINE OF WESTCOTT AND HORT

The Scripture

It is clear that neither Westcott nor Hort held anything even faintly resembling a conservative view of Scripture. According to Hort's son, Dr. Horts Own Mother (a devout Bible believer) could not be sympathetic to his views about the Bible. Westcott wrote to Hort that he overwhelmingly rejected the "idea of the infallibility of the Bible". Hort says the same thing, the same week, in a letter to Bishop Lightfoot.

When Westcott became the Bishop of Durham, the Durham University Journal welcomed him with the praise that he was "free from all verbal or mechanical ideas of inspiration".

Salvation

Hort called the doctrine of the substitutionary atonement

"immoral". In doing so he sided with the normal doctrine of the High Church Party of the Church of England .The Low Church Party was generally evangelical, teaching salvation through personal faith in Jesus Christ. They High Church Party taught salvation by good works including baptism and church membership.

Westcott and Hort wrote may commentaries that include references to classic passages about salvation. Repeatedly their commentary is vague and unclear. Westcott taught that the idea of "propitiating God" was "foreign to the New Testament". He taught that salvation came from changing the character of the one who offended God. This is consistent with his statement that, "A Christian never is but always becoming a Christian."

Again and again, Westcott's vague comments about salvation are easy to interpret as teaching universal salvation.

The Doctrine of Christ

It was common in the days of Westcott and Hort for those in the Church of England who denied the Deity of Christ to speak in vague terms! To clearly deny the Deity of the Christ was to jeopardize your position in the Church of England. Many High Church modernists learned to speak of the Deity of Christ in unclear terms as a way to avoid trouble. Many statements by both Westcott and Hort fall into that category of "fuzzy" doctrinal statements about Christ. Westcott and Hort were brilliant scholars. Surely they were capable of expressing themselves clearly on the doctrine of Christ if they wanted to. At best they are unclear; at worst, they were modernists hiding behind the fundamental doctrinal statement of the Church of England.

Other Teachings of Westcott and Hort

There are many other areas that cause fundamental Bible believers to have serious questions about Westcott and Hort. Westcott denied that Genesis 1 through 3 were historically true. Hort praised Darwin and his theory of evolution. Both Westcott and Hort praised the "Christian socialist" movement of their day. Westcott belonged to several organizations designed to promote "Christian socialism" and served as President of one of them (the Christian Social Union).

Both Westcott and Hort showed sympathy for the movement to return to the Church of England to Rome. Both honored rationalist philosophers of their time like Samuel Taylor Coleridge, Dr. Frederick Maurice, and Dr. Thomas Arnold. Both were serious students of the Greek philosophers Plato and Aristotle.

There is much about the teaching of Westcott and Hort to deeply trouble any objective Bible believer.

WERE WESTCOTT AND HORT SAVED MEN?

The evangelical defenders of Westcott and Hort are quick to assert that they were saved men even if some of their ideas seem a little strange in our day. They remind people that both were ordained preachers in the evangelical Church of England.

However , there is no doubt that there were many Church of England preachers that were not true evangelicals. The High Church party was well known to teach salvation by works. Within the Church of England there was a vigorous debate between true evangelicals and those who taught baptismal regeneration or some other system of works for salvation. In their lengthy writings, neither Westcott nor Hort ever give an account of their own conversation. They never identified with the evangelicals in the Church of England. They were never accepted by the evangelicals in the Church of England. They were associated with various occult figures, but never with evangelicals.

While Westcott and Hort praised evolutionists, socialists, and modernists, they were bitterly critical of evangelical soulwinners. Westcott criticized the work of William Booth and the Salvation Army. Hort Criticized the Crusades of D. L Moody. Hort Criticized the soul winning Methodists.

Both criticized evangelicals. Neither gave anyone reason to believe that he ever trusted Christ as his personal Saviour.

THE WORK OF THE ENGLISH REVISION COMMITTEE

In 1870, the English Parliament authorized a revision of the Kings James Bible. Two teams of translators were hired. Most translators were from the church of England but there were also seven Presbyterians, four Congregationalists, two Baptists, two Methodists and one Unitarian. The Translators were instructed to make as few alterations to the King James Bible as possible.

A similar committee was developed in the United States at the same time. The two committees exchanged copies of their work. Several thousand Church of England preachers signed a petition protesting the inclusion of a Unitarian, Dr. Vance Smith, on the Revision Committee. They felt that only saved men should be involved in translating the Bible. Proper translation required the illumination of the indwelling Holy Spirit.

Both Westcott and Hort defeded Smith and lobbied for his presence on the committee. Westcott threatened to quit if Smith was not included. Westcott and Hort supplied everyone working on the Committee with a private copy of their new Greek text. Hort lobbied (some would say intimidated) committee members to follow the Westcott and Hort text. Westcott, Hort and Bishop Lightfoot pressured the committee to go beyond their mandate for doing a revision of the King James Bible. Dr. Frederick Scrivener opposed many of the changes to be made on the basis of the new Westcott and Hort Greek Text. Committee meetings were referred to as"… a kind of critical duel between Dr. Hort ad Dr. Scrivener." Arthur Hort describing the right reading of the text as "to settle the question by the light of his own inner consciousness". Dean Burgon spoke of Hort's method as deciding by "the right of genuineness". Hort was far more concerned about his feelings than he was about the textual debate over any passage. Westcott referred to the debate over textual readings as "hard fighting" and " a battle royal". The original chairman, Bishop Samuel Wilberforce, resigned after referring to the project as "this most miserable business".

Westcott and Hort eventually won most of the debates. After the new English Revision was published, both Scrivener and Burgon published lengthy refutations of the Revision. Burgon attacked the Revision strongly, calling it "excursions into cloud land" and "blowing smoke". The people of England largely rejected the new translation. Attempts to make it the new Authorized Version of the Church of England met with such protest that Queen Victoria abandoned the idea.

Neither the English nor the American Revision sold very well. They were both soon replaced by other versions. However, the multitude of new English versions were all based upon the same Westcott and Hort Greek text and upon the theories of Westcott and Hort. Their English translation failed but their principles won the day. Even though evangelicals rejected the English Revision and the Westcott and Hort text, it did find supporters. Modernists and rationalists, both within and without the Church of England, praised their work. Theosophy founder, Helen Blavatsky, wrote at great length in praise of the new Greek text.

The defenders of Westcott and Hort claimed that the evangelicals were too simple-minded and unlearned to understand the work of Westcott and Hort and other English "scholars". Evangelicalism was presented as unscholarly. After a generation, many evangelicals began to feel uncomfortable at always being labeled as unscholarly and uneducated. Some evangelical leaders began to look for ways to reconcile the historic Christian faith with the theories of Westcott and Hort.

These theories and the Greek text of Westcott and Hort began to find their way into evangelical seminaries and Bible colleges on both sides of the Atlantic Ocean.

Two generations after the failure of the English Revision, the theories of Westcott and Hort had become majority opinion in evangelical Bible colleges and seminaries in both the United States and England. Their theories were universally accepted in modernist seminaries. The Jehovah's Witnesses and other cults bragged about having Bible translations based upon the Westcott and Hort theory.

Compromising evangelicals were suddenly proud of having "scholarship" accepted by the world. They used the same Greek text as the Roman Catholic Church, the modernists and the cults.

A relative handful of Bible believers refused to accept the Greek text and theory of Westcott and Hort. Such holdouts became an irritation to the "scholarly" evangelicals. As study of the issue increased, opposition to the Westcott and Hort theory grew. "Westcott and Hort only" no longer seemed an adequate reason for abandoning the King James Bible. The "scholarly evangelicals" began to react harshly to their "King James only" critics.

The "Westcott & Hort Only" Controversy

WERE WESTCOTT AND HORT SECRET PRACTITIONERS OF THE OCCULTS?

In 1993, Gail Riplinger published New Age Bible Versions. In this book, she alleges that Westcott and Hort were practitioners of the occult. It is indicated that they provide a bridge between apostate Christianity and the occult and the New Age Movement.

This charge created a sensation and generated a tremendous amount of criticism for Mrs. Riplinger. It is, of course, a very important charge. An objective look at the evidence for such a charge is important.

Along with Bishop Edward White Benson, Westcott and Hort founded the Ghostly Guild. This club was designed to investigate ghosts and supernatural appearances. The club was based upon the idea that such spirits actually exist and appear to men. According to The Encyclopedia of Occultism and Parapsychology, the members of the Ghostly Club would "relate personal experiences concerned with ghosts.

This club would eventually become the Society for Psychical Research. According to James Webb in The Occult Underground and W.H. Solter, The S.P.R. - An Outline of It's History, this club became a major factor in the rise of spiritualism among the elite of English society in the late 1800's. Many leading occult figures belonged to the Society.

Along the way, Westcott and Hort dropped out of the Ghostly Guild. However, they had plenty of opportunity to be exposed to the occult and demonism before they withdrew.

Westcott's son refers to his father's life long faith in spiritualism (Archbishop Benson's son referred to Benson in the same way.)

The Unbroken Bible

Communion with spirits became quite fashionable in the late 1800's in British society. Even Queen Victoria, who normally led a responsible Christian life, dabbled in spiritualism. However, it was considered unseemly for Church of England clergymen, and Wescott had to keep his ideas quiet. According to Wescott's son, Arthur,   Dr. Wescott practiced the Communion of the Saints. This was a belief that you can fellowship with the spirits of those who died recently.

Bible translator J.B. Phillips also believed in the Communion of Saints. He believed that the spirit of C.S. Lewis visited him after his death. According to Arthur Westcott, Bishop Westcott also had such experiences with spirits. His son writes, " The Communion of Saints seems particularly associated with Peterborough. He had an extraordinary power of realizing this Communion. It was his delight to be alone at night in the great Cathedral, for there he could meditate and pray in full sympathy with all that was good and great in the past... There he always had abundant company." Wescott's daughter met him returning from one of his customary meditations in the solitary darkness of the chapel of Auckland castle. She said to him, " I expect you do not feel alone?" "Oh, no," he said, "It is full."

Either Dr. Westcott's children lied about him or Dr. Westcott was used to meeting with spirits. Bible believers recognize these spirits as demons. Westcott and Hort both joined a secret society called, The Apostles. It was limited to 12 members. One of the other members was Henry Sidgwick. He was also stated to have led several professors at Trinity College into secretly practicing the occult. Westcott, his close friend, was also a professor at Trinity College. Strange company for a Christian teacher and Bible translator.

In 1872 Westcott formed a secret society, the Eranus Club. Members included Hort, Sidgwick, Arthur Balfour (future prime minister of England), Archbishop Trench and Dean Alford.

Both Trench and Alford would be involved in Bible revision work. Balfour became famous for his seances and practice of spiritualism. The Eranus Club would eventually become known as an occult secret society.

Westcott's defenders point out that Wescott also eventually dropped out of Eranus. Still he was certainly allied with practitioners of the occult in a secret society for a period of time.

Balfour and Sidgwick were involved in several occult organizations, socialism and Theosophy. How many Christians have so many friends prominent in the practice of the occult?

Balfour would also be involved in the founding of the League of Nations and in forming a secret society with Cecil Rhodes (the Round Table and the Council of Foreign Relations).

The evidence for Mrs. Riplinger's assertions is strong. Would Westcott and Hort's defenders accept anyone today who had such connections? They were clearly in contact with people who were "familiar" with spirits. There is every reason to suspect that they might also have been in contact with spirits. Based upon their associations, there is no clear reason to reject the suggestion that they were involved in the occult. The balance of evidence creates, at the very least, a strong suspicion of occult influence on both Westcott and Hort (especially Dr. Westcott).

THE FUNDAMENTALIST DEFENDERS OF WESTCOTT AND HORT

There are fundamentalists who refuse to accept the characterization of Westcott and Hort as liberals (much less occultists)! J.B. Williams writes, "I have three of Westcott's commentaries in my library, and I challenge anyone to find one sentence that would be a departure from Fundamentalist doctrine."

Keith Gepart writes, "In reality, Westcott had made clear statements affirming orthodox doctrines such as the deity of Christ. In no way was he guilty of heresy and apostasy." In responding to a critic of Westcott and Hort, Gephart wrote this, "I cannot help but suspect that… some blinding presupposition… drives you to prove him a heretic at any cost."

Dr. Stewart Custer writes, " Especially when these men had written in their mature years book after book defending the conservation interpretation of scripture, it is unjust to characterize their whole ministries by a few misinterpretations that they may have been guilty of."

Evangelist Robert Sumner admits that Westcott and Hort were liberal in theology but he still believes that they were trustworthy to "restore the original text."

It would be easy to ask at this point if everyone is reading from the same books. How can there be such a difference of opinion about what these men believed and wrote?

It is true that these men (especially Westcott) wrote commentaries in which they used the great doctrinal terms of the Christian faith in a positive way. They used terms that were part of the official doctrinal position of the Church of England (in which they both held prominent positions).

Almost all denominational liberals use the terms expected of them. This is important in maintaining their income, position and influence. The important thing is how they explain those doctrinal terms (or fail to explain them).

Unless you are determined not to see it, it is clear from their commentaries that they put a liberal interpretation on many Christian doctrines. Both of their sons admit that they were accused of heresy because of their books. This understanding of these statements in their commentaries are supported by several external facts.

Westcott and Hort identified with the High Church Party (Broad Party) within the Church of England. In contrast with the more evangelical and conservative Low Church. Modernism found its home in the High Church Party.

Westcott and Hort constantly praised theological liberals, socialists and other radicals like Coleridge and Darwin.

No similar praise is found for evangelicals or fundamentalists, either in or out of the Church of England. They are normally ignored! When they are mentioned at all, like D.L. Moody, it is with disdain!

Their private correspondence reveals their liberal drift much more clearly than their commentaries. Of course, it was safer for them to admit what they really believed in this forum. Their correspondence also shows that they had concerns that they could not afford to have all of their beliefs known by the general public.

The biographies of Westcott and Hort written by their sons clearly reveal that they were not in harmony with the official positions of the Church of England. Their sons had no reason to lie about them. Certainly their sons had no King James only bias.

It is interesting that some men can't face the real record about Westcott and Hort. In fact, some who are quick to attack even minor differences with living preachers, take a blind eye to Westcott and Hort.

However, this is easy to understand. Their campaign to replace the King James Bible has been based upon the work of Westcott and Hort only. To admit these men were not trustworthy would be to admit that they have been wrong in a major premise of their entire ministry.

Perhaps we must be forced to suspect that some blinding presupposition drives them to prove that Westcott and Hort were not heretics at any cost. It appears that "scholarship" requires only a shallow reading of Westcott and Hort and ignorance of their personal letters and correspondence. Their defenders do not spend any time quoting their personal correspondence of the biographies written by their sons. Their defenders never recount the testimonies of their conversion because no such testimonies exist.

KING JAMES ONLY OR WESTCOTT AND HORT ONLY?

Dean John Burgon was a contemporary and acquaintance of both Westcott and Hort. He was a firm opponent of the Westcott and Hort theory, their new Greek text and the revision of the English Bible that they so heavily influenced. In an article entitled " The Secret Spanking of Westcott and Hort" Burgon wrote: "the text of Drs. Westcott and Hort is either the very best which has ever appeared or else is is the very worst; the nearest to the sacred autographs or the furthest from them. There is no room for both opinions, and there cannot exist any middle view." In others words, "things that are different are not the same."

Millions of professing evangelicals have never heard of Westcott and Hort. None the less, their approach to the Scripture is based upon the theory of Westcott and Hort--Westcott and Hort only. No matter how many books, professors, colleges and denominational leaders these theories are filtered through, they are still the work of Westcott and Hort only.

Those who challenge the primacy of the king James Bible in the English speaking world depend on the work of Westcott

The "Westcott & Hort Only" Controversy

and Hort.

Westcott and Hort are not a sufficient basis to reject the Textus Receptus or the King James Bible. Their objectivity, scholarship and doctrine are all at best "suspect." There is no reason to believe that they were saved men. There is more reason to believe that they were influenced by the occult than there is to believe that they were influenced by the Holy Spirit.

Perhaps the "King James Only Controversy" is misnamed. It is really a "Westcott and Hort Only" controversy.

Are you willing to abandon the historic contributions of the Textus receptus and the King James Bible for Westcott and Hort Only?

The Unbroken Bible

PART TWO

The Unbroken HISTORY

The History of the English Bible
The Real Story of King James

The Unbroken Bible

4

The History of the English Bible

In the late Twentieth Century, English has become the most important language in the world. It is the language of international diplomacy and of world-wide trade. It is spoken by over one billion people (even though only one-third of them speak English as their mother tongue). Of the 2,700 languages in the world, English is the richest in vocabulary. The Oxford English Dictionary lists 500,000 English words (compared to 185,000 German words and 100,000 French).

English has reached this prominence despite being called a "mongrel" language. It is not one of the basic root human languages. English has developed as a "polyglot" language. Several languages were merged as a result of changing political circumstances in the British Isles.

Some of the earliest inhabitants of the British Isles were the Celts. Their language and dialects are the earliest on record in the British Isles. A Celtic language is still spoken by many of the inhabitants of Wales. Many Celtic words remain in the English language.

Between 55 BC and 410 AD the British Isles experienced several invasions and eventually were conquered by the Roman Empire. By this time Latin (the language of the Roman Empire) had absorbed many Greek words. During this period of Roman rule, many Latin and Greek words were mixed into the Celtic language.

By the year 449 AD three Germanic tribes (the Angles, Saxons, and the Jutes) had begun to invade the British Isles. These tribes eventually ruled most of Britannia. They became known as the English (a corruption of the name Angles). The Anglo-Saxon language was a Germanic language with words that came from the Celtic, Latin and Greek languages. This language was referred to as "Old English". It became a separate language from that of the Germanic tribes on the European continent.

In AD 793 the Vikings began to raid England and eventually controlled large areas of the British Isles. Under Alfred the Great (AD 878) the English rallied and regained control of many areas. Alfred feared that the Norse (Viking) language would take over the land. Alfred sponsored the translation of several books into English to protect the English language. The English language did pick up several Viking words.

In the year 1066 the Normans conquered England. Normandy was a region of France that had been conquered by the Vikings. The Normans ruled England for almost 300 years. They made French the official language of England (though most of the common people still spoke English). During the Hundred Year War with France (1337-1454), French was abandoned as the official language. During this time the English language had picked up many French words.

The History of the English Bible

By now the English language had undergone many changes. This version of the English language is called "Middle English". Middle English is usually thought of as the language from AD 1150 to 1500.

Modern English developed during the Sixteenth Century. The administrations of Henry VIII, Elizabeth I and James I and their sponsorship of literary pursuits brought English to a new height of richness. The writing of Shakespeare and especially the Authorized Version of 1611 brought the English language to its most perfect form of expression.

Partial Versions of the Scriptures in Old English

There are at least ten partial translations of the Scriptures into Old English. These translators included a stable-hand, two bishops, one archbishop, two monks, two priests, a hermit and a king.

The first was a stable-hand named Caedmon (AD 680). He did not translate the Scriptures into writing, but turned Genesis, Exodus and a part of Daniel into long songs in English.

The second known translator was Eadhelm (640-709), a bishop in southern England. In 705 he translated the Psalms into old English. Another English bishop, Egbert translated the gospels into Old English in 705.

The historian and theologian Bede is often called the Venerable Bede and the Father of English History. Among his many accomplishments was a translation of the Gospel of John into Old English. H.S. Miller tells this story of how he finished his translation work:

"All the day before Ascension Day, 735, the good old monk of Jarrow-on-the-Tyne, North England, had been dictating his translation, for he said, 'I do not want my boys to read or lie, or to work to no purpose after I am gone.' The next day he was very weak, and suffered much. His scribe said, 'Dear master, there is yet one chapter to do, but it seems very hard for you to speak.' 'Nay, it is easy, take up thy pen and write quickly.' In blinding tears the scribe wrote on. 'And now, father there is just one sentence more.' Bede dictated it and said, 'Write quickly.' 'It is finished, master.' 'Ay, it is finished!' echoed the dying saint, and with the Gloria chant upon his lips he passed to the great Master whom he had loved and served so long. His name will live always in the story of the English Bible and the History and Literature of England."

Alfred the Great (King of England from 871-901) worked hard to put many books into the English language. He personally translated the Ten Commandments, Psalms and the Gospels into Old English. He also translated parts of the Old Testament Law and proclaimed these laws and the Ten Commandments as part of the law of England. He is quoted as saying, "that all the freeborn youth of his kingdom should employ themselves on nothing till they could first read well the English Scripture." Winston Churchill credits Alfred with establishing "a common Christian England."

Around 950 AD, an English priest named Alfred wrote an Old-English paraphrase of the gospels between the lines of a Latin text. This is known as the Lindifarne Gospels. Around 1000 AD, Aelfric (the Archbishop of Canterbury) translated the Gospels, the first 7 books of the Old Testament, Esther, Job and Kings.

During the Norman rule of England there were at least partial translations. In 1215 a monk named Orm translate of the Gospels and Acts. In 1320 a parish priest named William translated the Psalms. In 1340 a hermit named Role translated the Psalms.

The History of the English Bible

These few rare portions of the Bible in English were owned by universities and monasteries. The common people rarely had access to them. The few Bibles available in England were in Latin. Only a very few of the English could read them.

The Work of John Wycliffe

John Wycliffe was born in Yorkshire, England around 1320 AD. He became a professor of theology at Oxford University and also served at several churches. His lectures and classes were attended by large crowds. Wycliffe challenged the authority of the Pope in Rome, taught justification by faith and the priesthood of all believers. As a result he instituted and led a group of preachers who went throughout England preaching and teaching the people.

Because of his teaching about the priesthood of the believers, Wycliffe longed for all the English people to be able to read the Bible in their own language. The following is a modern language translation of a famous statement of Wycliffe on the subject (as reported by Winston Churchill), "Christian men and women, old and young, should study fast in the New Testament, for it is full authority, and open to the understanding of simple men, as to the points that be most needful to salvation…" Wycliffe stated that his goal was a complete English Bible "so that every man might read in the tongue wherein he was born the wonderful works of God."

Wycliffe and several associates spent 15 years translating the Scriptures from the Latin Vulgate into English. Despite harsh opposition from church leadership, hand-written copies of this translation spread rapidly throughout England. Historian J.H. Merle d' Aubigne described the influence of Wycliffe's translation this way.

"The reception of the work surpassed all expectations. The

The Unbroken Bible

Holy Scriptures exercised a reviving influence over men's hearts; minds were enlightened; souls were converted; the voices of the "poor priests" had done little in comparison with this voice; something new had welcomed this new era with acclamations; the highborn curious curiously examined the unknown book; and even Anne of Bohemia, wife of Richard II, prompted perhaps by the popular interest, began to read the Gospels diligently. She did more than this: she made them known to Thomas Arundel, archbishop of York and chancellor, and afterwords a persecutor, but who now, struck by the site of a foreign lady - of a queen, humbly devoting her leisure to the study of 'such virtuous books,' commenced reading them himself, and rebuked the prelates who neglected his holy pursuit. 'You could not meet two persons on the highway,' says a contemporary writer, 'but one of them was Wycliffe's disciple.'"

To produce one copy of the Wycliffe's Bible took ten months of full time effort by a scribe. It took an amount slightly greater than a year's salary for an average English workman to purchase a copy of the Wycliffe Bible.

For 145 years the Wycliffe translation was the only complete translation into English. It changed a nation. Forty years after his death the ecclesiastical authorities had his body dug up and burnt at the stake. In 1408 the Catholic Church forbid any new translations.

Wycliffe's translation was in Middle English. It would serve the English people well until the language changed.

The Ministry of William Tyndale

In 1450 Johan Gutenberg of Germany invented the printing press. In 1454 he invented movable type. These inventions opened up great new possibilities for the distribution of God's Word.

The History of the English Bible

William Tyndale was born around 1484. Tyndale attended Oxford and Cambridge where he became skilled in Greek, Latin, Hebrew, Italian, Spanish and Dutch. He then attended Cambridge where he studied Greek under Erasmus (the great Greek scholar largely responsible for preparing the Textus Receptus. Erasmus taught him the importance of translating the Bible into the common languages so that everyone could read them.

As Tyndale began to promote the idea of a new Bible translation in English he began to experience opposition from church leadership. One Roman Catholic priest said to him, "We were better without God's law than without the Pope's." Tyndale replied, "I defy the Pope and all his laws; if God spares my life, ere many years I will cause a boy that driveth the plough shall know more of the Scripture than thou doest."

Tyndale moved to London and took a pastorate there. He began to seek the sanction and protection of the Lord Bishop of London for his translation project. The law forbidding private translation work had been repeated many times but it was legal to do translation work if authorized by the church. Tyndale continued to do translation work but no printer would dare print it. Tyndale chose to move to the European continent to gain a chance to have his translation printed.

Tyndale traveled to Germany and met with Martin Luther. He settled in Cologne, Germany and continued his translation work. He used Erasmus' Greek New Testament, the Latin Vulgate and Luther's German translation as the basis for his English New Testament.

Printing had already started on an order of 3,000 New Testaments when the city council ordered the printers to stop printing. Tyndale and his assistant fled to the German city of Worms. Soon 10,000 New Testaments were in print. Thousands were smuggled into England. They were hidden in bales for cloth, salt-barrels, sacks of flour and corn and in every way possible. There was a ready market for copies of the Bible in English. The English Church began to buy copies for the purpose of burning them. A new printing was made and soon another 18,000 were on their way to England.

The English Church sought to buy up these New Testaments. A friend of Tyndale's named Packington made arrangements to buy them from Tyndale and sell them to the Bishop of London. He reasoned that the Bishop would get them and burn them anyway. This way Tyndale would at least have money to print more. Thousands of copies of Tyndale's New Testament were smuggled into England. Strict laws against reading the Tyndale Bible were issued in England and Bible distributors and independent preachers were persecuted. Still new copies of the New Testament were produced and appeared all over England.

Tyndale began to roam Germany, trying to avoid agents sent to arrest or kill him. He translated several books of the Old Testament.

A secret agent of the Roman Catholic Church, Henry Phillips, pretended to be Tyndale's friend. He made arrangements to go to dinner with Tyndale but in reality he led him to several officers who seized him.

Tyndale was put on trial, convicted and sentenced to death. On Friday, October 6, 1536 he was burned alive. His last words were, "Lord, open the King of England's eyes."

The Old Testament translation was finished by others. Forty editions were published and by AD 1566, 50,000 copies of the New Testament were printed.

Tyndale is remembered as "the Father of the English Bible."

The History of the English Bible

A Rapid Succession of New English Bibles

Nine new English versions of the Bible were released during the next 85 years. The Coverdale Bible was released in 1535 under license granted by Henry the VIII. Coverdale was an evangelical Church of England preacher. He had been Tyndale's friend and proofreader. In 1535 he was asked by the Church of England to make an English translation of the Scriptures. He used the Italia Bible (Old Latin), Luther's German translation, the new Swiss Bible and Tyndale's translation as his basic sources. He was not familiar with either Greek or Hebrew. The Coverdale Bible was largely a reproduction of Tyndale's Bible.

The Matthew's Bible was released in 1537. The primary editor was John Rogers. He became acquainted with William Tyndale in Holland. He produced an edition of the Bible under the name Thomas Matthews. He used Tyndale's New Testament. He took some books of the Old Testament from Tyndale's translation and some from Coverdale's. The King authorized the sale of this new English edition of the Scriptures (probably without realizing that much of it was the same as Tyndale's outlawed translation).

J.H. Merle d' Aubigne described the influence of the Matthew's Bible:

"In many places there were meetings for reading; poor peopled clubbed their savings together and purchased a Bible, and then in some remote corner of the church, they modestly formed a circle, and read the Holy Book between them. A crowd of men, women and young folks, disgusted with the barren pomp of the altars, and with the worship of dumb images, would gather round them to taste the precious promises on the Gospel. God Himself spoke under the arched roofs of those old chapels or time-worn cathedrals, where for generations nothing had been heard but masses and litanies. The people wished, instead of the noisy chants of the priest; to hear the voice of Jesus Christ, of Paul and of John, of Peter and of James. The Christianity of the apostles reappeared in the Church."

John Rogers was eventually burnt at the stake by "Bloody Mary", during her attempt to restore Roman Catholicism in England.

Eleven years after Tyndale's New Testament was publicly burned, one year after he was burned at the stake, his New Testament and parts of his Old Testament were published with the King's license.

The Great Bible was released in 1539. Miles Coverdale was asked by the King of England to prepare another edition of the Bible. He took the Old Testament from the Matthew's Bible and the New Testament from Tyndale's. Both were slightly revised after consulting the work of Erasmus. It was called the Great Bible because of its size. It's pages were 13 ¼ inches by 7 ½ inches. Henry VIII licensed this new Bible, decreed that it be read publicly, ordered every church to have a copy and make it available to be read to the people. The Bibles were chained to the pulpit.

In 1539 The Taverner's Bible was released. Richard Taverner was an Oxford Scholar, a lawyer and a Greek scholar. He had been associated with Tyndale's New Testament and had been persecuted as a result. His translation was based upon the Matthew's Bible and the Latin Vulgate. Only two editions were released because of the popularity of the Great Bible.

The Geneva Bible was released in 1560 (the New Testament in 1557). In 1543 Henry VIII had given into pressure and agreed to limit the English Bible to persons considered "highly-educated" by the Church. Three years later Coverdale's Bible was outlawed and hundreds of Tyndale's and Coverdale's Bibles were publicly burnt. In 1554 Mary became Queen of England and began to persecute all the non-Catholic elements of English religion. Bibles in English were outlawed and hundreds of people were put to death.

The Geneva Bible was edited by William Whittingham, (an Englishman related to John Calvin by marriage). He was aided by many able scholars meeting in Geneva, Switzerland. Many were exiles from England. Members of the translation committee included Miles Coverdale, John Knox. Theodore Beza and John Foxe (author of "Foxe's Book of Martyrs"). They studied Greek and Hebrew manuscripts and revised the Great Bible. It was dedicated to Queen Elizabeth (who had succeeded her sister Mary as Queen). It was the first English translation to omit the Apocrypha. Queen Elizabeth gave consent to its distribution and over 160 editions were released between 1560 and 1644.

The importance of the Geneva Bible has been described this way, "The Scriptures had always been chained to reading stands in churches and libraries. But the Geneva Bible quickly became "the people's Book." It was used at home by the English common folk; and it became the backbone of the newly developing Puritanism, a movement to simplify or "purify" the liturgy, vestments, and government of the Church of England. Some Puritan shopkeepers even kept an open copy of the Geneva Bible on their counters for all to see."

The Bishops Bible was released in 1568. Since the Geneva Bible was being recognized of the Bible of the common man, some of the church leaders felt that the clergy should have its own Bible. A committee of nine bishops was formed to undertake a revision. The Great Bible was compared with some Greek, Hebrew and Latin manuscripts. Many maps, lists and tables were added. This edition was issued in 40 printings from 1568 to 1606. It was the least popular of the English Bibles with the people.

The Unbroken Bible

The Rheims Douay Bible was released in 1609 (the New Testament in 1582). It was produced by professors from a college for English Roman Catholics in France. This was primarily a translation of the Latin Vulgate. The Rheims Douay Bible has been retranslated several times but it has never found acceptance outside of Roman Catholic circles.

The King James Bible

During the reign of Queen Elizabeth (1558-1603) the English church was very divided. The church had three main factions. The Romanists wanted to return to the Roman Catholic church. The Anglo-Catholics wanted to maintain an independent English church but keep many of the doctrines, ceremonies and traditions of the Catholic church. The Puritans wanted to "purify" the church of Catholicism and maintain an evangelical state church.

King James I (1603-1625) did not identify with any of the three groups. He wanted to see all three groups held in check by the best translation of the English Bible possible. King James felt that the Geneva Bible, and especially its marginal notes, favored the Puritans.

A Puritan leader, John Rainolds, approached King James and asked him to authorize a new translation. King James was himself a great linguist and had translated the Psalms and Revelation into English.

Rainolds was President of Corpus Christi College at Oxford. He persuaded King James to sponsor this new translation. Because of this Rainolds is often called, "the Father of the King James Bible".

King James appealed to the English bishops to nominate learned Greek and Hebrew scholars for the translations committee. All of the previous translations had been limited by being the work of an individual or a small number of people. This committee would represent a large number of outstanding scholars. Soon fifty-four scholars had been selected. They would eventually engage the help of at least twenty-one more people.

Tyndale had died to provide the people translation of the Bible in English. Now King James was authorizing one. Truly the Lord had opened the King of England's eyes.

The translators were professional scholars and/or church leaders. Few were married or had families. They were granted leaves by their colleges and churches so that they could be full time translators.

The translators were divided into six teams. Two met in Westminster, England, one to work on the Old Testament, one on the New Testament. Two teams met at Oxford, England, one for each Testament. Two teams met at Cambridge. One worked on the Old Testament, one on the Apocrypha.

The teams met regularly for about six years. John Selden described how they checked their translation work, "The translation in King James' time took an excellent way. That part of the Bible was given to him who was most excellent in such a tongue (as the Apocrypha to Andrew Downes) and then they met together, and one read that translation, the rest holding in their hands some Bible, either of the learned tongues, or French, Italian, Spanish &c. If they found any fault, they spoke; if not, he read on."

An additional team was chosen to review the final work. Two members from each of the three groups were picked. They spent a year carefully checking the entire work.

Dr. Miles Smith reviewed the work for grammar. He placed

the commas, colons, and made the final verse and chapter divisions. Finally Smith to clear they were ready "to deliver God's book unto God's people in a tongue which they understand".

Robert Parker, the "Royal Printer", had exclusive right to print all English editions of the Bible. Miles Smith and Thomas Bilson proofed all the type set by the royal printers. The new translation was so well received that they immediately issued a second edition - both in 1611. These first two editions were designed for use in the church -- they were too large for the home or personal use. People began to beg for copies of the King James Bible. The third edition was printed in a small enough format to be used at home. Soon the King James Bible was being read by firesides all over England. The King James Bible soon became the "book" in England. As the English colonies developed on the east coast of North America, the King James Bible soon became of "the book" there as well.

Russell Kirk describes the influence of the King James Bible in the new world,

> "The book that was to exert a stronger influence than any other in America was not published until 1611. A few years after the first Virginian settlement: the "King James" translation of the Bible, the Authorized Version was prepared by English scholars for King James I. Read from American pulpits and in the great majority of American households during colonial times, the Authorized Version shaped the style, informed the intellect, affected the laws, and decreed the morals of the North American colonies."

There have been many secular testimonies to the importance of the King James Bible. Wendell Bartlett wrote,

> "The King James Bible, is probably the greatest

masterpiece of translation in the world; it has exercised on the thought and the language of English-speaking peoples an influence which cannot be overestimated."

Dr. William Faber wrote,

"It lives on the ear like a music that can never be forgotten, like the sound of church bells, which the convert hardly knows how he can forego. Its felicities often seem to be almost things rather than mere words. It is pert of the national mind and the anchor of national seriousness. The memory of the dead passes into it. The potent traditions of childhood are stereotyped in its verses. The power of all the grief and trials of a man is hidden beneath its words.It is the representative of his best moments; and all that there has been about him of soft, and gentle, and pure, and penitent, and good speaks to him forever out of his English Bible."

H.L. Mencken wrote:

"It is the most beautiful of all the translations of the Bible; indeed, it is probably the most beautiful piece of writing in all the literature of the world. Many attempts have been made to purge it of its errors in obscurities. An English Revised Version was published in 1885 and an American Revised Version in 1901, and since then many learned but misguided men have sought to produce translations that should be mathematically accurate, and in the plain speech of every day. But the Authorized Version has never yielded to any of them, for it is palpably and overwhelmingly better than they are, just as it is better than the Greek New Testament, or the Vulgate, or the Septuagint. Its English is extraordinarily simple, pure, eloquent, and lovely. It is a mine of lordly and incomparable poetry, at once the most stirring and the most touching ever heard of."

Even skeptic Bernard Shaw wrote:

> "In all these instances the Bible means the translation authorized by King James the First... The translation was extraordinarily well done because to the translators what they were translating was not merely a curious collection of ancient books written by different authors in different stages of culture, but the Word of God divinely revealed through His chosen and expressly inspired scribes. In this conviction they carried out their work with boundless reverence and care and achieved a beautifully artistic result. It did not seem possible to them that they could better the original texts; for who could improve on God's own style? And as they could not conceive that divine revelation could conflict with what they believed to be the truths of their religion, they did not hesitate to translate a negative by a positive where such a conflict seemed to arise, as they could hardly trust their own fallible knowledge of ancient Hebrew when I contradicted the very foundations of their faith, nor could they doubt that God would, as they prayed, take care that His message should not suffer corruption at their hands. In this state of exaltation they made a translation so magnificent that to this day the common human Britisher or citizen of the United States of North America accepts and worships it as a single book by a single author, the book being the Book of Books and the author being God."

A Multiplication of New English Translations Based Upon a New Source

In the mid-Nineteenth Century a group of textural scholars and Church of England preachers and college professors began to question the devotion of the previous transcribers and translators. These men believed that the early churches did not value the very words of Scripture. They claimed that the early church scribes freely made changes in the words of the text. Previously rejected manuscripts were found and these scholars claimed that these unusual manuscripts were superior.

Two leaders in this movement were B.F. Westcott and F.J.A. Hort. Westcott and Hort produced a new Greek text heavily influenced by newly appreciated texts. They claimed their work represented a new level of scholarship and accuracy. Their work was refuted by Dean John Burgon. He clearly demonstrated that the texts they relied on were inferior manuscripts that had been set aside because they were corrupt. Preachers, Bible teachers, Church of England clerics and professors were soon divided over which Greek Text to use.

In 1881 the English Revised Version New Testament (from Westcott and Hort's text) was published. It met with little positive response from the general public. The people of England pressured Queen Victoria to reject the suggestion that she declare the Revised Version the new Authorized Version of the English church. Since 1881 over two hundred translations have been made into English based upon Westcott and Hort's text and theories. Gradually their theories gained popularity until they were accepted by even a majority of doctrinal conservatives.

Some of the new translations were popular for a brief period of time. However they all soon faded. Meanwhile the King James Bible remained a consistent best seller year after year.

Many private translations into the English language were made. Cults developed their own translations. Translations were developed to promote modernism (Revised Standard Version, Good News for Modern Man, etc.). Translations were designed to promote specific doctrines (salvation by works - The New International Version). Personal paraphrases were developed

The Unbroken Bible

(The Living Bible).

Only a few people maintained the inspiration of the Greek Received Text and the superiority of the King James Bible. Yet no translation could match the sales of the King James Bible for very long. Doctrinally conservative preachers usually still feel obligated to use the King James Bible in the pulpit.

The 1970s, 1980s and 1990s have seen a revival of faith in the King James Bible. Modern scholars have expanded on the work of John Burgeon and have clearly demonstrated the superiority of the Received Text. Scholarly works refuting the work of Westcott and Hort are available to anyone with an open mind.

The difference in the Greek texts is dramatic. Everett Fowler writes about the differences:

> If the Bible Society's text is assumed to be the nearest to the original text, then we have in the King James Version, translated from the Received Text, 17 whole verses, 145 significant portions of verses, and over 760 other portions of verses, which were not in the original manuscripts and therefore could not be considered as verbally inspired by God. Stated another way, if the Bible Society's text is assumed to be the nearest to the verbally inspired original text, then the Received text has over 2,165 Greek words that were not inspired of God, and does not have over 215 words that were inspired of God. All of these Greek words are words which affect the translation into English. Also on this basis the King James version has over 2,100 words that are not inspired of God, and it does not have over 200 words that were inspired of God."

Many in the evangelical world have rethought their support

of Westcott and Hort and the English translations based upon their work. Perhaps the most dramatic evidence is in the change of position of Dr. Frank Logsdon, Co-Chairman of the New American Standard Bible translation committee:

> "I must, under God, renounce every attachment to the New American Standard Version. I'm afraid I'm in trouble with the Lord... We laid the groundwork; I wrote the format; I helped interview some of the translators; I sat with the translator; I wrote the preface... I'm in trouble; I can't refute these arguments; it's wrong, terribly wrong; it's frighteningly wrong; and what am I going to do about it.
>
> When questions began to reach me at first I was quite offended... I used to laugh with others... However, in attempting to answer, I began to sense that something was not right about the New American Standard Version. I can no longer ignore these criticisms I am hearing and I can't refuse them... The deletions are absolutely frightening... there are so many... Are we so naive that we do not suspect Satanic deception in all of this?
>
> Upon investigation, I wrote my very dear friend, Mr. Lockman, explaining that I was forced to renounce all attachments to the NASB. The product is grievous to my heart and helps to complicate matters in these already troublous times... I don't want anything to do with it."
>
> [T]he finest leaders that we have today... haven't gone into it [the new versions' use of a corrupted Greek text], just as I hadn't gone into it... that's how easily one can be deceived... I'm going to talk to him [Dr. George Sweeting, president of Moody Bible Institute] about these things.

The Unbroken Bible

[Y]ou can say the Authorized Version [KJV] is absolutely correct. How correct? 100% correct!...I believe the Spirit of God led the translators of the Authorized Version."

Conclusion

Throughout English history (and American history is part of English history) great men have dedicated themselves to get "God's book to God's people in a tongue they can understand". Heroes like King Alfred, John Wycliffe, William Tyndale, John Rainolds and hundreds of others whose names we know and thousands whose names we don't know, have struggled to carry out this great task. The King James Bible is the ultimate achievement of this great work of God.

The History of the English Bible

The Unbroken Bible

5

The Real Story of King James

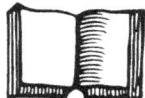

I never with God's grace shall do anything in private which I may not without shame proclaim upon the tops of houses. - King James I, 1603

And there must go much more to the making of a guilty man, than rumor. - Ben Johnson, 1605

USING THE PERSON OF KING JAMES TO ATTACK THE KING JAMES BIBLE

King James was a homosexual... Was a bitter persecutor of our forefathers... King James chose the King James translators, instructed the King James translators, approved and disapproved portions of the translators. . . . How can Baptist preachers believe the King James Version to be without error? King James was

The Unbroken Bible

a homosexual![1] - Baptist evangelist J. H. Melton.

Many critics of the King James Bible are deeply condescending towards the defenders of the King James Bible. This is seen in the statement by James White in his book, *The King James Only Controversy*:

> The KJV Only controversy feeds upon the ignorance among Christians regarding the origin, transmission, and translation of the Bible. Those who have taken the time to study this area are not likely candidates for induction into the KJV Only camp"[2]

But, the truth is that the defenders of the King James are often those who have studied the origin, transmission and translation of the Bible the most. Many books have been published on the issue over the last few years. Often King James Bible defenders are easily able to shatter the shallow attacks on the King James Bible. It is not unusual for those who have just found their pet arguments shattered to retreat to an argument like this, "Well, after all King James was a homosexual you know!"

But was he? Is this just a very historically shallow, unsound repetition of gossip and rumor or is it a historical fact? It must be admitted that many historians report that King James was a homosexual. But what is the evidence for such a charge? If King James was not a homosexual, his memory has been done a great injustice.

The real King James was a very different man than the one described by the critics of the King James Bible.

---

1 Ken Johnson, *A Response to J. H. Melton*, (Lubbock, Tabernacle Baptist Church), p. 14-15.

2 James R. White, *The King James Only Controversy*, (Minneapolis, Bethany House, 1995), introduction p. V and Vi.

The Real Story of King James
A BRIEF BIOGRAPHY OF KING JAMES

James was born in Edinburgh, Scotland, on June 19, 1566. He was the only son of Mary, Queen of Scots. His father, Lord Darnley, was assassinated in an explosion when James was only eight months old. When James was one year old, his mother abdicated the throne of Scotland and James officially became king. She never saw her son again.

James was supervised during his childhood by several Scottish lords. He had several tutors, all evangelical Protestants. He became fluent in Greek, French, and Latin and received classical instruction in all three of these languages as well as English. He was kept fairly isolated until age 14. He developed a great fondness for books. Even as a teenager he was recognized as a serious scholar.

James was slender and of average height. He enjoyed horseback riding and hunting. His thin legs, narrow jaw, and long tongue prompted some to mock his appearance.

In 1589 James was married to Anne, the daughter of Frederick II king of Denmark. They had eight children together. When Queen Elizabeth (his mother's cousin) died, James was next in line for the throne of England. In 1603 he was crowned King of England. He was officially King James VI of Scotland and King James I of England. He quickly ended the English war with Spain and England was to live in peace during his reign.

James survived four assassination attempts, the most famous of which was the Gunpowder Plot of 1605. A Roman Catholic agent, Guy Fawkes, has planted several barrels of gunpowder in the basement of Parliament. He planned to blow up the Parliament building while James was addressing the Parliament. His plot was disclosed and defeated. The English still celebrate the survival of James and the Parliament with a national holiday

The Unbroken Bible

- Guy Fawkes Day.

Even though James had many opponents among the nobility and the clergy, he remained popular among the English people. England experienced both peace and prosperity during his rule.

James was a strong advocate of the doctrine of the divine right of kings. Many Protestants felt that he took this concept much farther in his teaching and in his pronouncements than the Scripture warranted. However, he ruled in a generally kind and benevolent manner rather than as a royal despot. His many enemies were never able to generate any grassroots support among the people of England for their criticism of James.

The English program to colonize the Atlantic seaboard, begun under Queen Elizabeth, was strengthened under the influence of King James. Jamestown, the first enduring English settlement in the new world, was named after King James.

King James' most conspicuous claims to fame were the formation of Great Britain (England, Scotland, Wales, and Ireland under one throne) and the sponsorship of the King James' translation of the Bible.

Even King James' most loyal supporters acknowledged that he was sometimes unwise in his selection of advisors and cabinet ministers. Historian George McCauley wrote: "...he could never tell a good man from a rogue or a wise man from a fool."[3] As a result, he was surrounded by plots and intrigues, especially the last few years of his life.

In 1625 King James passed away peacefully at his country estate in Hertfordshire.

---

3 George McCauley, *History of England*, volume 8, (London, Matthews Co, 1965), p. 72.

THE ORIGINS OF THE ATTACK ON KING JAMES

There is no record of anyone accusing King James of homosexual behavior during his lifetime. If you read most modern historians, you would believe that King James's homosexuality was open and widely recognized but this is far from the truth. There are absolutely no contemporary accounts alleging homosexuality on King James's part though there are contemporary accounts praising him for his moral virtue.

Sir Anthony Weldon was an officer in the royal household of King James. He was knighted by King James in 1617. He was eventually dismissed from the royal court by King James. He vowed to get his revenge against King James.

Welden supported the anti-monarchy forces during the English Civil War. Twenty-five years after the death of King James, (one year after the execution of Charles I, King James's son) Welden made the first accusations of homosexuality against King James. His statements were widely rejected at the time because there were still too many living people who had known King James personally and who dismissed the allegations as ridiculous.

Evangelist Al Lacy describes this attack

> As for the books...James I died in 1625. These people wrote their books after King James had been dead for 350 years. What was their source of proof? A "document" written by a man named Anthony Weldon TWENTY-FIVE YEARS after James had died. Sour grapes was what it was.[4]

---

[4] Al Lacy, *Can I Trust My Bible*, (Littleton, Al Lacy Publications, 1991), p. 156.

The Unbroken Bible

The truth is that Weldon once served in the king's court. The two had a falling out, and James fired him. Weldon swore revenge. If he raised a finger against the king, however, he would be in real trouble. The people of Great Britain loved their king. So Weldon waited until James was long dead, then produced his "Document" claiming the king had been a homosexual. Sorta hard for a fella to defend himself when he's dead, wouldn't you agree? The common decent people of England abhorred homosexuality just like the common decent people of America abhor it today. Yet the British people loved and adored King James (who is on record as a monarch who fought immorality in his domain during his entire reign) and highly respected him.[5]

Disgruntled courtiers and political opponents picked up the allegations against King James and began to use innuendo to hurt his reputation. While not accusing him directly of homosexuality, they tried to create questions about his loyalties to his close friends and associates. These seventeenth century critics seem to fall into two groups. Some had their political and personal ambitions thwarted by King James. Others opposed his policy of uniting Scotland and England into one kingdom. All of these allegations come from people with a strong bias against James and they all were made a long time after his death.

Some historians began to repeat these attacks against King James without investigation. Soon vague allegations, rumor, innuendo and speculations were reported as historical fact. While some historians have sifted through the rumors to get the facts, many just repeated the statements of previous historians without any examination.

In the eighteenth century, the primary reporters of King

---

5 Al Lacy, <u>Can I Trust My Bible</u>, (Littleton, Al Lacy Publications, 1991), p. 156.

James's homosexuality, were those who opposed the union of Great Britain and also Roman Catholics who resented the support that James had given Protestants. In the twentieth century two different groups have clung to the allegations about King James and propagated them in defiance of the facts.

Homosexual activists have been determined to claim King James as one of their own. These are the same activists who claim that Abraham Lincoln, William Shakespeare, the Biblical King David and Jonathan and even Jesus Christ were really homosexuals. Historical facts means nothing to these people. They care only about their political and social agenda. It is a travesty when evangelicals quote their books as credible sources.

The second group which refuses to be persuaded by the facts about King James are those who wish to use King James supposed homosexuality to discredit the King James Bible.

In 1985, Moody Monthly magazine alerted the evangelical world to the allegations that King James was a homosexual. These charges came in an article entitled *The Real King James* by Karen Ann Wojahn. No evidence was provided. The article was accompanied by *The Bible That Bears His Name* by Leslie Keylock. This article was an attack on the King James Bible. Numerous attempts have been made to get Moody Monthly to either document or withdraw the charges made in these articles but neither has been done.

Despite the lack of evidence (and in spite of the evidence to the contrary) some evangelicals are quick to use the baseless accusations against King James to bolster their attacks on the King James Bible. But facts are contrary things! King James never claimed to be a homosexual. He was never accused of being one during his lifetime. No one ever claimed to see James in a homosexual situation. The accusations against him, past and present, stem from bias and not from fact.

The character and record of King James clearly refutes the charges of homosexuality against King James.

CONTEMPORARY REFERENCES TO THE MORAL CHARACTER OF KING JAMES

In 1602, Sir Henry Wotton wrote of King James, "...<u>Among his good qualities none shines more brightly than the chastness of his life</u>, which he has preserved without stain down to the present time contrary to the example of almost all his ancestors..."[6]

Sir Edward Coke, the famous English jurist was a contemporary of King James. He was often a political opponent of King James. Historian Jasper Ridley called Sir Edward the leader of the "lawyers opposition" to the king.[7] He had been appointed by James as the chief justice of the Court of the King's Bench. A number of his judicial rulings went against the king. He considered himself the defender of the English common law against the doctrine of the divine right of kings. James eventually had him dismissed from the English high court.

In his legal commentary, Coke maintained the common law position about homosexuality, "Buggery is a detestable and abominable sin, ...Against the ordinances of the Creator and the order of nature." Coke was no friend of homosexuality and no political ally of the king. Yet in reference to the personal character of King James he wrote "and I knowing the sincerity of his (James's) justice, (for which he is the most renowned king in the Christian world)..."[8]

---

[6] Steven A. Coston Sr., *King James Unjustly Accused,* (St. Petersburg, Koingswort, 1996), p. 39.

[7] Jasper Ridley, *The History of England*, Barrnes -- (New York, Barnes & Noble, 1981), p. 171.

[8] Steven A. Coston Sr., *King James Unjustly Accused,* (St. Petersburg,

Sir Arthur Wilson was a historian during the time of James. He opposed James and the concept of the monarchy. He wrote harshly about James in some areas. However, in his Dictionary of National Biography, he has these references to King James. He states that James' life was "decidedly pure" and "his own life was pure." He also stated that James did not "come into conflict with the Presbyterian clergy" in the area of "morality." [9] The Presbyterian preachers had opposed his mother, Mary Queen of Scots, on the grounds of her adulteries. They found no reason to oppose King James on moral grounds.

Bishop Godfrey Goodman lived during the time of King James. He publically preached against moral sins. He opposed King James and was denied opportunities for advancement by King James. James suspected him of sympathy towards Roman Catholicism. However, when Anthony Welden began to question James' morality, Bishop Goodman refuted him. According to English historian Charles Williams, Goodman wrote, "the king himself was a very chaste man."[10]

It is a rare political leader whose morality and virtue is praised even by his contemporary opponents.

Dr. Miles Smith was chosen by the King James' translators to write the preface to the King James Bible, "The Translators to the Readers." In this preface he says very complimentary things about King James. Some have suggested that this was simply the custom of the times and others have questioned the sincerity of the translators because of these comments. In reality these were devout Bible believing men who were not afraid to disagree

---

Koingswort, 1996), p.232.

9 IBID, p. 284.

10 Charles Williams, *James I*. (London, Morrison & Gibbs Limited, 1945), p. 296.

with the king. Many of them spoke publicly against King James' position on the divine right of kings. Had there been any reason to believe that he was a homosexual, they would have openly condemned him for it. Yet their estimate of his spiritual character and moral leadership is reflected in statements such as this one from the preface to the King James Bible:

> Great and manifold were the blessings, most dread sovereign which Almighty God, the Father of all mercies, bestowed upon us the people of England, when he first sent your Majesty's Royal Person to rule and reign over us." The preface also praises King James for "maintaining the truth of Christ, and propagating it far and near is that which hath so bound and firmly knit the hearts of all your majesty's loyal and religious people unto you, that your very name is precious among them. Their eye doth behold you with comfort, and they bless you in their hearts, as that sanctified Person, who, under God is the immediate author of their true happiness.

The Puritans were not frightened, helpless preachers who were scared into praising a wicked monarch. When James' son, Charles I, became king, the Puritans thundered against his perceived immoralities like John the Baptist against Herod. Yet they had nothing but praise for King James' moral and spiritual character.

Not all historians have blindly repeated the slander against King James. Isaac Disraeli (1863) wrote:

> Perhaps no sovereign has suffered more by that art, which is described by an old Irish proverb of killing a man by lies. "the surmises and the insinuations of one party, dissatisfied with the established government… the misconceptions of more modern writers…And the anonymous libels…vilify the Stuarts. <u>These cannot</u>

be treasured as authorities of history." Much can be substantiated in favor of the domestic affections and habits of this pacific monarch: and those who are more intimately acquainted with the secret history of the times will perceive how erroneously the personal character of this sovereign is exhibited in our popular historians, and often even among the few who, with better information, have re-echoed their preconceived opinions.[11]

In 1891, F. A. Inderwick wrote (Side Lights on the Stuarts) about King James:

> I think only justice to say, that much of scurrilous abuse to which he has been subjected appears to be without warrant, and that he was personally a man of good moral character, a quality which he was probably much indebted to the strict and careful training he received from his Presbyterian tutors…[12]

Historian Robert Chambers (1830) published two volumes on the life of King James. Chambers calls him "greatly loved and greeted", and "very much beloved by his people." He also calls him a "monarch whose character was good." He also says that his "conduct was every thing that could be expected of a good Christian."[13]

Historian Samuel Rawson Gardiner wrote of King James, "His own life was virtuous and upright."[14]

---

[11] Steven A. Coston Sr., *King James Unjustly Accused*, (St. Petersburg, Koingswort, 1996), p. 301-302.

[12] IBID, p. 303.

[13] IBID, p. 307-312.

[14] Samuel Rawson Gardiner, *Epochs of Modern History*, (London, Matthews, 1928), p. 24-25.

KING JAMES' OWN STATEMENTS ON HOMOSEXUALITY

King James' book <u>Basilicon Doron</u> (the Kingly Gift) was written in 1599. It contained instructions to his son about how to properly carry out the responsibilities of the king. Included among his instructions are this statement: "<u>there are some horrible crimes that ye are bound in conscience never to forgive: such as witchcraft, willful murder, incest, and sodomy...</u>"[15]

In July of 1610 James was asked to pardon a number of criminals. He did pardon several on the list but refused to pardon those convicted of sodomy. He advised his son to stay away from "effeminate ones." James repeatedly referred to homosexuality as the "horrible crime!" These are indeed strange statements from someone given to homosexuality. James routinely listed homosexuality with witchcraft and murder (just as the Bible does).

The King James Version translation of the Bible, which was authorized by King James, does not in any way weaken the Biblical statements about homosexuality. Some modern English translations like the RSV and the NIV weaken or delete Biblical statements condemning homosexuality. The King James Bible is clear in reflecting the Bibles' strong statements condemning homosexuality.

KING JAMES' MARRIAGE AND MORAL TEACHING ABOUT MARRIAGE

King James was married to Anne of Denmark in 1589. They remained married until her death in 1619. King James modern critics say that this means nothing since homosexual rulers have

---

[15] Steven A. Coston Sr., *King James Unjustly Accused*, (St. Petersburg, Koingswort, 1996), p. 48.

often maintained wives for public appearances sake.

However, King James spent much time with his wife (more than most monarchs), was openly affectionate to her in public and wrote her many love poems and sonnets. He greatly mourned her passing. <u>More significantly James and Anne had eight children together</u>.

The unmarried Puritan preacher John Rainolds questioned the use of the phrase "with my body I thee worship" in the standard English wedding ceremony. King James openly teased him about this. He said, "Many a man speaks of Robin Hood who never shot his bow; if you had a good wife yourself, you would think that all the honor and worship you could do her would be well bestowed. He then spoke of his queen as "our dearest bedfellow."[16]

In 1603 James wrote the following to Anne:

> ...I thank God I carry that love and respect unto you which, by the law of God and nature, I ought to do to my wife and mother of my children...For the respect of your honorable earth and descent I married you; but the love and respect I now bear you for that ye are my married wife and so partaker of my honour, as of all my other fortunes...Where ye were a king's or cook's daughter ye must be all alike to me being one my wife...[17]

D. H. Wilson wrote the following about King James's love poems to his wife:

---

[16] Gustavus S. Paine, *The Men Behind the King James Version*, (Grand Rapids, Baker Book House, 1959), p. 4.

[17] Steven A. Coston Sr., *King James Unjustly Accused*, (St. Petersburg, Koingswort, 1996), p. 30.

He remained infatuated with his bride, whose praises he sang in sonnets and in other verse. Her beauty, he wrote, has caused his love, 'Long smoldering as fire hidden among coals, to burst into sudden blaze.' She inspires his verse, and her approbation spurs him to preserve, though government brings stormy cares. But she is a sweet physician who can soothe and cure his ills.[18]

In fact, James did something almost unique for a royal monarch. He taught that the king should be a moral person, faithful to his wife and should set a moral example for his people. It was common for kings to have a number of mistresses. In France, the king's mistress was considered an official member of the royal court. <u>In fact, the lack of mistresses in King James's Court is often used as proof that he was a homosexual. However, a lack of mistresses is also a sign of a godly man leading a clean moral life.</u>

James further writes:

> Marriage is one of the greatest actions that a man does all his time…When you are married, keep inviolably your promise made to God in your marriage, which all stands in doing of one thing. And abstaining from another, to treat her in all things as your wife and the half of yourself, and to make your body (which then is no more yours but property hers) common with none other. <u>I trust I need not to insist there to dissuade you from filthy vice of adultery, remember only what solemn promise you made to God at your marriage.</u>" "And for your behavior to your wife, the Scripture can best give you counsel therein. Treat her as your own flesh, command her as her lord, cherish her as your helper, rule her as your pupil, please her in all things reasonable, but teach her not to be curious in things that belong not to her. You are the head,

---

18 IBID, p. 41.

she is your body, it is your office to command and hers to obey, but yet with such a sweet harmony as she should be as ready to obey as you to command, as willing to follow as you to go before, your love being wholly knit unto her, and all her affections lovingly bent to follow your will.[19]

James repeatedly taught the importance of morality and marriage. James wrote in <u>*Basilicon Doron*</u>:

> But the principal blessing that you can get of good company will stand, in your marrying of a godly and virtuous wife...being flesh of your flesh and bone of your bone...<u>Marriage is the greatest earthly felicity</u>... without the blessing of God you cannot look for a happy marriage.[20]

James instructed his son:

> <u>Keep your body clean and unpolluted while you give it to your wife whom to only it belongs for how can you justly crave to be joined with a Virgin if your body be polluted?</u> Why should the one half be clean, and the other defiled? And suppose I know, fornication is thought but a venial sin by the most part of the world, yet remember well what I said to you in my first book regarding conscience, and count every sin and breach of God's law, not according as the vain world esteems of it, but as God judge and maker of the law accounts of the same: hear God commanding by the mouth of Paul to abstain from fornication, declaring that the fornicator shall not inherit the kingdom of heaven, and by the mouth of John reckoning out fornication among other grievous sins that declares the commiters among dogs

---

19 IBID, p. 45.

20 IBID, p. 43.

and swine.

James notes the end thereof is a "man give over to his own filthy affections."[21]

Because of King James' strong moral teaching and personal example, Disraeli wrote: "James had formed the most elevated conception of the virtues and duties of a monarch."[22] Few English monarchs used the moral authority of the throne to teach morality and demonstrate it by example. Those who did, like King James and Queen Victoria, generated great resentment from those who were convicted by their moral teachings. In both cases, after their death, their enemies attacked them with vicious moral slanders. The real King James was an outstanding moral example and a clear moral teacher. In neither case was there any evidence to back up the accusations against these godly monarchs.

King James pointed out how many civil wars were started by the illegitimate sons of kings. He pointed out how many innocent lives could have been saved if kings had been moral people.

MISUNDERSTOOD CUSTOMS OF THE TIME

King James' critics ask: isn't it true that King James publicly kissed men on the cheek and called men affectionate names like darling and sweetheart? Didn't men routinely sleep at night in his bed? Didn't King James often lean on male members of the royal household? These allegations are true. Similar evidence is also used by modern homosexual activists to assert that William Shakespeare (a contemporary of King James) was a homosexual. But this is all a misreading of the customs of the time.

---

21 IBID, p. 44.

22 IBID, p. 54.

Assassination of royalty were a common event and it was a customary thing for kings to have bodyguards sleep in their bed. No one accuses the promiscuous, womanizer, Henry VIII of being anything but a heterosexual. Yet he routinely slept with bodyguards in the royal bed. King James survived two kidnappings and four violent attempts on his life. Such experiences did nothing to cause King James to break with the normal procedure of always keeping his bodyguards close at hand. In sharing his bed with royal bodyguards, King James was only following the normal practice of the royalty of his time.

Terms of affection like "sweetheart" and "darling" were normal terms used between men in the seventeenth century in England. In Psalm 22:20, God the Father calls Christ the Son "My Darling." He does so again in Psalm 35:17. In the 1990's, African-American women routinely called each other "girlfriend." This is not a homosexual term but a normal expression of the time. Anyone who presents the use of terms like "sweetheart" and "darling" as proof of homosexuality in seventeenth century England is a very shallow historian (or has a very vulgar mind). King James (or for that matter William Shakespeare) does not deserve such treatment.

Men kissing men as a form of greeting was a common innocent custom in seventeenth century England (just as it is in twentieth century France).

Erasmus wrote of the English:

> Wherever you come, you are received with a kiss by all; when you take your leave, you are dismissed with kisses: you return, kisses are repeated, They come to visit you, kisses again: they leave you, you kiss them all round. Should they meet you anywhere kisses in abundance: in

fine, wherever you move, there is nothing but kisses.[23]

Before evil minded men are quick to present this as proof of homosexuality, perhaps they should remember that this was also a common custom in Bible times: *"Greet ye one another with a holy kiss."* I Corinthians 16:20 (see also Luke 7:45, Romans 16:16, II Corinthians 13:12, I Thessalonians 5:26, I Peter 5:14, Acts 20:37).

Because of the weakness of his legs James often leaned on members of the royal staff as he was dealing with official business. Such a position is not unusual for a king (II Kings 7:2,17). John leaned on Jesus (John 13:23, 21:20). Homosexual activists try to claim this as proof of homosexuality on the part of Jesus but Bible believers are quick to see through such foolishness, (Titus 1:15).

Anyone interested in the truth would be willing to understand King James's behavior in the light of the customs of the day.

WAS KING JAMES A SAVED MAN?

James was around the preaching of the gospel and the teaching of evangelical theology from his early childhood. His coronation sermon was delivered by Reformation leader John Knox. Puritan theologian George Buchanan was one of James early tutors and later dedicated a doctrines textbook to him.

Historian Robert Chambers described James' Biblical knowledge this way, "He was deeply read in Scripture; he could quote its texts with great facility; knew it even with philological exactness."[24] James wrote to a friend and said, "Praying God that as you are regenerated and born in him anew, so you may

---

23 IBID, p. 104-105.

24 IBID, p. 311.

rise to him and be sanctified in him forever."[25] In his writings James often refers to salvation as a free gift, salvation by faith and regeneration. He refers to one day receiving "white garments washen in the blood of the lamb."

In only one area does James ever seem to differ doctrinally with his Scottish Presbyterian tutors - the doctrine of civil government.

James was trained by evangelical Christians, claimed to be an evangelical Christian, wrote about evangelical doctrine and was accepted as a saved man by the born again Christians of his time. Nothing documented in his life gives anyone reason to question his salvation. In fact the real King James showed an interest in morality and holiness that is almost unique among the royalty of the period. James wrote "Holiness being the first and most requisite quality of a Christian (as proceeding from true fear and knowledge of God)."[26]

There is no legitimate reason to question James's salvation. The real King James was a professing Christian with a good testimony.

KING JAMES' ROLE IN SPONSORING THE KING JAMES TRANSLATION

From January 14-18, 1604 A.D., the leaders of the church of England met at Hampton Court in London. This meeting was called by King James. The Church of England was divided into three main factions. The Anglo-Catholic faction wanted to keep all the trappings and much of the doctrine of Roman Catholicism without acknowledging the authority of the Pope. The Protestant fraction wanted the Church of England to be a

---

25 IBID, p. 300.

26 IBID, p. 55.

state Protestant Church like the Lutheran Church in Germany and the Reformed Church in Switzerland.

The Puritans were the most thoroughly evangelical and Biblically oriented of the three groups. They wanted a complete break with Catholicism and a greater degree of independence for local churches.

The three factions were at considerable odds with each other. King James attempted to moderate between the different factions. John Rainolds, representing the Puritans, made a formal request that King James sponsor a new English translation. The Bishop of London opposed this suggestion but John Rainolds eventually persuaded King James to give his blessing! Because of this Rainolds is remembered as the Father of the King James Bible.[27]

<u>King James became the first earthly monarch to successfully sponsor and encourage the distribution of the entire Word of God in the daily language of his people</u>. (King Alfred had made an attempt to get part of the Scripture in the language of the people of England centuries earlier).

William Tyndale, the Father of the English Bible had been used of God to bring an early translation of the Bible in English to the English people. For this crime he was declared to be a heretic and was burned at the stake. His last words were "Lord open the King of England's eyes." Now a born again English king was sponsoring an English Bible, produced openly on English soil for English churches and English Christians.

King James appointed 54 learned men to make "one more exact translation of the Bible." Later others would be invited to join them. King James encouraged financial gifts to this project and set the example by agreeing to underwrite the salary of

---

[27] S. Paine, *The Men Behind the King James Version*, p. 3.

several of the translators himself.

Even though the official name for this translation would be the Authorized Version, it was soon known as the King James Bible. It was uniquely made possible and promoted by the King of England - King James. Layman now had no fear of owning their own Bible - it was sponsored by the King for them. God had indeed opened the King of England's eyes!

THE LITERARY ACCOMPLISHMENTS AND SCHOLARSHIP OF KING JAMES

King James was fluent in Greek, Latin and French. He wrote a number of books and pamphlets on a wide variety of subjects. In his book *Great Britain's Solomon*, Maurice Lee, Jr. wrote:

> It would be difficult to imagine a more absorbing companion than this intelligent, learned, witty Scot, an author who wrote on subjects as diverse as theology, tobacco, witchcraft and the theory and practice of kingship and who was a poet to boot. And a king - a king almost from birth in his native Scotland, for forty of his forty-nine years and of England and Ireland for twenty-two. And be it said at once a successful king.[28]

King James did his own private translation of Psalms. He also wrote a commentary on the book of Revelation and a series of devotionals on the Lord's Prayer.

Tobacco use began in England during the time of King James. Tobacco was being introduced from England's new American colonies. King James wrote a small book about tobacco and condemned both the smoking and chewing of tobacco as disgusting habits. He wrote that "...a smoker and a non-smoker

---

28 Maurice Lee Jr., *Great Britain's Solomon*, (Chicago University of Illinois Press, 1990), p. 41.

cannot be equally free in the same room."

James wrote a book entitled *Demonology*. This book enraged the witches of England because it attributed their supernatural power to demon possession. They swore their eternal hatred of James.

James wrote often about moral matters including homosexuality. There is absolutely nothing in his writings to give evidence to the moral charges against King James and there is much to refute them.

King James wrote more books than any royal monarch of any nation. As a result he is the most often quoted royal monarch of all time. The real King James was a respected scholar and an influential author.

KING JAMES' POLITICAL ACCOMPLISHMENTS

King James was the first British monarch to bear the title "sacred majesty."[29]

King James united Scotland, England, Wales, and Ireland under one royal throne. This created the United Kingdom. How different the world might have been if the United Kingdom had not had the strength to resist first the German fascists and then the Russian communists in the twentieth century.

The leadership of King James was essential in planting an enduring English presence in the Western Hemisphere. These humble beginnings would lead to the foundation of the United States of America. Again, how different the world would have been in the twentieth century had the United States not been Great Britain's indispensable partner in resisting both fascism and communism in the twentieth century.

---

29 Coston, *King James Unjustly Accused*, p. 79.

The Real Story of King James

Certainly all the credit cannot be given to King James for the strength and development of the United Kingdom and the United States but he played an important and positive role in the history of each.

One of James contemporaries described his rule this way: "... for he lived in peace, died in peace and left all his kingdoms in a peaceable condition."

James is also credited with ending torture as a part of the English legal system. He also replaced burning at the stake as a means of execution.

When James became king it was a common thing for Baptists (among others) to be executed by the state for being religious nonconformists. This continued through the early years of the reign of King James but he put an end to this policy in 1612. He wrote, "I will never allow in my conscience that the blood of any man shall be shed for diversity of opinions in religion."[30]

The peace and prosperity enjoyed by England during James' rule would be a credit to any civil ruler.

Upon his death in 1625 James was compared (in his funeral sermon) to King Solomon.

> King Solomon is said to be *Brigentus Corm Matre Sua,* the only son of his mother, Proverbs 4:3. So was King James. Solomon had a complexion white and ruddy, Song of Solomon 5:10. So was King James. Solomon was an infant king, *Pver Parvulus*, a little child, I Chronicles 22:5 - So was King James, a King at the age of 13 months. Solomon began his reign in the life of his predecessor, I Kings 1:32, so by the force and compulsion of the state

---

30   Paine, The Men Behind the King James Version, p. 5.

(Scotland) did our late sovereign King James. Solomon was twice crowned and anointed a King. I Chronicles 29:22 - so was King James. Solomon's minority was rough, through the quarrels of the former sovereign; so was that of King James. Solomon learned above all the princes of the East, I Kings 4:20 - so was King James. Above all the princes of the universal world. Solomon was a writer in prose and verse, I Kings 4:32 - so in a very pure and exquisite manner was our sweet sovereign King James. Solomon was the greatest patron we ever read to church and churchman and yet no greater (let the house of Aaron now confess then King James). Solomon was honored with ambassadors from all Kings of the earth, I Kings 4 - And so you know was King James...Solomon died in peace, when he had lived about 60 years and so you know did King James.[31]

Sir Fernando Gorges, one of the founders of Jamestown, also compared James to Solomon.

This great monarch gloriously ascending his throne (1603) being born to greatness above his ancestors to whom all submitted as to another Solomon for wisdom and justice.[32]

KING JAMES -- UNJUSTLY ACCUSED

Slightly over half of the information in this chapter comes from one source - the book *King James the VI of Scotland and The I of England Unjustly Accused*. This book was written by Stephen Coston Sr. and published in 1996. This book does a masterful job of refuting the moral accusations against King James. Coston's work is unanswerable.

---

[31] Coston, *King James Unjustly Accused*, p. 56.

[32] IBID, p. 22.

CONCLUSION

King James spoke eloquently of the role of the King as a moral example:

> But it is not enough to be a good king, by the thralldom of good laws will execute to govern his people, <u>if he joins not therewith his virtuous life in his own person and in the person of his court and company, by his good example alluring his subjects to the love of virtue, and hatred of, vice…</u>[33]

King James believed his servant John Gibb had lost some important papers. In his anger he kicked him. Later he found out that Gibb had not lost them. In a display of humility, almost unheard of for a royal monarch, he knelt before Gibb and begged his forgiveness.[34]

As historian Steven Coston Sr. says "James was, no matter what tales some may tell, a virtuous man of good intentions, who did the best he could as God gave him strength."[35]

---

33 IBID, p. 52.

34 Lee, *Great Britain's Solomon*, p. 32.

35 Coston, *King James Unjustly Accused*, p. 24.

The Unbroken Bible

PART THREE

The Unbroken ACCURACY

The Accuracy of Biblical English
In Defense of 1 John 5:7
In Defense of Mark 16:9-20
In Defense of Acts 12:4

The Unbroken Bible

6

The Accuracy of Biblical English

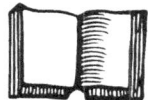

Seeing that we have such hope, we use great plainness of speech. - II Corinthians 3:12

My son, if thou wilt receive my words, and hide my commandments with thee; So that thou incline thine ear unto wisdom, and apply thine heart to understanding; Yea, if thou criest after knowledge, and liftest up thy voice for understanding; If thou seekest her as silver, and searchest for her as for hid treasures; Then shalt thou understand the fear of the Lord, and find the knowledge of God. - Proverbs 2:1-5

Next to Christianity itself the version of 1611 is the greatest book which a kind Providence has bestowed upon the human race. - Philip Schaff [1]

---

1 Theodore Letis, The Majority Text (Institute for Biblical Textual Studies, Grand Rapids, 1987) p. 98.

THE IMPORTANCE OF THE ENGLISH LANGUAGE IN THE WORLD TODAY

English is spoken and understood by over one billion people (even though it is the mother tongue of only 300,000,000). Only Chinese is spoken by more people. English has become the world's language of diplomacy, communication, trade, and entertainment.

English is a polyglot language (sometimes called a mongrel language); and largely because of this it has the richest vocabulary of any language in the world. Eighty percent of its vocabulary comes from words "borrowed" from other languages. Ralph Waldo Emerson wrote "The English language is the sea which receives tributaries from every region under heaven."[2]

There are over one million words common to the English language. By comparison German has 185,000 words and French 100,000.

English has become the language of trade and diplomacy because so many people speak English as a second language. Violence broke out all over India after the assassination of the prime minister, Mrs. Indira Gandhi. When her son, Rajiv Gandhi, went on television to appeal for an end to the violence, he did not use any of the Indian dialects. He spoken English. More Indians know English than know any single Indian dialect. Travelers can communicate in English in countries as widespread as India, Nigeria, and Japan.

English has become the world's second language through several means. Christian missionaries and early English colonists spread English all over the world. The entire world is anxious to

---
2 Robert McCrum, The Story of English, (Viking Books, New York, 1986) p. 11.

trade with both England and the United States. American and British radio programs, T.V. programs, and movies have spread around the world and are seen in almost every country.

THE DEVELOPMENT OF STANDARD ENGLISH

Standard English (the accepted usage of English words) was formed as various peoples intermingled in the development of the British Isles.

The Celtics were the first conquerors of England. Their Germanic root language merged with the language of the original inhabitants. Later, Roman legions brought Latin which was merged into the Celtic language.

Anglo-Saxon invaders brought their Germanic languages to the British Isles. They picked up enough Celtic and Latin words to create a new language referred to as English. Viking raiders would contribute many new words to this already polyglot language.

The Normans conquered the British Isles next. Their language was a poly-glot of various Viking dialects and French. The influence of their language would transform Old English into Middle English.

Words from Latin and Greek literature continued to be added to the English language. The language was gradually changed into modern English.

Some have suggested that this unusual polyglot language (formed from so many other languages of the world), so uniquely rich and vocabulary, is a providential language raised up as a special vehicle for the work of spreading the Word of God.

English became standardized during the reigns of Queen

Elizabeth and King James (1558 to 1625). Many great English authors (Shakespeare and Spenser, for example) contributed to the standardization.

THE CONCEPT OF BIBLICAL ENGLISH

One of the most frequently heard criticisms of the King James Bible is that it is based upon Elizabethan (1611) English, and thus it is out of date. However, even just a little bit of research would demonstrate how unscholarly and unsound that statement is.

English literature is flowing with material from this period - the writings of Shakespeare, Samuel Johnson and the many scholarly works of King James himself for example. These are all dramatically different in style and prose than the King James Bible. There are many sermons and writings available from the men who translated the King James Bible, and not one of them used a style like that of the King James Bible. This is made clear when you compare of the style of the Translators preface with the translation itself.

Bible scholar Edward Hills explains the distinctiveness of the language of the King James Bible this way:

> ...the English of the King James Version is not the English of the early seventeenth century. To be exact, it is not a type of English that was ever spoken anywhere. It is Biblical English which was not used on ordinary occasions even by the translators who produced the King James Version....Even in their use of thee and thou the translators were not following seventeenth century English usage but Biblical usage, for at the time these translators were doing their works these singular forms had already been replaced by the plural you in polite

conversations.³

A.T. Robertson makes the same point when he says:

> No one today speaks the English of the Authorized Version or ever did for that matter for though like Shakespeare it is the pure Anglo-Saxon yet unlike Shakespeare it reproduces to a remarkable extent the spirit and language of the Bible.⁴

O.T. Allis also stresses this truth when he says:

> It is quite obvious that the AV did not attempt to make the usage of the Hebrew and Greek conform to the usage of the Elizabethan or early Jacobean period it simply followed the biblical usage, despite the fact that for some three hundred years the trend had been increasingly away from it.⁵

Much of the King James Bible was not easy for the people of 1611 to understand That is because the translators were not interested in an easy translation they were interested in an accurate one. The translators stated their purpose this way "that out of the Original Sacred Tongues, together with comparing of the labors both in our own, and other foreign languages of many worthy men who went before, THERE SHOULD BE ONE MORE EXACT TRANSLATION OF THE HOLY SCRIPTURES INTO THE ENGLISH TONGUE." (Emphasis added)

These translators were not trying to create an "easy read";

---

3 Edward F. Hills, The King James Version Defended (Christian Research Press, Des Moines, 1956) p. 218.

4 A.T. Robertson, A Grammar of the Greek New Testament. (Broadman Press, Nashville, 1934) p. 56.

5 J.P. Thackway, Archaic or Accurate (the Bible League, Wiltshire) p. 45.

they were not looking for a marketing technique. They were not trying to put the Scriptures in the "language of their day"; they were trying to honestly translate the Word of God.

King James Bible critics are fond of referring to the use of thee and thou as proof that the King James Bible is trapped in 1611. In reality, thee's and thou's are the language of Old Testament Hebrew and New Testament Greek. In Hebrew and Greek, thee, thou, and thy are singular words; and ye and you are plural words. To change all these words to the generic English "you" is to miss the full meaning of the words in the Biblical text. The reader who can't cope with thee and thou had better be prepared to settle for less accurate Bible than the King James.

Almost all modern translations are based upon the "dynamic equivalence" method of translation. The translators give you the meaning that they think the words in the text communicate. The translator thus becomes a bridge between the reader and the Scripture. The translation is only as accurate as the honesty, objectivity, and scholarship of the translators allow. The translators become the priests for the reader. The King James Bible translators reproduced the Hebrew and Greek Scriptures into English. Thus the doctrine of the priesthood of each believer is maintained as each individual believer can study the Scripture directly. This literal approach to Bible translation stems from the doctrine of word-for-word literal Bible inspiration that the King James translators held to.

The truths of the Scripture are not always simple, consequently an accurate translation does not always contain simple words and easy to understand concepts. The truths of the Bible are universal, and they often cannot be captured and the unique expressions of an individual era. As a result, the translators of the King James Bible avoided the unique speech patterns of Elizabethan English and used a basic historic English that would be simple, timeless, and beautiful.

The Accuracy of Biblical English

By carefully choosing the English words which accurately rendered the Hebrew and Greek words of the Scripture, the King James translators created an enduring "Biblical English" which has survived all attempts to alter and replace it.

The KJV translators were aware that the Tyndale Bible was in the hearts and minds of the English people. The Geneva and Matthews Bibles and greatly reproduced the wording of the Tyndale Bible. Many words that Tyndale used had already fallen out of use in everyday English. The people remained familiar with these words only through their use of the Bible. The KJV translators stayed with these words, maintaining the accuracy of Scripture and creating a distinct category of the English language--Biblical English.

David Daiches, has written about the influence of previous English translations in the development of Biblical English:

> The style of the Authorized Version was in some degree archaic by now (at the time of its publishing), and the revisors were thus deliberately perpetuating a biblical style which was something apart from contemporary English prose, a style that had been forged in almost a century's experimentation. It was the culmination of the successive versions of which Tyndale's was the first. And though archaic in its time, it had a great influence on the rhythms and the vocabulary of the later English prose, especially in the seventeenth and nineteenth centuries.[6]

These Biblical scholars showed themselves much wiser than the current producers of "modern translations". I remember hearing about the new "Living Bible" during my high school days. It was supposed to be "cool", "hip", and a "with it" translation.

---

6 David Daiches, A Critical History of English Literature (Ronald Press, New York, Vol. 1) p. 470-471.

The Unbroken Bible

But its "modern figures of speech" are already as out of date as the Mod Squad and Happy Days. Biblical English was effective then, and it still is now.

Edward F. Hills asks how we can dare put the Bible in "the language of today":

> What is the language of today? The language of 1881 is not the language of today nor the language of 1901, nor even the language of 1921. In none of these languages, we are told. can we communicate with today's youth. There are even some who feel that the best way to translate the Bible into the language of today is to convert it into "folk songs." Accordingly, in many contemporary youth conferences and even worship services, there is little or no Bible reading but only crude kind of vocal music accompanied by vigorous piano and strumming guitars. But in contrast to these absurdities the language of the King James Version is enduring diction which will remain as long as the English language remains, in other words, throughout the foreseeable future.[7]

By accurately translating the Bible, the King James translators created Biblical English--the unique expressions, terms, and idioms that communicate God's truth to the English speaking world. By refusing to cater to the trends of the day, by refusing to subject their works to a marketing strategy, by prizing accuracy over popularity, they avoided the mistakes that poison the efforts of modern English translators.

Rousas J. Rushdoony sums up the issue well when he says:

> The issue is not that the Bible should speak everyday language, for this involves debasement, but that it should be understandable, and have, all arguments to

---
7 Hills, p. 219.

the contrary not withstanding that King James speaks a language which, while sometimes difficult because the matter itself is so, is the more often simple, clean cut and beautiful.[8]

A GUIDE TO THE SIGNIFICANCE OF BIBLICAL ENGLISH TERMS

Thou - designates the subject of a verb.

Thee - designates the object of a verb.

Ye - designates the subject of a verb.

You - designates the object of the verb.

T - a personal pronoun beginning with T is a singular pronoun, e.g. Thou, Thy, Thee, Thine.

Y - a personal pronoun beginning with a Y is a plural pronoun, e.g. Ye, You, Yours.

Est - indicates the second person singular (the one spoken to).

Eth - indicates the third person singular (the one spoken about).

Shall - refers to the first person with future tense.

Will - refers to the second or third person in the future.

All these shades of meaning are in the original Greek and Hebrew words. To replace these terms with a generic you or a generic will is to produce a translation with less meaning than

---

[8] The Journal of Christian Reconstruction, 1989, p 12-13.

the King James.

Famed scholar, J. Gresham Machen clearly believed that "thee" and "thou" were the only way to translate the Bible correctly and included this information in his Greek grammar for beginners.

D. A. Waite points out how important all this is to Biblical accuracy:

> The King James Bible, in their use of the pronouns, thee, thy, thyself, thou, the, ye, you, your, and yourselves, have rendered accuracy a great service. All the pronouns beginning with the letter "T" are singular. All the pronouns beginning with the letter "Y," are plural. In this way, the English reader can pick up the King James Bible, and unlike any of the other modern versions, he can tell immediately whether the second person pronoun is singular or plural.. you don't need to know Greek or Hebrew to find the answer.[9]

These terms are not archaic English just because most modern readers don't understand them. They are an accurate translation of the Hebrew and Greek.

Oswald T. Allis correctly states:

> It is a well-known fact that in contemporary English the forms THOU, THY, THINE have almost disappeared from secular use. They are largely restricted to the language of religious devotion, in which they are constantly employed, and which is largely formed by, and owes its peculiarities to, the Authorized Version. Consequently, it is often asserted

---

9 D.A. Waite, Defending the King James Bible, (Bible for Today Press, Collingwood, 1992) p. 255-256.

or assumed that the usage of the AV represents the speech of 300 years ago, and that now, three centuries later, it should be changed to accord with contemporary usage. But this is not at all a correct statement of the problem. The important factor is this: THE USAGE OF THE AV IS NOT THE ORDINARY USAGE OF THE EARLY SEVENTEENTH CENTURY. IT IS THE BIBLICAL USAGE BASED ON THE STYLE OF THE HEBREW AND THE GREEK SCRIPTURES.[10]

THE ACCURACY OF BIBLICAL ENGLISH IN REFERENCE TO GOD

Some have wanted to correct what they felt was improper English grammar in the Bible. However, sometimes God chooses to express Himself in ways that violate all the human rules of grammar, Greek, English, and Hebrew.

In referring to Himself, God often mixes singular, plural, and compound singular words. This, of course, would be grammatical nonsense if such terms were used in this way in reference to anyone but God. But God is greater than human rules of grammar. The Biblical doctrine of the Trinity is beyond human rules of grammar.

The very word translated God in the English Bible is the plural Hebrew word Elohim. Yet, it is properly translated (when referring to Jehovah) as the singular word God. God is simply three but one (I John 5:7). The classic verse on the nature of God, "Hear, O Israel: the LORD our God is One LORD" mixes the plural word God with the singular word LORD and the compound singular word (in the Hebrew one). This is grammatical nonsense unless you are talking about the Trinity.

---

10 Thackway, p. 37

Singular and plural words are also mixed in reference to God in Ezra 1:3, Daniel 5:26, Revelation 16:5, and every time the phrase Lord God is used. To "straighten out" the grammar would weaken the doctrinal teaching of the original Greek and Hebrew words that God gave the human writers of Scripture.

Some critics of the King James Bible have been unhappy because of Romans 8:16 refers to the Spirit "itself". Many modern translations try to correct this "error." However, the neuter "itself" is found in both the "critical" and "traditional" texts. This passage is not the only place that God uses neuter words contrary to the normal rules of human grammar. In Luke 1:34-35 and Revelation 5:6, Christ is referred to with neuter words. In John 4:21-22, God the father is referred to with a neuter word. Proverbs 18:22 refers to wives with a neuter term. These terms are not mistaken translations by the King James translators but accurate translations of the words that God used. God is greater than the rules of human grammar and is entitled to use any words that He chooses. An accurate translation values revelation and inspiration more than it does man-made rules.

THE SIMPLICITY OF THE KING JAMES BIBLE

Despite modern complaints to the contrary, the King James Bible is a model of simplicity. "Whereas Shakespeare ransacked the lexicon, the King James Bible employs a bare 8,000 words-- God's teaching in homely English for every man."[11]

Anyone who wishes to master any book has to become familiar with the distinctive language and terminology of that book. The King James Bible has a smaller vocabulary than any other book of its size. It is true that word definitions sometimes change or develop. But if you retranslate a book every time a few words change, you must retranslate that book every few months. You are left with a translation that is here today and

---

11 McCrum, p. 113.

gone tomorrow.

This constant process of re-translating is not done with Shakespeare, Spenser, Milton, Bunyan, or any of the great English classics.

If this process was followed, these classics would be in such a constant state of change that no one would become familiar with them or ever memorize any passages from these classics. In some circles this is exactly what is happening to the Bible. As William O. Einwechter points out, "Isn't it ironic that with the proliferation of all the modern language versions that are supposed to make the Bible 'more understandable,' are supposed to increase readership, that there is such a neglect of serious Bible reading and study and that there is such a profound theological ignorance in the average evangelical Christian as we see you today? There is a heavy price to pay when the Bible is made more understandable than it is in the original Hebrew and Greek and when people are deceived into thinking that the difficulty of Bible study is simply due to the 'archaic language' of the AV, and that all they need is a modern language Bible that reads like today's newspaper."[12]

In 1935 Maurice Price wrote:

> For almost three centuries the Authorized or King James version has been the Bible of the English-speaking world. Its simple majestic Anglo-Saxon tongue, its clear, sparkling style, its directness and force of utterance have made it the model in language, style and dignity of some of the choicest writers of the last two centuries. Added to the above characteristics, its reverential and spiritual tone and attitude have made it the idol of the

---

12 William O. Einwechter, The Excellence of the Authorized Version, (The Chalcedon Report, June 19197).

Christian church. for its own words have been regarded as authoritative and binding.[13]

THE KING JAMES BIBLE AND THE USE OF ITALICS

The differences in languages sometimes make it difficult to do a literal word for word translation. At times to do a proper formal equivalent translation, additional words are required. When the King James Bible translators found it necessary to do this, they designated the additional added words by marking them with italicized print.

Most new English translations fail to mark the added words in anyway. (Compare Psalms 23:1 in the KJV with Psalms 23:1 in the NIV.)

Joseph Philpot comments on the importance of using italics in this way:

> We cannot but admire the great faithfulness of our translators and so scrupulously adhering to the exact words of the Holy Spirit, and when they were necessarily compelled to supply the ellipses in the original, to point out that they had done so by marking the word in italic characters. By doing so, they engaged themselves, as by bond, to give the Word of God in its strict original purity; and yet, as thorough scholars in the original tongues, and complete masters of their own, they were enabled to give us a version admirable not only for its strict fidelity, but also for its eloquence, grandeur, and beauty.[14]

Jakob van Bruggen adds,

---

13 Maurice Price, The Ancestry of Our English Bible, (Harper, New York 1935) p. 282.

14 David Otis Fuller, True or False (Grand Rapids International, Grand Rapids 1973) p. 282.

The Accuracy of Biblical English

To a large extent, the KJV owes its authority to the rule that most inserted words were printed in italics. The Bible reader was thus able to see how carefully the translators treated God's Word. They were afraid to add even one word, but if they were not able to translate without adding a word for the sake of clarity, they indicated that it had been added.[15]

The importance of italics can be seen in the matter of who slew Goliath. I Chronicles 20.5 proves that Elhanan killed a brother of the giant Goliath. I Samuel 17 states that David killed Goliath. The Hebrew text of 2 Samuel 21:19 is obscure. The New American Standard Bible and the New International Version translate 2 Samuel 21:19 as stating that Elhanan killed Goliath thus creating a contradiction in the Bible. Through the use of italics the KJV translators end this confusion without using any secrecy or subterfuge.

THE ENGLISH LANGUAGE AT ITS BEST

Literary scholars are in almost unanimous agreement that the modern English language was at its height in the Elizabethton period. The reigns of Queen Elizabeth I and her successor, James I, are the high point of this is seen in Bacon in natural science, Shakespeare in literature, Spenser and Sidney in poetry, English literature Raleigh in civil government, and Hooker in theology.

The *Story of English* declares about this period, "During their reigns, about seventy years, the English language achieved a richness and vitality of expression that even contemporaries marveled at."[16]

---

15 Jakob Van Bruggen, The Future of the Bible (Institute for Biblical Textual Studies, Grand Rapid, 1970), p. 246-247.

16 McCrum, p. 91.

Most language scholars would also recognize that the English language is in a state of deterioration in the early 21st century.

This raises the question, Should the standard English translation of the Bible come from the height of the English language or from its depths? David Otis Fuller answers this question.

> We are now come, however, to a very striking situation which is a little observed and rarely mentioned by those who discuss the merits of the King James Bible. The English language in 1611 was in the very best condition to receive into its bosom the Old and New Testaments. Each word was broad, simple, and generic. That is to say, words were capable of containing in themselves not only their central thoughts, but also all the different shades of meaning which were attached to that central thought.
>
> Since then, words have lost that living, pliable breadth. Vast additions have been made to the English vocabulary during the past 300 years, so that several words are now necessary to convey the same meaning which formerly was conveyed by one. It will then be readily seen that while the English vocabulary has increased in quantity; nevertheless, single words have lost their many shades, combinations of words have become fixed, capable of only one meaning, and therefore less adaptable to receiving into English the thoughts of the Hebrew which likewise is a simple, broad, generic language. New Testament Greek, is, in this respect, like the Hebrew. When our English Bible was revised, the Revisers labored under the impression that the sacred writers of the Greek New Testament did not write in the everyday language of the common people. Since then the accumulated stores of archaeological findings have demonstrated that the

The Accuracy of Biblical English

language of the Greek New Testament was the language of the simple, ordinary people, rather than the language of scholars, and is flexible, broad, generic, like the English of the 1611 version.[17]

The period in which the King James Bible was translated is clearly the best period in the English language to produce a standard English Bible Certainly it takes some work to understand the King James Bible, but any great work of literature requires more work to understand it than a newspaper, comic book, or pulp fiction. The Holy Scriptures certainly require that a person be willing to study and work hard.

Since some of the English words of the King James Bible have become relatively unfamiliar to most modern readers, it is good to have appropriate study aids available. Several good study aids, produced by men respectful of the Word of God, are available.

The Defined King James by D. A. Waite provides the King James text with helpful word definitions as foot notes. Archaic Words and the Authorized Version by Laurence M. Vance defines and explains every word in the King James Bible that has been labeled as archaic. The King James Bible Dictionary by David Cloud defines many words used in the King James Bible.

The Webster's 1828 dictionary, which is still in print, is keyed to the King James Bible and contains all 8,000 words used in the King James Bible.

As F. G. Kenyon notes, "The English of the Authorized Version is the finest specimen of our prose literature at a time

---

[17] David Otis Fuller, Which Bible (Institute for Biblical Textual Studies, Grand Rapids, 1970), p. 246-247.

when English prose wore its stateliest and most majestic form."[18]

English literacy giant J.R.R. Tolkien even blamed the modern deterioration of the English language on a wrong attitude toward the Bible:

> I think that this writing down flattening, Bible-in-basic-English attitude is responsible for the fact that so many older children and younger people have little respect and no love for words and very limited vocabularies and alas! little desire left (even when they had the gift which has been stultified to refine or enlarge them.[19]

THE LANGUAGE OF WORSHIP AND RESPECT

The cry that the Bible should read like the daily newspaper, that Christian music should sound like folk songs, and that prayer should sound like casual conversation is a new one. It arises from a time that has lost its respect for the sacred.

Oswald T. Allis gives the warning about the desire to trivialize the sacred:

> It is only in very recent days that Christian people have raised objections to the former language of devotion and worship. When the present century began, people did not raise objections to what we may call a scriptural and biblical style as the language of devotion and worship. They liked it. They did not want the Bible to readjust like any other book, to have the up-to-the-minute style of the daily newspaper. They loved its quaint, if you wish to call it that, its distinctive, its Biblical way of putting

---

18 F. G. Kenyon, Our Bible and The Ancient Manuscripts (New York, 1941), p. 307.

19 Humphrey Carpenter, The Letters of J.R.R. TOLKIEN (Houghton, Boston, 1981), p. 310-311.

things.[20]

CONCLUSION

Many great Bible teachers have commented on the role that the King James Bible and its distinctive Biblical English have played in so many lives.

Dean John Burgon wrote:

> Whatever may be urged in favor of Biblical Revision, it is at least undeniable that the undertaking involves a tremendous risk. Our Authorized Version is the one religious link which at present binds together ninety millions of English-speaking men scattered over the earth's surface. Is it reasonable that so unutterably precious, so sacred a bond should be endangered, for the sake of representing certain words more accurately,--here and there translating a tense with greater precision,--getting rid of a few archaisms? It may be confidently assumed that no 'Revision' of our Authorized Version, however judiciously executed, will ever occupy the place in public esteem which is actually enjoyed by the work of the Translators of 1611,--the noblest literary work in the Anglo-Saxon language. We shall in fact never have another 'Authorized Version.'[21]

Joseph Philpot wrote:

> The present English Bible (Authorized Version) has been blessed to thousands of the saints of GOD; and not only so, it has become part of our national inheritance which we have received unimpaired to our children. It

---

20 Thackway, p. 45.

21 John Burgon, The Revision Revised (Joan Murray, London,), p. 225.

is, we believe, the grand bulwark of Protestantism; the safeguard of the Gospel, and the treasure of the Church; and we should be traitors in every sense of the word if we consented to give it up to be rifled by the sacrilegious hands of the Puseyites, concealed papists, German Neologians, infidel divines, Arminians, Socinians, and the whole tribe of the enemies of God and godliness.[22]

Literary experts have also commented on the importance of the King James Bible and its Biblical English.

J. Isaacs, in his essay "The Authorized Version and After" (1940), exclaims:

> The Authorized Version is a miracle and a landmark. Its felicities are manifold, its music has entered into every blood and marrow of English thought and speech, it has given countless proverbs and proverbial phrases even to the unlearned and the irreligious. There is no corner of English life, no conversation ribald or reverent it has not adorned. Embedded in its tercentenary wording is the language of a century earlier. It has both broadened and retarded the stream of English speech. It is more archaic in places than its forerunners, and it is impossible for us to disentangle from our ordinary talk the phrases of Judea, whether Hebrew or Greek, whether of the patriarchs, the prophets, the poets, or the apostles, Only the closest scrutiny can give precision to the rhapsodical vagueness with which the Authorized Version is worshiped at a distance.[23]

Joseph Addison, famous eighteenth-century British essayist,

---

22 Joseph Philpot, The Authorized Version--1611 (Gospel Standard, April 1857).

23 J. Isaacs, The Authorized Version and After, (Greenwood, Westport, Ct., 1940) p. 160.

The Accuracy of Biblical English

dramatist and political leader wrote:

> It happens very luckily, that the Hebrew idioms run into the English tongue with a particular grace and beauty. Our language has received innumerable elegancies and improvements, from that infusion of Hebraism, which are derived to it out of the poetical passages in Holy Writ. They give a force and energy to our expressions, warm and animate our language, and convey our thoughts in more ardent and intense phrases, and any that are to be met with in our own tongue...How cold and dead does a prayer appear that is composed in the most elegant and polite forms of speech which are natural to our tongue when it is not heightened by the solemnity of phrase which may be drawn from the sacred writings.[24]

Historians have also commented on the importance of the King James Bible and its Biblical English. Sir Winston Churchill wrote:

> In the crowded emigrant ships which sailed to the New World of America there was little room for baggage. If the adventurers took books with them, they took the Bible, Shakespeare, and later The Pilgrim's Progress; and the Bible they mostly took with them was the Authorized Version of King James I. About ninety million complete copies are thought to have been published in the English language alone. It has been translated into more than seven hundred and sixty tongues. The Authorized Version is still the most popular in England and the United States. This may be deemed James's greatest achievement, for the impulse was largely his, The Scottish pedant built better than he knew. The scholars who produced this masterpiece are mostly unknown and unremembered.

---
24 Letis, p. 95.

But they forged an enduring link, literary and religious, between the English-speaking peoples of the world.[25]

John Richard Green writes:

> No greater moral change ever passed over a nation than passed over England during the years which parted the middle of the reign of Elizabeth from the meeting of the Long Parliament. England became the people of a book, and that book was the Bible. It was as yet the one English book which was familiar to every Englishman. it was read at churches and read at home, and everywhere its words, as they fell on ears which custom had not deadened to their force and beauty, kindled a startling enthusiasm.[26]

In an address at Royal Albert Hall in 1961, Dr. Martin Lloyd Jones sums up the matter well:

> I suppose that the most popular of all the proposals at the present moment is to have a new translation of the Bible...The argument is that people are not reading the Bible any longer because they do not understand its language--particularly the archaic terms--what does your modern man... know about justification, sanctification, and all the biblical terms? And so we are told the thing that is necessary is to have a translation that Tom, Dick, and Harry will understand, and I began to feel six months ago that we had almost reached the stage in which the Authorized Version was being dismissed, to be thrown into the limbo of things forgotten, no longer of nay

---

25 Winston Churchill, History of the English Speaking Peoples, (Barnes and Noble, one volume edition), p. 160.

26 John Richard Green, Short History of the English People (Harper, New York, 1892, V. 3), p. 933.

The Accuracy of Biblical English

value. Need I apologize for saying a word in favour of the Authorized Version...

It is a basic proposition laid down by the Protestant Reformers, that we must have a Bible "understood of the people." That is common sense...we must never be obscurantist. We must never approach the Bible in a mere antiquarian spirit..but it does seem to me that there is a very grave danger incipient and so much of the argument that is being presented today for these new translations. There is a danger, I say, of our surrendering something that is vital and essential.

Take this argument that the modern man does not understand such terms as justification, sanctification and so on. I want to ask a question. When did the ordinary man ever understand those terms?... Did the colliers to whom John Wesley and George Whitefield preached in the 18th century understand? They had not even been to a day school...They could not read, they could not write. Yet these were the terms that were used. This was the version that was used—The Authorized Version. The common people have never understood these terms. we are concerned here with something that is spiritual: something which does not belong to this world at all, which, as the apostle Paul reminds us. the princes of this world do not know. Human wisdom is of no value here--it is a spiritual truth. This is the truth about God primarily, and because of that it is a mystery...

Yet we are told--it must be in such simple terms and language that anybody taking it up and reading it is going to understand all about it. My friends, this is sheer nonsense. What we must do is to educate the masses of the people up to the Bible, not bring the Bible down to their level. One of the greatest troubles today is that everything is being brought down to the same level: everything is cheapened. The common man is made the standard of authority; he decides everything, and everything has to be brought down to him…

Are we to do that with the Word of God? I say no! What has happened in the past has been this. Ignorant, illiterate people, in this country and foreign countries, coming into salvation have been educated up the to book and have begun to understand it, to glory in it, and to praise God for it, and I say that we need to do the same at this present time. What we need is therefore, not to replace the Authorized Version. ... . We need rather to reach and train people up to the standard and language, the dignity and the glory of the Old Authorized Version.[27]

---

[27] Quoted in the Trinitarian Bible Society Quarterly, July-September 1981.

The Accuracy of Biblical English

The Unbroken Bible

7

In Defense of 1 John 5:7

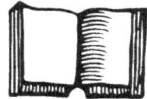

On 1 John 5:7 the Old Scofield Reference Bible marginal notes read, "It is generally agreed that v.7 has no real authority, and has been inserted."

The Jehovah's Witness Watchtower magazine says of 1 John 5:7, "Another reference that speaks of the three together is found in some older Bible translations at 1 John 5:7. Scholars acknowledge, however, that these words were not originally in the Bible but were added much later."

Many serious students of the Word of God are shocked to find Jehovah's Witnesses at the door quoting the marginal notes of the Old Scofield Reference Bible but it is a common occurrence. Young Christians often have their faith weakened when they hear that 1 John 5:7 doesn't really belong in the Bible that they have been taught is the Word of God.

A clear view of 1 John 5:7 is important for Christians. The

purpose of this chapter is to present the evidence for the inclusion of 1 John 5:7 in the New Testament Text.

The serious Bible student consulting numerous commentaries by well-known authors, finds a challenge when it comes to 1 John 5:7. Cultists, modernists and naturalistic textual critics dispute the authority of 1 John 5:7, but they are not alone. Bible scholars known to be evangelical, known to hold to "conservative" doctrine of Inspiration , known to normally oppose modernism, also also challenge the authenticity of 1 John 5:7.

The disputed verse in 1 John 5:7 reads, "For there are three that bear record in heaven , the Father, the Word, and the Holy Ghost,: and these three are one." This verse is often called the Johannine Comma.

However, the issue is not as simple as the many critics of 1 John 5:7 claim. It is interesting how many people reject 1 John 5:7 in the name of scholarship, - yet their own scholarship is so shallow that they are unaware of the arguments for 1 John 5:7.

THE CONSERVATIVE ATTACKS ON I JOHN 5:7

On I John 5:7, Adam Clarke writes, " It is likely that this verse is not genuine. It is wanting in every manuscript one excepted."[1]

The Jamieson, Fausett and Brown one volume commentary on the Bible claims that the Johannine Comma is spurious because it lacks "two or three witnesses."[2]

J. Vernon McGee approvingly quotes A.T. Robertson as saying that this verse is not in "the better manuscripts." He

---

1 Adam Clarke, Commentary on the Bible, Grand Rapids, Baker Book House, 1967 (abridged edition), p. 1324.

2 Robert Jamieson, A.R. Fausett, David Brown, Commentary on the Whole Bible, Grand Rapids, Zondervan, 1961 (revised edition), p. 1509.

further adds, "Evidently some scribe put what we have as verse 7 in the margin and then later on another scribe came along and thought it was to be included in the text."[3]

Arno Gaebelein wrote, "The seventh verse has no business in our Bibles, it must be stricken out. It is an interpolation and all the historical evidences are against it."[4]

Kenneth S. Wuest writes, "There is general agreement among textual critics that the contents of this verse are spurious and do not belong to the original text."[5]

B.H. Carroll wrote, "Let us take out of the King James Version all the 7th verse and the words "in earth" of the 8th verse. They are unquestionably an interpolation. They do not appear in any of the ancient manuscripts and our standard version leaves them out."[6]

Craig S. Keener writes, "The trinitarian formula found in the KJV of I John 5:7 is orthodox but not part of the text."[7]

In the Liberty Bible commentary, edited by Jerry Falwell, it reads "The rest of verse 7 and and the first nine words of verse 8 are not original and are not considered as part of the Word of

---

[3] J. Vernon McGee, Thru the Bible with J. Vernon McGee, Nashville, Thomas Nelson, 1983, p. 816 (volume 5).

[4] Arno C. Gaebelein, Gaebelein's Concise Commentary on the Bible, Neptune New Jersey, Loizeaux, 1985 (revised edition), p. 1185.

[5] Kenneth S. Wuest, Wuest's Word Studies From the Greek New Testament, Grand Rapids, Eerdmans, 1954, p. 176.

[6] B.H. Carroll, The Pastoral Epistles, Nashville, Broadman Press, 1916, p. 326.

[7] Craig S. Keener, The Inter Varsity Press Bible Background Commentary, Downers Grove, Inter Varsity Press, 1993, p. 745.

The Unbroken Bible

God (refer to the marginal notes in any reference Bible)."[8]

Warren Wiersbe writes, "Most scholars agree that I John 5:7 of the Authorized Version does not belong in the letter, but omitting it does not affect the teaching at all."[9]

The New Scofield Reference Bible has a footnote on I John 5:7 that reads, "It is generally agreed that this verse has no manuscript authority and has been inserted."[10]

The New King James Version has a footnote on I John 5:7 that reads, "The Nu-Text and M-Text omit the words from 'in heaven' (verse 7) through 'on earth' (verse 8). Only four and five late Greek manuscripts contain these words."[11]

There are countless other examples. It is also interesting to note how many commentaries on I John ignore verse 7. They do not offer commentary on the verse but do not explain why.

Even Peter Ruckman admits that I John 5:7 is the most questionable verse in the A.V. 1611 text (though he concludes it is absolutely authentic), "The most questionable of any of these is the Johannine Comma (I John 5:7), ..."[12]

It would appear that many scholars think that I John 5:7 is a closed issue, that all the evidence is in and the verdict has

---

[8] Jerry Falwell, executive editor, Liberty Bible Commentary, Lynchburg, Old Time Gospel Hour, 1983, p. 2638.

[9] Warren W. Wiersbe, Be Real, Wheaton, Victor Books, 1972, p. 176.

[10] New Scofield Reference Bible, New York, Oxford University Press, 1967, p. 1346.

[11] The New King James Version, Nashville, Thomas Nelson, 1979, p. 1197.

[12] Peter S. Ruckman, The Christian's Handbook of Manuscript Evidence, Pensacola, Pensacola Bible Press, 1970, p. 127.

been reached. However, there is much more to this issue than the above quotations would seem to indicate.

As Michael Maynard has written,

> A marginal note with more justice in the treatment would be, a few late Greek manuscripts, at least four Old Latin manuscripts, over eight Church Fathers (including Cyprian who died A.D. 258), four Syriac editions, Slavic and Armenian manuscripts, over 600 distinct editions of the Textus Receptus from 1522 to 1881, 18 pre-Lutheran Bibles, and thousands of Vulgate manuscripts read... Further of those Greek manuscripts which do omit this verse, 97% are late manuscripts, dated from the 10th century and later.[13]

HOW I JOHN 5:7 GOT INTO THE TEXTUS RECEPTUS!

The Textus Receptus is the Greek text from which the King James Bible is primarily translated. This is the text that the Protestant Reformation was based upon and from which all the great Protestant translations were made. The Sixteenth Century scholar Erasmus compiled this text based upon his study of the Traditional Greek Text and the Traditional Latin Text. These were the Bibles being used by God's people throughout Europe.

In his first edition of the Textus Receptus, Erasmus omitted the Johannine Comma. There was an outcry of protest from Bible students. Most Bible students used the Latin Bible which contained this verse. It had been used, quoted and commented on for centuries. Under pressure, Erasmus agreed to include the verse if one Greek manuscript could be produced which included the verse.

---

13 Michael Maynard, The Debate Over I John 5:7-8, Tempe Comma Publications, 1995, p. 247.

A Greek manuscript (now known as 61 and kept at Trinity College in Dublin) was presented which included I John 5:7. True to his word, Erasmus added the verse in his third edition of the Textus Receptus. This is the edition used in the translation of the King James Bible. The King James Bible translators were the greatest Hebrew, Greek and Latin scholars in England. There was no shortage of manuscripts available to them but they choose to accept the Third Edition of the Textus Receptus, including I John 5:7.

It is important to note that many commentators act as if I John 5:7 was a marginal note introduced by mistake into the Bible in the Sixteenth Century and that modern scholars in their great wisdom can now correct the mistake. It is important to realize that this verse had been in the Bibles used by God's people, the priesthood of believers, that caused this verse to be placed in the Textus Receptus.

Edward F. Hills comments on this process,

> But whatever may have been the immediate cause, still, in the last analysis it was not trickery which was responsible for the inclusion of the Johannine Comma in the Textus Receptus but the usage of the Latin-speaking Church. It was this usage which made men feel that this reading ought to be included in the Greek text and eager to keep it there after its inclusion had been accomplished. Back of this usage, we may well believe, was the guiding providence of God.[14]

---

14 Edward F. Hills, Believing Bible Study, Des Moines, Christian Research Press, 1967, p. 211.

In Defense of 1 John 5:7

BACKGROUND INFORMATION NECESSARY TO UNDERSTAND THE DEBATE OVER I JOHN 5:7

There are more issues in the debate than just the issue of which Greek text a person has faith in. Most people will never see an ancient Greek text of the Bible. People had to develop principles by which they would evaluate claims about the text of Scripture. In order to properly develop such principles, a person needs to be familiar with certain issues.

The Concept Of The Common Faith: The Priesthood Of Believers

There is little controversy over the accurate text of the Old Testament. The transmission of the Old Testament text was committed to the priests of Israel and Levites (Deut. 31:24-26, 17:18, Proverbs 25:1, and Romans 3:2). These Old Testament priests and their later descendants have been widely praised for their very careful and accurate copying techniques. This praise has come not only from Jews and Christians, but also from secular linguistic scholars. The Holy Spirit preserved the Old Testament text by guiding the priests to gather the parts of the Old Testament into one canon and to maintain the purity of the Old Testament texts.

The New Testament was given to a different type of priesthood. All New Testament believers are priests (I Peter 2:1-7). No secular or ecclesiastical organization is in charge of preserving the New Testament Scriptures. Routinely scholars recognize that the New Testament canon was established by the common consent of believing Christians. When the canon is discussed, it is recognized that the Holy Spirit guided individual believers and that their common consent established the canon of the New Testament. Hills applies this principle of the priesthood of believers as it relates to the subject of the transmission of the New Testament Text,

Just as the divine glory of the new Testament are brighter far than the glories of the Old Testament, so the manner in which God has preserved the New Testament text by means of something physical and external, namely, he Aaronic priesthood. God has preserved the New Testament text by means of something inward and spiritual, namely the universal priesthood of believers. Hence the preservation of the New Testament text is not due to the decisions of any ecclesiastical organization or council or committee. All such attempts to deal with the New Testament text are bound to fail. God has preserved the New Testament text in the New Testament way which is free from any traces of Old Testament bondage, namely, through the guidance of the Holy Spirit operating in the hearts of individual believers and gradually leading them, by common consent, to reject false readings and to preserve the true. But this God-guiding usage of believers the true New Testament text has been preserved and is now found in the vast majority of the Greek New Testament manuscripts, in the Textus Receptus, and in the King James Bible and other faithful translations of the Textus Receptus.[15]

The concept of the universal priesthood of believers (not just professing Christians) influences your attitude toward the Biblical text. Those who believe that the text of Scripture is to be determined by a handful of language scholars criticize Erasmus for responding to the faith of God's people about I John 5:7. Those who accept the universal priesthood of believers find something providential in the acceptance of I John 5:7 by the average Christian throughout the centuries.

---

15 Ibid, p. 35.

In Defense of 1 John 5:7

The Traditional Text

There are many sources for determining the identity of the New Testament Test. There include 5,366 Greek manuscripts and 2,209 Greek lectionaries.[16] Dean John Burgon compiled over 87,000 quotations of the New Testament scriptures from the early centuries of Christianity.[17] There are many other early Bibles in the Old latin, the Syriac, Coptic and Ethiopian languages.

The overwhelming number of these manuscripts, quotations, lectionaries and ancient language Bibles are in basic agreement with each other. Well over 90 percent of the Greek manuscripts are in agreement with each other. An overwhelming majority of the quotations agree with this text.[18] This was the common text for people who read Greek. Because the vast majority of Greek texts are of this type, it is called the Majority Text. Because it was normally accepted by believers, it is called the Traditional Text. Because it was preserved in Greek speaking and writing Byzantine Empire, it is sometimes called the Byzantine Text. Because it was the text accepted by the priesthood of believers, it is sometimes called the Common Text (reflecting the common faith that unites believers-Jude 3). Because it was received by the vast majority of orthodox believers and churches, it is called the Received Text. From the beginning, there were texts available which differed from the Traditional Text. These texts almost always omitted words and even whole sentences- sometimes thousands of them. Sometimes this was thought to be the result of copying errors. Sometimes it was clear that texts were

---

16 G.A. Riplinger, New Age Bible Versions, Munroe Falls, Ohio, A.V. Publications, 1993, p. 471.

17 Ibid, p. 471.

18 Pickering, The Identity of the New Testament Text, Nashville, Thomas Nelson, 1977, p. 67-68.

purposely corrupted. Teachers like Marcion and Origen simply left out words, phrases and sentences that were inconvenient to their theology. These texts were routinely rejected by believers who were familiar with the whole text. There are no ancient copies of the Traditional Text. As the Bible was faithfully read and studied, copies were worn out and new ones had to be made The only copies that survived the centuries were those that were rejected and placed in a storage or in libraries. As a result, the oldest manuscripts available are those that were rejected by the priesthood of believers for general use. During the Nineteenth Century, the unusual view was advanced that God's Word had been preserved in the tiny number of minority texts that had been previously rejected. It was suggested that the priesthood of believers had been wrong for centuries and that their Bibles had been translated from deficient manuscripts. According to this view,Only a handful of scholars could now tell the Christian world what the true text of Scripture was. The most influential of these scholars were B.F Westcott and F. J.A Hort. These men produced a Greek text based upon the previously rejected minority of manuscripts. Their work was hailed as great scholarship. The cults and naturalistic and modernistic Christians immediately accepted their work. After all it is much easier to teach heresy if certain words and phrases are removed from Scripture. For example, it is much easier to deny the trinity if John 5:7 is removed from the Bible. Both Westcott and Hort were accepted members of the Church of England. Neither was considered part of the evangelical segment (low church) of the Church of England. Each Man had a son who would later write a biography of his life. Both sons claimed that their fathers privately rejected Church of England doctrine and practiced spiritualism.

Surprisingly, these men and their works were also warmly received by many evangelical and doctrinally conservative teachers,denominations and Christian organizations. In over one hundred years two hundred English translations have been produced based upon their textual work. None of these translations have been able to replace the English translation based upon the Traditional Text- the King James Bible. Not one of these new translations acknowledge 1 John 5:7 as part of Scripture. Even though the premise for the works of Westcott and Hort is easily and simply refuted, many evangelicals cling to it in the name of scholarship. It is hard to imagine that God would allow the priesthood of believers to be deceived about the true text of Scripture for centuries, but would reveal it to Westcott and Hort. At best, Westcott and Hort were non-evangelical traditionalists in the Angelo-Catholic wing (high church) of the Church of England. At worst, they were practitioners of the occult publicly pretending to be Christian preachers.

Latin Bibles

Many of the Christians in the early centuries did not read Greek. As a result, the Old Latin Bibles were very important, A traditional or majority Latin text developed out of the use of these Bibles. The Traditional Latin Text includes at least 10 passages that are found in only a few Greek Majority Text manuscripts. 1 John 5:7 is one of those passages. During this time, more Bible believing Christians were reading the Scriptures in Latin than in Greek. Many teachers believed God was using both Traditional Greek Text and Traditional Latin text to preserve the true words of scripture. All of these ten passages eventually ended up in the Textus Receptus.

1 John 5:7 is routinely found in the Old Latin Bibles. It is also found in a few Greek manuscripts. When Jerome published his Latin Vulgate in the Fifth Century, he excluded 1 John 5:7 But this statement was already so commonly considered as Scripture by the people that later editions of the Vulgate were forced to include it. The priesthood of believers had spoken. As Edward Hills writes, "In these rare instances, God called upon the usage of the Latin- speaking Church to correct the usage of

the Greek speaking Church."[19]

The Work Of Erasmus

In the sixteenth Century, Erasmus was determined to provide a text which would be purchased by the general public. Erasmus was both a Greek and Latin scholar. Influenced by the long standing independent churches and the new Protestant reformers. People everywhere were rejecting Catholicism.

People wanted to read the Bible for themselves. There was a great need for a new Greek text. Erasmus remained in the Catholic Church but he had little respect for its hierarchy and doctrine. His many books clearly reflected as a respect for the historic faith of the believers.

Erasmus believed that the true text of Scripture could be determined from a diligent comparison of the Traditional Greek texts and the Traditional Latin texts. This was also the position of the later King James translators.

Erasmus was influenced by the common Christian tradition. When he consented to include 1 John 5:7 in his third edition of the Textus Receptus, he was reflecting the common idea that the Holy Spirit was using both Greek and Latin texts to preserve the Scripture.

DISCOVERING THE NEW TESTAMENT TEXT: BURGON'S SEVEN NOTES OF TRUTH

The changes made popular by Westcott and Hort did not go unchallenged. Dean John William Burgon, one of the greatest (some would say greatest) Greek scholars of the Nineteenth Century wrote and spoke extensively challenging Westcott and Hort. He thoroughly refuted the basis for their Greek text. He

---
19 Hills, Believing Bible Study, p. 214.

also opposed their sense of final authority.

Hort claimed that the final determining factor is deciding which reading of a particular verse to accept was its "ring of genuineness."[20] In other words, the final authority was simply how Westcott and Hort felt about a passage. They now exercised the authority that the priesthood of believers had previously exercised.

There was no room for 1 John 5:7 in Hort's Bible. According to his son, he wrote (in a private letter). "It could be gotten rid of…"[21] This was not based upon textual argument, but upon his feeling that the verse didn't "ring true". Burgon felt that this was much too subjective and that was contrary to the priesthood of the believer and the sole authority of Scripture.

Burgon devised his now well known seven "Notes of Truth" These were seven objective tests for determining the authenticity of reading scripture. The seven Notes of truth are:

- The antiquity of the reading
- The number of the witnesses to the reading.
- The variety of types of readings.
- The respectability (weight) of the witnesses.
- The continuity of (unbroken tradition of acceptance) of the passage.
- The context of the entire passage.
- Internal considerations (or reasonableness) of the passage.

These tests can be applied to 1 John 5:7.

APPLYING THE SEVEN NOTES OF TRUTH TO 1 JOHN 5:7

---

20 Pickering, The Identity of the New Testament Text, p. 27.

21 Riplinger, New Age Bible Verisons, 1993, p. 380.

The Unbroken Bible

Antiquity

Those who claim that 1 John 5:7 is spurious because it was unknown before a Fifteenth Century Greek manuscript simply haven't done their research.

The Verse is found in an Old Syriac manuscript from around A.D. 170.[22] It is found in an Old Latin manuscript from around A.D. 200.[23] According to Gaussen (in his classic book on inspiration, *Theopneustia*) it is quoted or referred to by several Latin church fathers in the Second, Third, Fourth and Fifth Centuries.[24] It was quoted in the Second Century by Tatian,[25] by Tertullian around A.D. 200,[26] and Cyprian around A.D 250.[27] It was quoted by Athanasius in A.D. in 350[28] and by both Priscillian and Idacius Clarus in A.d. 385.[29]

The verse is found in copies of the Latin Vulgate from the Fifth Century (Gaussen reminds his readers that these manuscripts predate most Greek manuscripts).[30]

In A.D 415, the verse was included in the resolutions of the

---

22 Ibid, p. 381.

23 Ibid, p. 381.

24 L. Gaussen, Theopneustia: The Plenary Inspiration of the Holy Scriptures, London, Passmore and Alabaster, 1896, p. 194.

25 Riplinger, New Age Bible Versions, p. 381.

26 Ibid, p. 381.

27 Hills, Believing Bible Study, p. 211.

28 Riplinger, New Age Bible Versions, p. 381.

29 Hills, Believing Bible Study, p. 211.

30 Gaussen, Theopneustia, p. 194.

In Defense of 1 John 5:7

Council of Carthage.[31] In 484A.D., the King of the Vandals demanded the Bishops of North Africa prove the Doctrine of the Trinity. He was an Arian. He denied the Trinity and considered the bishops all heretics. Four hundred bishops signed a Confession of Faith that included a defense of the Trinity. This defense quoted 1 John 5:7 and discussed it at length.[32] It was quoted by Cassiodorus in Italy in 480 A.D.[33]

Other quotations or references include Vadmarium A.D. 380, Cassian A.D.435, Jerome A.D. 450, Vigilius A.D 484, Victor-Vita A.D 489 and Fulgentius A.D 533. It was also quoted in a document called Liber Apologeticus in A.D 350.[34]

The Textus Receptus reading of 1 John 5:7 is not only seen in antiquity it was obviously widespread in antiquity.

The Consent of Witnesses

1 John 5:7 is found in the Greek text designated 61, the text designated 629, in the margin of the text 88 and in the codex Ravianus. While this is only a small percentage of the Greek texts, the passage is found in the vast majority of Latin Bibles. It is legitimate to carefully study this passage because of the discrepancy between the Greek texts and the Latin texts but it is not legitimate to say the verse is only found in one or two texts. Including the Latin texts, it is found in thousands of manuscripts.

Variety of Evidence

1 John 5:7 is widely quoted, it is found in official statements

---

31 Riplinger, New Age Bible Versions, p. 381

32 Gaussen, Theopneustia, p. 194 and Hills, Believing Bible Study, p. 211.

33 Hills, Believing Bible Study, p. 211.

34 Riplinger, New Age Bible Versions, p. 381.

of church councils, in a limited number of Greek manuscripts and in a large number of Latin manuscripts. It is found in both North Africa and Europe. The reading is not limited to a group sect or geographic area.

The Respect of the Witnesses

The readings of 1 John 5:7 are not limited to quotations by obscure unknown writers or isolated texts. It was used by well known leaders like Cyprian. Tertullian, Jerome and Athanasius. It was so widely used in the Latin speaking church that it was commonly accepted as Scripture. It is completely wrong to compare 1 John 5:7 to disputed readings of Scripture that have been rejected because they have only isolated support.

Unbroken Tradition

References can be found to 1 John 5:7 from the Second Century forward. Again, these references are not isolated but are in the Bibles being used by the majority of Bible believers.

In 1120, the Waldenses quoted 1 John 5:7 in their doctrinal creed: "We must believe in God the Father Almighty, the Creator of Heaven and earth, for which God is one Trinity, as it is written in the law. "Hear O Israel the Lord thy God is one',and Isaiah 'I am the Lord and there is none else, neither is there any God besides me' and St. Paul, in the fourth of the Ephesians: ' One Lord, one faith, one baptism, one God and Father of all.' And St. John, 'There are three that bear witness in heaven; the Father, the Son and the Holy Ghost; and these three are one.'"

Context

Grammatically, I John 5:8 makes no sense without verse 7. In verse eight, the word three is in the masculine in the Greek language. The previous three nouns spirit, water, and blood are all neuter. The rules of Greek grammar make it impossible (and nonsensical) for the word three to refer back to spirit, water, and blood. "Three" clearly refers to the Father, the Word, and the Holy Ghost of verse 7. In 1828, Bishop Middleton of Cambridge wrote an eighteen page article names *The Doctrine of the Greek Article*. He makes it clear how the wording of verse 8 demands the wording of verses 7 to proceed it.[35] Without the Johannine Comma, the passage is incomplete and is grammatical nonsense.

Internal Considerations

By this test, Burgon meant asking if the proposed reading was on the subject being discussed in the passage and if the doctrine taught was consistent with the rest of Scripture. The subject was the Deity of Christ. What could be more relevant than a clear statement about the Trinity. What could be more consistent with the Biblical doctrine of Scripture than this statement: "For there are three that bear record in heaven, the Father, the Word, and the Holy Ghost: and these three are one."

Those that accept I John 5:7 as genuine have more scholarly arguments on their side than those who simply reject it without studying the issues involved.

THE DOCTRINAL IMPORTANCE OF I JOHN 5:7

I John 5:7 is called "the famous Trinitarian proof text."[36] It is certainly possible to prove the Trinity from many other passages of Scripture. But cultists and modernists have found ways to twist the other passages. No one can find a way to twist I John 5:7. The Jehovah's Witnesses were quick to embrace Westcott and Hort's abandonment of I John 5:7. Cultists and modernists rejoice in declaring that it has been proven that I John 5:7 is not really

---

35 Gaussen, Theopneustia, p. 195.

36 Riplinger, New Age Bible Versions, p. 389.

part of Scripture. Many doctrinal conservatives, evangelicals, fundamentalists (and even independent Baptists) unknowingly give them aid and comfort by repeating this assertion.

In the name of scholarship many unthinkingly quoted the opinions of "authorities" who reject I John 5:7. But rejecting a passage approved for centuries under the concept of the common faith is no minor step. Surely it must involve more than quoting a few scholars. No one should even think about rejecting a passage approved throughout the centuries without undertaking their own full and careful study. The doctrinal implications of this verse are important. Modernists and unbelievers are uncomfortable with any Bible that contains this verse. Bible believers should be uncomfortable with any version that omits this verse.

Summary

John Calvin carefully studied the work of Erasmus and concluded that I John 5:7 was genuine.[37] The noted language scholar, Theodore Beza (1519-1605), carefully studied I John 5:7 and concluded, "It seems to me that this clause ought by all means to be retained."[38] Early German Bibles included I John 5:7. Martin Luther did not include it in his New Testament, but soon after his death it was included in the official German Lutheran Bible. The people simply demanded it. John Wesley included it in his English New Testament.[39]

I John 5:7 appeared in every standard translation of the English Bible until the English Revised version of 1881 omitted it. I John 5:7 was included in the Wycliffe Bible in 1380, the Tyndale Bible in 1535, the Matthew's Bible in 1537, the

---

37 Hills, Believing Bible Study, p. 203.

38 Ibid, p. 205.

39 Jasper James Ray, God Wrote Only One Bible, Junction City, Oregon, 1955, p. 34.

In Defense of 1 John 5:7

Taverner Bible of 1539, the Great Bible of 1539, the Geneva New Testament of 1557, the Bishop's Bible of 1568, and the King James Bible of 1611.

Many scholarly defenses of I John 5:7 have been written. Gaussen, Burgon, Middleton and Hills have already been mentioned. In 1815 Frederick Nolan wrote, An Inquiry into the Integrity of the Greek Vulgate or Received Test of the New Testament. He included a clear defense of I John 5:7.

Robert L. Dabney (1891) wrote a defense of I John 5:7 in which he said:

> First, if it be made, the masculine article, numeral, and particle... are made to agree directly with three neuters- an insuperable and very bald grammatical difficulty. But if the disputed words are allowed to stand, they agree directly with two masculines and one neuter noun... Where, according to a well known rule of syntax, the masculines among the group control the gender over a neuter connected with them...

> Second, if the excision is made, the eighth verse coming next to the sixth, gives us a very bald and awkward, and apparently meaningless, repetition of the Spirit's witness twice in immediate succession.

> Third, if the excision is made, then the proposition at the end of the eighth verse, [and these three agree in one], contains an unintelligible reference... "And these three agree to that (aforesaid) One," ... What is that aforesaid unity to which these three agree? If the seventh verse is excinded, there is none... Let the seventh verse stand, and all is clear: the three earthly witnesses testify to that aforementioned unity which the Father, Word,

and Spirit constitute.[40]

It is amazing how little those who claim scholarship as the grounds for rejecting I John 5:7 know of the available scholarship on the subject.

Matthew Henry, noted Puritan Bible Commentator, addressed the passage well when he wrote,

> We are stopped in our course by the contest there is about the genuineness of v. 7. It is alleged that many old Greek manuscripts have it not. We shall not here enter into the controversy. It can scarcely be supposed that, when the apostle is representing the Christian's faith in overcoming the world, and the foundation it relies upon in adhering to Jesus Christ, he should omit the supreme testimony that attended him (v.9). Upon our present reading here is a noble enumeration of the several witnesses and testimonies supporting the truth of the Lord Jesus.
>
> The apostle, having told us that the Spirit that bears witness to Christ is truth, shows us that he is so, by assuring us that he is in heaven, v 7.
>
> Here is a trinity of heavenly witness, such as have testified and vouched to the world the authority of the Lord Jesus in his claims. The first that occurs in order is the Father; he set his seal to the commission of the Lord Christ all the while he was here. The second witness is the Word, a mysterious name. He must bear witness to the human nature, or to the man Christ Jesus. The third witness is the Holy Ghost. True and faithful must he be to whom the Spirit of holiness sets his seal. These are

---

[40] R. L. Dabney, Discussions of Robert Lewis Dabney, Carlisle, Bonnie of Trust, 1967, p. 378.

witnesses in heaven; and they bear record from heaven; and they are one.

To these there is opposed, though with them joined, a trinity of witnesses on earth, v. 8. Of these witnesses the first is the spirit. The regeneration or renovation of souls is a testimony to the Savior. It is a testimony on earth, because it continues with the church here. To this Spirit belong not only the regeneration and conversion of the church, but it's progressive sanctification, victory over the world. The second is the water. This was before considered as a means of salvation, now as a testimony to the Savior himself, and intimates his purity and purifying power. And so it seems to comprehend the testimony of John's baptism, who bore witness of him and to the purity of his own doctrine, by which souls are purified and washed. The baptism that he has appointed for the initiation of his disciples. The third witness is the blood; this he shed, and this was our ransom. This testifies for Jesus Christ; in that it demonstrated unspeakable love to us; and none will deceive those whom they entirely love. In that it lays obligation on his disciples to suffer and die for him. This shows that neither he nor his kingdom is of this world. These are signified and sealed in the institution of his own supper. Such are the witnesses on earth. These three witnesses agree in one, in one and the same thing among themselves.[41]

---

[41] Matthew Henry, The Matthew Henry Commentary, Grand Rapids, Zondervan, 1961 (revised edition), p. 1061-2.

The Unbroken Bible

8

In Defense of Mark 16:9-20

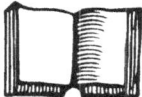

"It is easy to join the critics and say Mark's original manuscript ended with verse 8, it is impossible to satisfactorily support this statement." - Dean J. Burgon

IS IT OR ISN'T IT?

Many modern evangelical "scholars" find themselves unsure of whether Mark 16:9-20 is really part of the Bible. Many Bible students have puzzled over the note about Mark 16:9-20 in the Old Scofield Reference Bible. This note reads, "The passage from verse 9 to the end is not found in the two most ancient manuscripts, the Sinatic and Vatican, and others have it with partial omissions and variations. But it is quoted by Irenaeus and Hippolytus in the second and third century."

Can you imagine the confusion that a young Christian has when they read this note? Does this mean that it is to be considered as spurious or is there a reason to trust this passage?

The Unbroken Bible

The Scofield Reference Bible raised the question, but never answered it!

Many evangelical preachers seem sure that it makes no difference at all. The King James has the passage but the NIV rejects it as Scripture. Many evangelicals will assure you that the NIV and the King James are so much the same that it doesn't make any difference which one you use.

But if you believe in the verbal inspiration of Scripture, every word matters. We are forbidden to add to Scripture and we are forbidden to subtract from Scripture. (Revelation 22:18-19). Either someone committed a terrible act by trying to remove eleven verses of previous Scripture from the Bible or someone perpetrated a horrible fraud by trying to add eleven verses written by men to the Bible. You can't have it both ways. Things that are different are not the same.

Some evangelical scholars are not so indecisive. They are sure that Mark 16:9-20 is spurious:

A.T. Robertson, Studies in Mark- "It is impossible that the last leaf of Mark was lost before any copies were made of it. If Mark did write more of his gospel (after verse 8) and if copies were made of the autograph before it perished, then someday we may see the true ending of Mark's Gospel."[1]

Howard F. Vos, A Study Guide Commentary- "The very best manuscripts stop at verse 8." The great scholar Eusebius, writing in the 4th century, said that nearly all copies of Mark's Gospel ended in verse 8. Jerome said almost the same thing. Many argue that verses 9-20 are not in the same style as the rest of the Book, so the tendency of modern textual scholars is to omit these

---

[1]

verses."[2]

Tyndale, NT Commentary- "Verses 9-20 are not found in some important witnesses. This longer ending shows knowledge of John 20, Luke 24, and Matthew 28. This is an early attempt to 'round off' a Gospel whose original ending has become in some way maimed or lost. These verses were perhaps derived from the other Gospels, a patchwork of pieces from the other Gospels."

THE ARGUMENTS FOR REJECTING MARK 16:9-20

Argument Number One:

Mark 16:9-20 is not found in the two manuscripts, Sinaticus and Vaticanus, that Westcott and Hort (and most modern critics) put their faith in. These two manuscripts serve as the primary authority for many of the "scholars" of the evangelical world.

Argument Number Two:

Eusebius, church historian for Constantine and devoted disciple of Origin, wrote about the ending of Mark 16. He challenged the integrity of the long ending and declared that he used texts without this ending. His work was acknowledged by Jerome. Some have claimed that this was an endorsement on Jerome's part, but he clearly acknowledged Mark 16:9-20 as Scripture. He simply stated that such texts as Eusebius referred to existed. The debate over Mark 15 is not a new one.

Argument Number Three:

Some scholars claim that the type of Mark 16:9-20 is too different from the rest of the book of Mark. There are some

---
2

words found in mark 16:9-20 that are not found in the rest of the book.

The reading of the overwhelming majority of the manuscripts of the book of Mark have been rejected based upon these arguments.

CRITICAL ENDINGS

So how do the modern textual critics believe that Mark 16 should end? The more theologically modernist critics usually believe that verse 8 is the real ending of Mark. For them the last words of Mark are "for they were afraid."

A few "scholars" and some cults accept a short ending for Mark which was found in one Latin manuscript.

Many "evangelical scholars" believe that the original ending of Mark has been lost. They hope that is may be found again some day. In their thinking god inspired the "originals" but He never promised to preserve His word. They have no problem with the idea that the genuine God given ending for Mark has been lost and is currently not available. Not only do they not have a problem with this position-- they seem to take real comfort in it. (See chapter one)

If the God-given ending of Mark is lost then that pesky doctrine of preservation is "done away with: and "scholars" have become the final authority for believers today.

VARIOUS VERSIONS AND MARK 16

The RSV

The Revised Standard Version has a note that says that Mark 16:9-20 is not found "in some manuscripts."

It also offers an alternate two verse ending which reads, "v 9-10 The women quickly told Peter and his friends what had happened. Later, Jesus sent the disciples to the east and to the west with his sacred and everlasting message of how people can be saved forever."

The Phillips New Testament

J.B. Philips translates the verses, but he provides a heading that lists them as "an ancient appendix" to the book of Mark.

The New World Translation

The Jehovah's Witness translation provides both the long and short endings to Mark 16 with notes that explain to Mark 16 with notes that explain that both have some support in "certain manuscripts."

The Williams New Testament

Williams provides a note that says verse 8 ends the book of Mark in the two best manuscripts.

The Beck New Testament

The New Testament in the Language of Today (Beck) provides a note at verse 8 that says" The two oldest and best manuscripts do not have Mark 16:9-20 but end Mark's Gospel with verse 8."

The Living Bible

The Living Bible provides a note at verse 8 that reads, "Verse 9-20 are not found in the most ancient manuscripts but may be considered an appendix giving additional facts.:

The Weymouth Translation

Weymouth provides brackets around verses 9-20.

The Moffat Translation

Dr. Moffat adds a footnote that says the reader has a choice of two endings- each an appendix written in the second century attempting to complete what Mark left undone.

The NEB

The New English Bible provides a note after verse 8 that reads, "At this point some of the most ancient witnesses bring the book to a close"

The NASV

The New American Standard Version prints Verse 9-20 in brackets and provides a note that reads " Some oldest manuscripts omit verse 9-20".

The NIV

The New International Version places this note between verse 8 and verse 9. " The most reliable early manuscripts and other ancient witnesses do not have Mark 16:9-20."

The New King James Bible

The New King James Bible provides this note at the end of verse 20,"Verses 9-20 are bracketed in Nu-Texts as not original. They are lacking in Codex Sinaticus and Codex Vaticanus, although *nearly all other manuscripts of Mark contain them.*

THE MANUSCRIPT EVIDENCE FOR MARK 16:9-20

Of the five manuscripts that Westcott and Hort considered the oldest, two (Vaticanus and Sinaiticus) do not contain Mark 16:9-20. The other three do contain this passage.

Of the next fifteen manuscripts generally considered the oldest all fifteen contain the full ending of Mark.

Out of 600 minuscule manuscripts, all 600 contain Mark 16:9-20, 618 out of 620 manuscripts often considered most important by most evangelical scholars contain Mark 16:9-20.

These verses are found in all ancient Latin copies of the book of Mark except one.

The Earliest ancient translations, Latin, Gothic and Coptic all include these verses, Among the Syrian translations, all but one (the Sinaitic Syriac) contains this passage.

QUOTATIONS FROM ANCIENT CHURCH LEADERS AND ORGANIZATIONS

These Verses were quoted as Scripture by many church leaders. Some of the quotes were made 150 years before Sinaticus and Vaticanus were produced. Justin Martyr (AD 150), Irenaeus (AD180), Tation (AD 170), and Hippolytus (AD 250) all quote Mark 16:9-20 as Scripture.

Jerome (AD 331-420) acknowledges that some people were using Greek manuscripts that don't contain Mark 16:9-20. However, he quotes it as Scripture and included this passage in his Latin Vulgate translation.

Augustine (AD 395-430) quotes these verses as Scripture

often. So do Nestorius (AD 430),Cyril of Alexandria (AD 444), and Hesychius of Jerusalem (AD430).

Victor of Antioch (Ad 425-450) stated that the last few verses of Mark had been deliberately omitted by certain copyists. He was clear that there was no good reason for this but some teachers omitted them because they wanted to. He pointed out that the vast majority of manuscripts contained these verses and that he was convinced that they were genuine.

Lectionaries in common use among Eastern and Western Churches routinely contained Mark 16:9-20 This is true in lectionaries used by Catholic, Orthodox, Monophysite and Gothic Churches. Mark 16:9-20 was also routinely used in church liturgies among all different professing Christian groups.

THE ABSURDITY OF AN ABRUPT ENDING AT MARK 16:8

To end Mark 16 at verse 8,with no account of the resurrection and the disciples trembling in fear, destroys any meaningful purpose for the book. Even liberal textual critic J.J Griesbach wrote: "No one can imagine that Mark cut short the thread of his narrative so ineptly."

Evangelical Bible teacher, Arno Gabelein wrote:

> "Higher criticism declares that the proper ending of the Gospel of Mark is verse 8. They disputed the genuineness of verses 9-20. Another hand, they claim, added later these verses. That spurious translation, which goes under the name of The Twentieth Century New Testament (wholly unsatisfactory), also gives this portion as a late appendix. It is not. Mark wrote it and some of the best scholars have declared that it is genuine. How foolish to assume that the blessed document, which

begins with the sublime statement 'The Gospel of Jesus Christ, the Son of God' could end with 'they were afraid!' The trouble with these critics is that they approach the Word of God with doubt and reject its inspiration."

G. Campbell Morgan, J. Vernon McGee, R.H Lenski, Bruce McClaren, and Albert Barnes have all written refuting the liberal attempt to end Mark 16 with verse 8.

WHAT ABOUT THE ARGUMENT CONCERNING WRITING STYLE?

Liberals are always reflecting on the possibility that the style of writing of some passages prove that it wasn't written by just one author. They tell us Deuteronomy was written by four authors and that Isaiah was finished by Deutero-Isaiah. They tell us that Daniel was compilation and that Paul couldn't have written Ephesians. They assure us that different men wrote I and II Peter. They speculate that the John of the Gospel of John and the John of the book of Revelation are different men.

However their arguments are always subjective and personal. They believe these things simply because they want to!

In 1946 R.H Lenski wrote five pages about the arguments concerning literary style and the ending of Mark 16. He demolished the arguments of the liberals. He pointed out every chapter of the book of Mark contains at least one word that is unique to that chapter. Liberals reject the ending of Mark 16 over the issue of literary style for one reason -they want to!

THE STRANGE BLANK IN THE VATICANUS MANUSCRIPT

Following Mark 16;8 in the Vaticanus manuscript (one of the two authorities for rejecting Mark 16:9-20) there is a blank space of 42 empty lines before Luke 1 begins. This is the only blank area in the entire 759-page manuscript.

Dean John Burgon comments on the importance of this unusual blank space:

> The older manuscript from which Codex B was copied must have infallibly contained the twelve verses in dispute. The copyist was instructed to leave a blank space in memoriam rei. Never was blank more intelligible! Never was silence more eloquent!
>
> By this simple expedient, strange to relate, the Vatican Codex is made to recite itself even while it seems to be bearing testimony against the concluding verses of St. Mark's Gospel, by withholding them: for it forbids the inference which, under ordinary circumstances, have been drawn from that omission.
>
> It does more. By leaving room for the verses it omits, it brings into prominent notice at the end of fifteen centuries and half, a more ancient witness than itself. The venerable author of the original codex from which Codex B was copied, is thereby besought to vie. And thus, our supposed adversary (Codex B) proves our most useful ally; for it procures us the testimony of an hitherto unsuspected witness. The earlier scribe unmistakably comes forward at this stage of inquiry, to explain that he at least is prepared to answer for the genuineness of these twelve concluding verses with which the later scribe, his copyist, from his omission of them, might unhappily be thought to have been unacquainted."[3]

N. CLAYTON CROY

---

[3] Fuller, Counterfeit or Genuine, P. 67-68

In 2003, N. Clayton Croy's book, *The Mutilation of Mark's Gospel*, was published. It is compendium of all the different views of the ending of Mark.

He considers the rejection of Mark 16:9-20 by Westcott and Hort as proof that these verses do not belong in the Bible. For him, clearly Sinaiticus and Vaticanus are authoritative.[4]

He admits that the vast majority of all manuscripts contain the traditional ending and that it was accepted throughout the centuries.[5]

He completely refutes the idea that Mark 16 could have ended at verse 8. However, since he is sure that the Traditional Text and the King James Bible couldn't possibly be right, he concludes that the true ending of Mark 16 must be lost. Since he doesn't believe in the doctrine of preservation this is not a problem for him.

He approvingly quotes the statement of Fenton Hort about Mark 16:9-20:

> There is…. No difficulty in supposing …(1) that the true intended continuation of vv. 1-8 either was very early lost by the detachment of a leaf or was never written down; and (2) that a scribe or editor, unwilling to change the words of the text before him or to add words of his own, was willing to furnish the gospel with what seemed a worthy conclusion by incorporating with it unchanged a narrative of Christ's appearance after the Resurrection which he found in some secondary record then surviving from a preceding generation. If these

---

[4] p.21.

[5] Croy, p.19.

suppositions are made, the whole tenure of the evidence becomes clear and harmonious. Every other view is, we believe, untenable.[6]

Hort was not bound by any belief in divine preservation of Scripture.

"WHAT ABOUT DIVINE PRESERVATION?"

David Otis Fuller, in his introduction to Burgon's The Last Twelve Verses of Mark writes:

> Every faithful Christian must reckon seriously with the teaching of Christ concerning the providential preservation of Scripture. Our Lord evidently believed that the Old Testament Scriptures had been preserved in their original purity from the time of their first writing down to His own day that this providential preservation would continue until the end of ages.[7]

Are the last verses of Mark lost? If they are, is there any more Scripture lost? Can anyone be sure that we are not missing passages from every other book? If Mark 16:9-20 is spurious, is our Bible full of other false passages?

Your perspective will be determined by your doctrine The evidence for Mark 16:9-20 is overwhelming. But if you are determined to protect Vaticanus or sinaiticus you just won't face the evidence. If you are determined to protest Westcott and Hort you will find it easy to reject the evidence.If you are determined not to admit that you and your fellow "scholars" are wrong about one of your fundamentally important beliefs then you will claim that you can't find one verse in the Bible about

---

6 Westcott and Hort, The New Testament in the Original Greek, p.46

7 Fuller, David Otis. The Last Twelve Verses of Mark.

diving preservation-so it is no problem if the ending of Mark is lost.

If you trust what the Bible says about divine preservation you will find it easy to face the facts of history and the overwhelming manuscript evidence for Mark 16:9-20.

WHY MAINTAIN THE ATTACK ON MARK 16:9-20?

The evidence for the genuineness of Mark 16:9-20 is compelling. So why do so many cling to the discredited attacks against Mark 16:9-20?

Modernists desperately cling to the idea that Mark 16 ends with verse 8. This is important to them. They deny the essence of the Christian faith (the bodily resurrection of Christ),but they want to be accepted within Christianity anyway. If you end Mark 16 at verse 8 there is no account of the resurrection in Mark 16. Liberals claim that Mark shared their doubts about the resurrection. If you recognize Mark 16:9-20 as Scripture their argument is finished.

Many "evangelical scholars" also have a vested interest in denying Mark 16:9-20. For almost one hundred years, "evangelical scholarship" has accepted the idea that the Sinaiticus and the Vaticanus manuscripts are the "older and better manuscripts." This has become a fundamental of the faith for many modern evangelicals. If you do not believe this you are rejected as an unscholarly, unsound fanatic. You are dismissed as a "simpleton."

Every day in the classrooms of the vast majority of evangelical (and independent Baptist) Bible colleges and seminaries, the traditional Text and the King James Bible is corrected based upon the authority of the Sinaticus and Vaticamus texts. Commentaries have been published which cover every verse by verse by correcting the King James reading with the older and better manuscripts.

In the matter of ending the book of Mark, these manuscripts disagree dramatically with the majority Text (textus Receptus, Byzantine Text.) They also disagree with the vast majority of other Alexandrian texts. Their approach to the ending of Mark is virtually unique. On this matter, they are either the very best of all texts or the very worst.

In his article, *The Secret Spanking of Westcott and Hort*, Dean Burgon makes this point. These two manuscripts are either the very closest to the originals that we have or the ones that are farthest away. Things that are different are not the same!

If we face the facts about Mark 16:9-20 we must admit that these two texts are inferior. If that is true then the very foundation for teaching the Bible in most of our colleges and seminaries has been false for almost a century. Pride won't allow many to make that admission, no matter what the facts are.

If Mark 16:9-20 was given by God, then many modern "evangelical scholars" are found to be less than scholarly. Their criticism of the Traditional Text has for years been based upon a false premise. Their agreement with unsaved textual critics about the text of the Bible is found to be unsound.

A PERSONAL TESTIMONY

I was saved in 1963 as a ten-year-old. I was a "bus kid" attending a non-denominational church in inner-city Indianapolis. My Sunday school teacher taught me that the Bible was the word of God. Every word of it. I accepted it, including Mark 16:9-20, without question.

When I was seventeen, I surrendered to the call to preach. By this time. I was attending an independent Baptist Church.

In Defense of Mark 16:9-20

Our church recommended that everyone use and Old Scofield Reference Bible. I requested one for Christmas and my mother bought me one. Imagine my surprise to discover that I John 5:7 was not inspired and that Mark 16:9-20 was questionable. .

I attended four years of Bible College and never heard the text issue or Bible debate discussed. This subject was so completely ignored that I now wonder if the professors were instructed to ignore it to avoid controversy!

After graduating from college I found myself teaching a Sunday School class on the book of Mark. I carefully studied all the commentaries available to me. Almost all agreed that Mark 16:9-20 was spurious. I wanted to be a serious student and share the best scholarship with my Sunday School students. However, I couldn't get peace about telling them that the King James ending of Mark was false. I ignored the subject and taught through Mark 16:9-20, but felt guilty about it!

A number of years later, I began a serious historical study of the different text types underlying the various translations of the New Testament. I realized how shallow the phrase "older and better manuscripts" is. If a corrupted copy of Mark 16 was made the day after God gave the original, and if we found that copy today, it would be the oldest copy of part of the N.T. ever found. It would be "older and more corrupt". I realized that "modern evangelical scholarship" was based upon "theological political correctness" and not on history, reason and evidence.

I accepted the Traditional Text and the King James Bible by faith. I now had the same view of the Bible I had when I was a bus kid! I believed every word of the Bible that God was using. I had come full circle.

I am still fascinated by the arguments that people use for rejecting the Textus Receptus and King James readings. I am amazed at how history, reason and logic are consistently ignored in the attempt to be considered "scholarly" (theologically correct). I now understand why the Textus Receptus and the King James Bible has withstood all the attacks of the centuries and why they have survived unscathed.

I now teach Mark 16:9-20 as the absolute, verbally inspired Word of God without any question or guilt. The evidence will always support the Scripture if we are not blinded by our desire to be accepted by men who don't accept the scriptures.

In 1907 the Frer Manuscript (now known as Codex W) was discovered in Egypt. It dates back to the fourth century. It contains Mark 16:9-20 with wording exactly like the of the Traditional Text.

Samuel Zwemer, *The Last Twelve Verses of the Gospel of Mark*, writes:

> After all this we are content to turn to the text of the authorized English version, to scores of translations made by the Bible Societies into hundreds of languages and rejoice to find in them no break and no mutilation of the Mark text.[8]

I wonder how many thousands of "bus kids" today understand Mark 16:9-20 better than many of our independent Baptist seminary professors.

---

8 Samuel Zwemer, *The Last Twelve Verses of the Gospel of Mark*, 1918

In Defense of Mark 16:9-20

The Unbroken Bible

9

In Defense of Acts 12:4

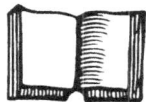

EASTER OR PASSOVER?

One of the most consistent attacks on the King James Bible is that the use of the word *Easter* in Acts 12:4 is an obvious mistake.

"Perhaps there was never a more unhappy, not to say absurd translation than that in our text." - Adam Clark

"The word Easter should be Passover." - J.V. McGee

Acts 12:4 in the KJV says Herod was planning 'after Easter' to bring Peter out. The KJV translates this same Greek word as 'Passover' 28 times. This is the only time they translate this Greek word as 'Easter'. Either the translators were wrong 28 times or they are wrong in Acts 12:4. The NASB translates this Greek word as

Passover all 29 times.[1] - James White

The word that the KJV translates as 'Easter' appears 29 times in the New Testament. In each of the other 28 instances the KJV translates the phrase as 'the passover'. For example, in John 19:14, "And it was the preparation of the passover, and about the sixth hour: and he said unto the Jews, Behold the King!' And there is no reason for confusion as to what Luke is referring to here, for the preceding verse said, 'Then were the days of unleavened bread.' The days of unleavened bread, of course, were connected with the Passover celebration. Yet in this one place the AV contains the anachronistic term 'Easter'. Luke's reference to the days of 'unleavened bread' makes it clear that he is referring to the Jewish Holiday season, not to some pagan festival that did not become known by the specific term 'Easter' for some time to come.[2]

Some consider the utilization of 'Easter' in place of passover in Acts 12:4 in the KJV to be an implementation of dynamic equivalency.[3]

THE PRINCIPLE OF POLYSEMY

"The capacity of a word to have two or more different meanings is technically known as polysemy."[4]

Many words or phrases have more than one possible meaning. This is called polysemy. The proper meaning is determined by

---

1 Robert Joyner, King James Only, p. 14

2 James White, The King James Only Controversy, p. 233

3 Calvin George, the Battle for the Spanish Bible, p. 83.

4 David Black, Linguistics for Students of New Testament Greek, p. 124-125.

"context"- the way the words are used in a given situation. In the dictionary several possible definitions for a polysemic word will be listed. The most common definition will be listed first, then the second most common and so forth. Context will often rule out many translations or definitions that are linguistically possible.

Hebrew, Greek and English are polysemic languages. Polysemic languages are often humorous to people with nonpolysemic languages (see Russian comedian Yakov Smirnov's famous comedy skit "The Door is Ajar").

POLYSEMY AND THE BIBLE

There are many places in the Bible where the principle of polysemy and context play an extremely important role in translation and/or interpretation.

In Isaiah 7:14, virgin is one linguistically possible translation for the Hebrew word *almah*. Another is young maiden. Context requires the use of the word virgin. This is confirmed by the Greek quotation of Isaiah 7:14 in Matthew 1:23. Virgin is the only possible translation for the Greek word *parthenos* used in Matthew 1:23.

The King James translation uses the word virtue in Mark 5:30, Luke 6:19, 8:46. Most modern translations use the word "power". Either is possible linguistically but the context demands "virtue". There are more than just the power of a magician involved.

The Hebrew word *Elohim* (or is Aramaic equivalent) can mean God, gods, or judges. As a result, it is translated God when it refers to the Creator God (Genesis 1:1) or gods when it refers to the pagan gods (many times in the Old Testament). Context dictates what the proper translation is. In Psalm 136:2, it is translated two different ways in the same phrase - context demands it. In Exodus 22:28, the word gods clearly refers to human judges (people who tend to think that they are gods).

In Daniel 3:25, one of several translations is linguistically possible; a son of the gods, or a son of God, or the Son of God, or the son of the gods. Context demands that it be the Son of God - or Daniel 3 becomes a nonsense passage (see v. 28).

POLYSEMY AND BIAS

It is in dealing with polysemic words that the personal and theological bias of translators and interpreters becomes very clear. If you don't believe in the virgin birth, it is very tempting to use the term "young woman" in Isaiah 7:14, even though context demands otherwise. If you don't believe in the Deity of Christ, it is very tempting to translate Daniel 3:25 "a son of the gods" - even though context demands otherwise.

If you are gripped by a prejudice against the King James Bible, you are tempted to pick any translation that is linguistically possible just as long as it is different from the King James Bible. A graphic example is Hosea 3:1.

The Hebrew phrase "flagons of wine" could also be translated "cakes of raisins". This is linguistically possible but is a nonsense translation.

God condemns Israel for drunkenness in chapters 1, 2, 4, and 5 of Hosea. He is clearly doing the same in Hosea 3:1! But an anti-KJB bias makes some people willing to grasp at any possible translation as long as it is different from the KJB.

So the Revised Standard Version reads "and love cakes of raisins," the Contemporary English Versions reads "and enjoy cakes with fruit". The New American Standard Version reads, "and love raisin cakes," the New World Translation reads, "loving raisin cakes" and the New International Version "and love the sacred raisin cakes". That's right, these modern translations have God condemning Israel for liking raisins. Anything to keep from agreeing with the KJB.

The Living Bible ignores the Hebrew words completely and uses the phrase "turned to other gods and offered them choice gifts". The New King James Version tries to get out of this amazing mess by adding words: "and love the raisin cakes of the pagans". They admit they added the words "of the pagans" by putting them in italics. The New English Bible reads "and loves raisin cakes offered to idols". No reader of the NEB could tell that the last three words were added to the text. Some are so biased against the KJB that they will believe anything that doesn't match the KJB.

The King James translators referred to flagons of wine because the context demanded it.

EASTER AND POLYSEMY

In the New Testament times, the Greek word "pascha (or pasche)" is used to refer to religious holiday feasts. So are its Hebrew and Aramaic equivalents.

Its most common usage in Greek literature was in reference to the pagan feast of Ishtar. This feast was later adopted by the Roman Catholics and the name changed to Easter. The pagan festival of Ishtar had been around for centuries before Rome tried to "Christianize" it. "Easter is nothing else than Astarte, one of the titles of beltis, the queen of heaven".[5]

The second most common usage was in reference to the Jewish feast of the Passover.

---
5 Alexander Hislop, The Two Babylons, p. 103

The Unbroken Bible

The third most common usage referred to a pagan holiday feast in the fall.

The fourth most common usage referred to a pagan feast in December (later adopted by the Roman Catholics as Christmas). Each time the word was used, the context determined which holiday feast it referred to.

According to the New Oxford English Dictionary, the word paschal: (1) relates to Easter, and (2) relates to the Jewish Passover.

According to Webster's Dictionary, the word Easter originally referred to a pagan spring festival almost coincident in the date with the Passover Festival.

The Roman Catholic church tried to merge the pagan holiday of ishtar with the Jewish Passover to create a new Christian holiday- Easter. This created confusion in the mind of many in the Christian world.

The word pascha is used 29 times in the New Testament. In most early English Bibles, it is translated Easter every time. This was consistent with Catholic usage. Easter is the most common definition of the word in Greek literature.

However, the King James translators did not follow this policy (as they mention on page 11 of their preface).

In 28 of 29 cases the context demands the translation, Passover. The Jewish holiday is clearly in view. They rejected the Catholic idea of always translating the word pascha as Easter. Recognizing the principle of polysemy, they turned to the second most common definition of the word pasche- passover.

However, in one place they retained the word Easter because the Jewish Passover was clearly not being referred to.

The holiday referred to clearly takes place during or after the feast of the unleavened bread (Acts 12:3-4). The days of the unleavened bread take place for the first seven days AFTER the Passover - see Exodus 12; Ezra 6:19-22; II Chronicles 30:15-21; Deuteronomy 16:1-3; NUmbers 28:16-17; Leviticus 23:5-6; Joshua 5:10-11.

This holiday feast took place after the Passover- to call it the Passover would clearly be a mistake.

The word pascha could not refer to the holiday feasts in September or December because this "pascha" followed closely after the Passover which took place in April. Practicing the principle of polysemy, considering the immediate context of Acts 12 and the whole context of Scripture, the KJB translators knew exactly which word to pick. Only the pagan festival of Ishtar (Easter) fits the context. Ishtar was celebrated in the spring. They chose the word Easter precisely because Easter is the only possible correct word here. They used Easter because it was the pagan Easter feast in view in this passage. Their scholarship far outshines the scholarship of their critics.

As Sam Gipp writes:

> This we see that it was God's providence which had the Spirit-filled translators of our Bible to correctly translate 'pascha' as 'Easter'. It most certainly did not refer to the Jewish passover. In fact, to change it to 'passover' would confuse the reader and make the truth of the situation unclear.

The Unbroken Bible
THE TRANSLATORS ON POLYSEMY

"Another thing we think good to admonish thee of (gentle Reader) that we have not tried ourselves to an uniformity of phrasing, or to an identity of words, as some peradventure would wish that we had done, because they observe, that some learned men somewhere, have been as exact as they could that way. Truly, that we might not vary from the sense of that which we had translated before, if the word signified that same in both places (for there be some words that be not the same sense everywhere) we were especially careful, and make a conscience, according to our duty. But, that we should express the same notion in the same particular word; as for example, if we translate the Hebrew or Greek word once by PURPOSE, never to call it INTENT; if one where JOURNEYING, never TRAVELING; if one were THINK; never SUPPOSE; of one where PAIN, never ACHE; if one were JOY, never GLADNESS, etc. This to mince the matter, we thought to savour more of curiosity than wisdom, and that rather it would breed scorn in the Atheist than bring profit to the godly Reader."- King James Translators, from the Preface to the King James Bible

In Defense of Acts 12:4

The Unbroken Bible

PART FOUR

The Unbroken LEGACY

The Cultural Legacy of the King James Bible
The Linguistic Legacy of the King James Bible
The Spiritual Legacy of the King James Bible

The Unbroken Bible

10

The Cultural Legacy of the King James Bible

The influence of the King James Bible can be traced in many areas. Its legacy is unmatched in Western Civilization. According to Vanderbilt University Press, the King James Bible is the best-selling book of all times.[1] According to historian Adam Nicholson, more than five billion copies of the King James Bible have been sold over the last 399 years.[2] According to Nelson publishers, the King James Bible is the most frequently quoted document in existence.[3] Donald L. Brake calls the KJB the "most famous and influential Bible in English history."[4] The Story of English, (a history of the English

---

1 Allen, Ward, Translating for King James, Vanderbilt Press, 1969, back cover.

2 Nicholson, Adam, 2003 Interview with Given Ifill, Online News Hour.

3 Nelson Publishers, Advertisement for KJV400 Celebration in the History Channel Magazine.

4 Brake, Donald L., A Visual History of the English Bible, Baker books, 2008, p. 235.

language), goes even farther, calling the KJB "Probably the single-most influential book ever published in the English language."[5] This reference makes every other English Bible translation seem minor in significance.

Adam Nicholson describes the KJB "as the richest, most passionate (and most bought) of all works of English prose. It is full of grandeur and a vivid heart-gripping immediacy."[6] As the King James Bible approaches its anniversary, there is increasing focus of its incredible impact. In 2011, it will have been the dominant English Bible translation for four hundred years. Hundreds of English Bible translations have been offered to replace it. It outlasts them all. The KJB is used all over the world and its influence is felt everywhere. Christopher Anderson writes that the KJB "is the only version in existence on which the sun never sets."[7]

Every American president, except one (Franklin Pierce) has taken his oath of office with his hand on the King James Bible. Arthur Cleveland Coxe stated, "The Holy Scriptures, as translated in the reign of King James the First, are the noblest heritage of the Anglo-Saxon race."[8]

The 1995 edition of Compton's Encyclopedia calls the KJB "the most influential book in the history of English civilization."

THE BEAUTY OF THE KING JAMES BIBLE

C. S. Lewis complained that the KJB was too beautiful to

---

5 McCrum, Robert, The Story of English, 1986, p. 109.

6 Nicholson, Adam, The Greatest Story Ever Written, July 15, 2002, Internet article.

7 Thuesen, Peter J., In Discordance with the Scripture, Oxford, 1999, p. 36.

8 Coxe, Arthur Cleveland, An Apology for the Common English Bible, Vance Classic Reprints 48, 1857. p. 5.

serve as a common edition of the Bible.[9] Has such a "complaint" ever been made about any other English Bible translation?

The Merit Students Encyclopedia describes the KJB this way:

> The greatest English Bible is the Authorized, or King James, Version. Based on Tyndale's translation and original texts, it was produced in 1611 by six groups of churchmen at the command of King James I. The King James Bible became the traditional Bible of English-speaking Protestants. Its dignified and beautiful style strongly influenced the development of literature in the English language. The influence can be seen in the works of John Bunyan, John Milton, Herman Melville, and many other writers.

Actor Charlton Heston described the beauty of the King James Bible in his autobiography:

> . . .the King James translation has been described as 'the monument of English prose' as well as 'the only great work of art ever created by a committee'. Both statements are true. Fifty-four scholars worked seven years to produce the work from its extant texts in Aramaic, Hebrew, Greek, Latin, and English. Such an undertaking can be expected to produce great scholarship, but hardly writing as spare and sublime as the King James. . .

> The authors of several boring translations that have followed over the last fifty years mumble that the KJV is 'difficult' filled with long words. Have a look at the difficult long words that begin the Old Testament, and end in the Gospels: 'In the beginning God created the

---

9 Lewis, C. S., introduction to the Letters to Young Churches by J. B. Philips.

heaven and the earth. And the earth was without form, and void; darkness was upon the face of the deep.' And 'Now, of the other things which Jesus did, if they should be written every one, I suppose the world itself could not contain the books that would be written. Shakespeare aside, there's not comparable writing in the language, as has been observed by wiser men than I.

Over the past several centuries it's been the single book in most households, an enormous force in shaping the development of the English language. Carried around the world by missionaries, it provided the base by which English is about to become the lingua franca of the world in the next century. Exploring it during this shoot (Ten Commandments) was one of the most rewarding creative experiences of my life."[10]

H. L. Mencken wrote about the KJB, "It is the most beautiful of all the translations of the Bible; indeed, it is probably the most beautiful piece of writing in all the literature of the world."[11]

Dr. William Faber, a Roman Catholic priest, wrote about the KJB:

It lives on the ear like a music that can never be forgotten, like the sound of church bells, which the convert hardly knows how he can forego. Its felicities often seem to be almost things rather than words. It is a part of the national mind and the anchor of national seriousness. The memory of the dead passes into it. The potent traditions of childhood are stereotyped in its verses. The power of all the grief and trials of a man is

---

10 Heston, Charlton, In the Arena, Simon and Schuster, 1995, p. 554-5.

11 Paine, Gustavus S., The Men Behind the King James Version, Baker Book House, 1959, p. VIII.

The Cultural Legacy of the King James Bible

hidden beneath its words. It is the representative of his best moments; and all that there has been about him of soft, and gentle, and pure, and penitent, and good speaks to him forever out of his English Bible.[12]

Interestingly enough, a beautiful translation was not a conscious goal of the KJB translators. It was simply a by-product of an accurate translation.

Historian Alister McGrath writes:

> Yet there is no evidence that the translators of the King James Bible had any great interest in matters of literature or linguistic development. Their concern was primarily to provide an accurate translation of the Bible, on the assumption that accuracy was itself the most aesthetic of qualities to be desired. Paradoxically, the king's translators achieved literacy distinction precisely because they were not deliberately pursuing it. Aiming at truth, they achieved what later generations recognized as beauty and elegance. Where later translations deliberately and self-consciously sought after literary merit, the king's translators achieved it unintentionally, by focusing on what, to them, was a greater goal. Paradoxically, elegance was achieved by accident, rather than design."[13]

President Ronald Reagan described his feelings about the beauty of the King James Bible:

> "What would you say if someone decided Shakespeare's plays, Charles Dickens's novels, or the music of Beethoven could be rewritten and improved?.

---

12 Paine, Gustavus S., The Men Behind the King James Version, Baker Book House, 1959, p. VIII.

13 McGrath, Alister, In the Beginning, Doubleday, 2001, p. 254-5.

The Unbroken Bible

...Writing in the journal The Alternative, Richard Hanser, author of The Law and the Prophets and Jesus: What Manner of Man is This? has called attention to something that is more than a little mind boggling. It is my understanding that the Bible (both the Old and the New Testaments) has been the best-selling book in the entire history of printing.

Now another attempt has been made to improve it. I say another because there have been several fairly recent efforts to 'make the Bible more readable and understandable'. But as Mr. Hanser so eloquently says 'For more than three and a half centuries, its language and its images have penetrated more deeply into the general culture of the English-speaking world, and been more deeply treasured, than anything ever put on paper.' He then quotes the irreverent H. L. Mencken, who spoke of it as purely a literary work and said it was, 'probably the most beautiful piece of writing in any language'.

They were, of course, speaking of the Authorized Version, the one that came into being when the England of King James was scoured for translators and scholars. It was a time when the English language had reached its peak of richness and beauty.

Now we are to have The Good News Bible which will be in 'the natural English of everyday adult conversation'. I'm sure the scholars and clergymen supervised by the American Bible Society were sincerely imbued with the thought that they were taking religion to the people with their Good News Bible, but I can't help feeling we should instead be taking the people to religion and lifting them with the beauty of language that has outlived the centuries." (Radio address aired on September 6, 1977)

The Cultural Legacy of the King James Bible

J Issacs, in his essay, "The Authorized Version and After" (1940), exclaims:

> The Authorized Version is a miracle and a landmark. Its felicities are manifold, its music has entered into every blood and marrow of English thought and speech, and it has given countless proverbs and proverbial phrases even to the unlearned and the irreligious. There is no corner of English life, no conversation ribald or reverent it has not adorned. It has both broadened and retarded the stream of English speech. It is more archaic in places than its forerunners, and it is impossible for us to disentangle from our ordinary talk the phrases of Judea, whether Hebrew or Greek, whether of the patriarchs, the prophets, the poets, or the apostles. Only the closest scrutiny can give precision to the rhapsodically vagueness with which the Authorized Version is worshiped at a distance.[14]

Joseph Addison, famous eighteenth Century British essayist, dramatist and political leader wrote:

> It happens very luckily, that the Hebrew idioms run into the English tongue with a particular grace and beauty. Our language has received innumerable elegancies and improvements, from the infusion of Hebraism, which is derived to it out of the poetical passages on Holy Writ. They give a force and energy to our expressions, warm and animate our language, and convey our thoughts in more ardent and intense phrases, than any that are to be met within our own tongue . . . How cold and dead does a prayer appear that is composed in the most elegant and polite forms of speech which are natural to our tongue when it is not heightened by the solemnity of phrase

---

14 Bruce, Frederick. F., History of the Bible in English, Cambridge, 2002, p. 26.

which may be drawn from the sacred writings.[15]

Charles A Dinsmore, for many years professor at Yale Divinity School, in his great work, The English Bible as Literature, wrote of "the unique and sovereign greatness of our standard English Version," saying: "It is unlike any other book in our language, and in charm and power is above them all."[16]

Thomas B. Macaulay, the author of the classic multi-volume History of England, comments that the translators of the Authorized Version produced a book which: "...if everything else in our language should perish, would alone suffice to show the whole extent of its beauty and power."[17]

Many authors have remarked upon the beauty of the KJB. But the remarkable influence of the KJB goes far beyond its beauty.

THE INFLUENCE ON WESTERN CULTURE OF THE KING JAMES BIBLE

The Anglo-Christian culture, known as Western Civilization, has promoted prosperity and freedom around the world for almost four hundred years. This culture was created by the King James Bible and was made possible by the bonding influence of a shared Bible.

Professor Russell Kirk wrote:

---

[15] Rosenau, William, Hebraisms in the Authorized Version of the Bible, 1900, p. 14.

[16] Dinsmore, Charles, The English Bible as Literature, Houghton, Mifflin, 1931, p. VIII.

[17] Price, Ira M., The Ancestry of Our English Bible, Harper and Brothers, 1906, p. 4.

The Cultural Legacy of the King James Bible

The book that was to exert a stronger influence than any other in America was not published until 1611, a few years after the first Virginian settlement: the 'King James' translation of the Bible, the Authorized Version prepared by English scholars for King James I. Read from American pulpits and in the great majority of American households during colonial times, the Authorized Version shaped the style, informed the intellect, affected the laws, and decreed the morals of the North American colonies.[18]

Barrett Wendell, a professor of composition at Harvard for twenty years, observes,

> The King James Bible is probably the greatest masterpiece of translation in the world; it has exercised on the thought and the language of English-speaking peoples an influence which cannot be overestimated.[19]

The influence of the King James Bible on the development of the United States of American is hard to over-estimate. In *the Bible of America*, P. Marion Simms wrote, "No nation in all history was ever founded by people so dominated by the Bible as America."[20] Primarily, that Bible was the King James Bible.

Historian Paul Johnson wrote:

> "Hence Americans never belonged to the religious category who seek certainty of doctrine through clerical

---

18 Kirk, Russell, America's British Culture, Transaction Publications, 1993, p. 22

19 Wendell, Barrett, A Literary History of America, T. Fisher Union, 1901, p. 5

20 Simms, P. Marian, The Bible in America, Wilson-Erickson, 1936, p. 14.

hierarchy; during the whole of the colonial period, for instance, not a single Anglican bishop was ever appointed to rule flocks there. What most Americans did belong to was the second category; those who believe that the knowledge of God comes directly to them through the study of Holy Writ. They read the Bible for themselves, assiduously, daily. Virtually every humble cabin in Massachusetts colony had its own Bible. Adults read it alone, silently. It was also read aloud among families, as well as in church, during Sunday morning service, which lasted from eight till twelve (there was more Bible-reading in the afternoon). Many families had a regular course of Bible-reading which meant that they covered the entire text of the Old Testament in the course of each year. Every striking episode was familiar to them, and its meaning and significance earnestly discussed; many they knew by heart. The language and lilt of the Bible in its various translations, but particularly in the magnificent new King James Version, passed into the common tongue and script. On Sunday the minister took his congregation through key passages, in carefully attended sermons which rarely lasted less than an hour. But authority laid in the Bible, not the minister, and in the last resort every man and woman decided 'in the light which Almighty God gave them' what the Bible meant."[21]

Historian Benson Bobrick describes the impact of the KJB on western culture:

> "Next to the Bible itself, the English Bible was (and is) the most influential book ever published. It gave every literate person complete access to the sacred text, which helped to foster the spirit of inquiry through reading and reflection. These in turn accelerated the

---
21 Johnson, Paul, A History of the American People, Harper Collins, 1997, p. 40.

growth of commercial printing and the ever-widening circulation and production of books. Books 'formerly imprisoned in the libraries of monasteries' were, as one contemporary put it, 'redeemed from bondage, obtained their enlargement, and freely walked about in the light.'

Once the people were free to interpret the Word of God according to the light of their own understanding, they began to question the authority of their inherited institutions, both religious and secular, which led to reformation within the Church, and to the rise of constitutional government in England and the end of the divine right of kings. Although the vernacular Bible had begun as a pillar of support for England's monarchical authority and independence from the pope, in the end it contributed to and justified defiance of the monarchy itself.

Only in England was the Bible in any sense a 'national possession,' in that it seemed to exist apart in English as an original work of art. Indeed, not even Luther's version (despite its impact on the development of the German language) may be compared to the English Bible in this way. Englishmen looked to and cherished their Bible—as the ground and inspiration of their lives—overseas, even as it came to live in their own language with more abiding force 'than the greatest works to which their authors were giving birth.' In some indefinable way, it managed to incorporate into their own history 'a living memory of the central part of the world,' so that, over time, 'the deeds and thoughts of men who had lived thousands of years before in the eastern Mediterranean came to color the everyday thought and speech of Britons to the same degree,' wrote the great historian G. M. Trevelyan, 'as they are colored in our own day by the commonplace of the newspaper press.' Beyond the shores of Albion,

The Unbroken Bible

it fortified the spirit of the pioneers of New England, helped to shape the American psyche, and through its impact on thought and culture eventually spread the world over, 'as wide as the waters be.'"[22]

In Pen of Iron, Robert Alter wrote: "But it was in America that the potential of the 1611 translation to determine the foundational language and symbolic imagery of a whole culture was most fully realized."[23]

William Lyon Phelps wrote: "The Bible is not only the foundation of modern English; it is the foundation of Anglo-Saxon civilization.[24]

On the three hundredth anniversary of the King James Bible, Cleland Boyd McAfee wrote, *The Greatest English Classic, A Study of the King James Version of the Bible and Its Influence on Life and Literature.* He describes the influence of the King James Bible on western culture:

> And it would not be surprising if it should have such influence. It is the one great piece of English literature which is universal property. Since the day it was published it has been kept available for everybody. No other book has ever had its chance. English-speaking people have always been essentially religious. They have always had a profound regard for the terms, the institutions, the purposes of religion. Partly that has been maintained by the Bible; but the Bible in its turn has been maintained by it. So it has come about that English-speaking people,

---

22 Bobrick, Nelson, Wide as the Waters, Penguin Books, 2001, p. 11-12.

23 Robert, Pen of Iron, American Prose and the King James Bible, Princeton University Press, 2010, p. 1.

24 Phelps, William Lyon, Reading the Bible, Macmillan Company, 1919, p. 15.

The Cultural Legacy of the King James Bible

though they have many books, are essentially people of one Book. Wherever they are, the Bible is. Queen Victoria has it nearby when the messenger from the Orient appears, and lays her hand upon it to say that this is the foundation of the prosperity of England. But the poor housewife in the cottage, with only a crust for food, stays her soul with it. The Puritan creeps into hiding with the Book, while his brother sails away to the new land with the Book. The settler may have his Shakespeare; he will surely have his Bible. As the long wagon train creeps across the plain to seek the Western shore, there may be no other book in all the train, but the Bible will be there. Find any settlement of men who speak the English tongue, wherever they make their home, and the Bible is among them. When did any book have such a chance to influence men? It is the one undisturbed heritage of all who speak the English tongue. It binds the daughter and the mother country together, and gathers into the same bond the scattered remnants of the English-speaking race the world around. Its language is the one speech they all understand. Strange it would be if it had not a profound influence upon history."[25]

On the three hundredth anniversary of the KJB, President William Howard Taft wrote:

> "The publication of this version of the Holy Scriptures in 1611 associates it with the early colonies of the English people upon this continent. It became at once the Bible of our American forefathers. Its classic English has given shape to American literature. Its spirit has influenced American ideals in life and laws and government.
>
> I trust that this celebration may continue and deepen the influence of the Bible upon the people of this

---
25 McAfee, Cleland B., The Greatest English Classic

Republic."[26]

Men learned about limited government, liberty, personal faith in Christ, and responsibility to God from the King James Bible. Speaking about the tercentenary anniversary of the King James Bible, Woodrow Wilson said:

> The Bible is a book which reveals men unto themselves, not as creatures in bondage, not as men under human authority, not as those bidden to take counsel and command of any human source. It reveals every man to himself as a distinct moral agent, responsible not to men, not even to those men whom he has put over him in authority, but responsible through his own conscience to his Lord and Maker. Whenever a man sees the vision he stands up a free man, whatever may be.[27]

---

[26] From a statement released by the White House for Tercentenary Celebration of the King James Bible.

[27] From a speech delivered on the Tercentenary Anniversary of the King James Bible, in Denver on May 7, 1911.

The Cultural Legacy of the King James Bible

The Unbroken Bible

II

The Linguistic Legacy of the King James Bible

The KJB was a pioneer in English literature. It was the first example of major English prose to be based primarily upon Anglo-Saxon words rather than Latin words. This approach would become standard in the English language because of the influence of the KJB.

The King James Bible used short phrases joined together by conjunctions like and. We take this for granted today because it is basic English. However, before the KJB, English prose was much wordier and much harder to read.

Paul Cross writes: "Whether we live in England or America, Australia or Africa, Canada or the Caribbean, the English language was largely shaped by one book—the King James Version of the Bible."[1]

---

1 Cross, Paul, Spiritual Reflections: What's Been the Impact of the King James Bible? Sept, 17, 2010, Internet article.

The Unbroken Bible

In 1611 only one nation on the planet spoke English. Today dozens of nations have English as their official language and many more use English as a secondary language.

Literary figure Matthew Arnold wrote (of the KJB):

> He (the translator) will find one English book and one only, where, as in the Iliad itself, perfect plainness of speech is allied with perfect nobleness; and the book is the Bible.[2]

In 1906, Ira Maurice Price, writing in The Ancestry of Our English Bible wrote:

> "For almost three centuries the Authorized, or King James, Version has been the Bible of the English-speaking world. Its simple, majestic Anglo-Saxon tongue, its clear, sparkling style, its directness and force of utterance have made it the model in language, style, and dignity of some of the choicest writers of the last two centuries. Its phrasing is woven into much of our noblest literature; and its style, which to an astonishing degree is merely the style of the original authors of the Bible, has exerted very great influence in molding the ideal of simplicity, directness, and clarity which now dominates the writing of English. It has endeared itself to the hearts and lives of millions of Christians and has molded the characters of leaders in every walk of life. During all these centuries the King James Version has become a vital part of the English-speaking world, socially, morally, religiously, and politically."[3]

---

2 McGrath, Alister, In the Beginning, Doubleday, 2001, p. 218.

3 Price, Ira M., The Ancestry of Our English Bible, Harper and Brothers, 1906, p. 276-7.

The Linguistic Legacy of the King James Bible

The simple, direct, clear form of expression that English is famous for (or used to be famous for) is the product of the influence of the King James Bible. This directness is one reason (along with the financial influence of the U.S.A. and Britain and television) why English has become the second language to the world.

Robert Alter, wrote about Lincoln's Gettysburg Address, ". . .though one might argue that the very use of a language that is both plain and dignified, resonant in its very ordinariness, is in part inspired by the dictation of the King James Version."[4]

Alter also writes:

> The King James Version of the Bible, once justifiably thought of as the national book of the American people, helped foster, at least for two centuries, a general responsiveness to the expressive, dignified use of language, to the ways in which the rhythms and diction of a certain kind of English could move readers.[5]

Parataxis (the use of short, clear, complete sentences) became common in American literature and in everyday common American speech because of the influence of the King James Bible.

Historian Mark A Noll writes:

> Because the KJV was so widely read for religious purposes, it had also become a source of public ideals. Because it was so central in the churches, and because the churches were so central to the culture, the KJV

---

4 Chanes, Jerome, If English Was Good Enough for Jesus Christ, August 25, 2010, Internet article.

5 Altar, Robert, Pen of Iron, American Prose and the King James Bible, Princeton University Press, 2010, p. 41

functioned also as a common reservoir for the language. Hundreds of phrases (clear as crystal, powers that be, root of the matter, a perfect Babel, two-edged sword) and thousands of words (arguments, city, conflict, humanity, legacy, network, voiceless, zeal) were in the common speech because they had first been in this translation.[6]

The King James Bible became the source of "sacred linguistics" for western civilization. "With the Puritan adoption of the King James Bible, the words of 1611 became America's sacred lexicon, the language in which divinity addressed humanity."[7]

As Alister McGrath writes: "The Bible changed a nation, a language and a culture."[8]

THE LITERARY INFLUENCE OF THE KING JAMES BIBLE

Historian Alister McGrath declares of the KJB, "It did not follow literary trends; it established them." He also wrote:

> The two greatest influences on the shaping of the English language are the works of William Shakespeare and the English translation of the Bible that appeared in 1611. The King James Bible—named for the king of England who ordered the production of a fresh translation in 1604—is both a religious and literary classic. Literary scholars have heaped praise upon it. Nineteenth-century writers and literary critics acclaimed it as the 'noblest monument of English prose.' In a series of lectures at Cambridge University during the First World War, Sir

---

6 Noll, Mark, The American Biblical Tradition, July 7, 2006, Internet article.

7 Thuesen, Peter J., In Discordance with the Scriptures, Oxford Press, 1999, p. 30.

8 McGrath, Alister, In The Beginning, Doubleday, 2001, front page.

The Linguistic Legacy of the King James Bible

Arthur Quiller-Couch declared that the King James Bible was 'the very greatest' literary achievement in the English language. The only possible challenger for this title came from the complete works of Shakespeare. His audience had no quarrel with this judgment. It was the accepted wisdom of the age.

The King James Bible was a landmark in the history of the English language, and an inspiration to poets, dramatists, artists, and politicians. The influence of this work has been incalculable. For many years, it was the only English translation of the Bible available.[9]

William Lyon Phelps was the Lampton Professor of English Literature at Yale University for 41 years. He was a graduate of both Yale and Harvard. He was the author of numerous books about English and American Literature. In 1921 he wrote the following about the King James Bible:

> Priests, atheists, skeptics, devotees, agnostics, and evangelists, are generally agreed that the Authorized Version of the English Bible is the best example of English literature that the world has ever seen...

> Every one who has a thorough knowledge of the Bible may truly be called educated; and no other learning of culture, no matter how extensive or elegant, can, among Europeans and Americans, form a proper substitute. Western civilization is founded upon the Bible...I thoroughly believe knowledge of the Bible without a college course is more valuable than a college course without the Bible...

The Elizabethan period—a term loosely applied to the years between 1558 and 1642—is generally regarded

---
9 McGrath, Alister, In the Beginning, Doubleday, 2001, p. 1 and 3.

as the most important era in English Literature. Shakespeare and his mighty contemporaries brought the drama to the highest point in the world's history; lyrical poetry found supreme expression; Spencer's Faerie Queene was a unique performance; Bacon's Essays have never been surpassed. But the crowning achievement of those spacious days was the Authorized Translation of the Bible, which appeared in 1611. Three centuries of English literature followed; but, although they have been crowded with poets and novelists and essayists, and although the teaching of the English language and literature now gives employment to many earnest men and women, the art of English composition reached its climax in the pages of the Bible...

Now, as the English speaking people have the best Bible in the world, and as it is the most beautiful monument erected with the English alphabet, we ought to make the most of it, for it is an incomparably rich inheritance, free to all who can read. This means that we ought invariably in the church and on public occasions to use the Authorized Version; all others are inferior.[10]

He also wrote about the King James Version, "...it is the most important and the most influential book in English literature."[11]

The New World Encyclopedia declares this about the literary influence of the King James Bible:

"The King James Version has proved to have been an influence on writers and poets, whether in their literary style, or matters of content such as the images

---

10 Phelps, William Lyon, Human Nature in the Bible, Scribner and Sons, 1922, p. 13-14.

11 Phelps, William Lyon, Reading the Bible, Macmillan, 1919, p. 10.

they depicted, until the advent of modernism. Although influenced by the Bible in general, they likely could not have helped being influenced by the style of writing the King James Version used, prevalent as it was during their time. John Hayes Gardiner of Harvard University once stated that 'in all study of English literature, if there be any one axiom which may be accepted without question, it is that the ultimate standard of English prose style is set by the King James version of the Bible.' Compton's Encyclopedia once said that the King James Version '. . .has been a model of writing for generations of English-speaking people.

A general effect of the King James Version was to influence writers in their model of writing; beforehand, authors generally wrote as scholars addressing an audience of other scholars, as few ordinary peasants were literate at the time. The King James Version, as it was meant for dissemination among the ordinary man and to be read by preachers to their congregations, could not afford the luxury of using such a technique. The simpler, more direct style used by the translators of the King James Version so influenced authors that their prose began to address the reader as if he or she was an ordinary person instead of a scholar, thus helping create the idea of the general reader."

Author Robert Alter is well known for his book *Pen of Iron: American Prose and the King James Bible*.

Reviews of his book are very instructive:

Robert Alter's *Pen of Iron* is an expanded, book-length version of the Spencer Trask Lectures given by the author at Princeton University in April, 2008. The subject: the pervasive influence of the King James Bible in American literature from its

The Unbroken Bible

1611 publication in England to the present day.

Alter defines the influence of the King James Bible in two ways: As a rich source of ideas, images, and metaphors about God and man, and as a manual of style for a distinctive, classical way of writing. Alter pursues his thesis through a series of examples spanning American literature: Herman Melville's *Moby Dick*, William Faulkner's *Absalom, Absalom!*, Saul Bellow's *Seize the Day*, Ernest Hemingway's *The Sun Also Rises*, Marilynne Robinson's *Gilead* and Cormac McCarthy's *The Road*.

In each example, Alter traces elements of plot, language and style back to the bedrock of the King James Bible. As American culture has become more secular, these associations have become less distinct, but Alter argues the King James Bible continues to have an influence as part of our common literary heritage. Customer review:

> "As a leading scholar and translator of the Bible, who is also deeply knowledgeable about American literature, Robert Alter is ideally suited to study this complicated inheritance... Pen of Iron makes a convincing case that it is impossible to fully appreciate American literature without knowing the King James Bible—indeed, without knowing it almost instinctively, the way generations of Americans used to know it." (Adam Kirsch, New Republic)

> "Alter's intelligent treatments of several major works—principally *Moby Dick, Absalom, Absalom!, Seize the Day,* and Marilynne Robinson's justly applauded novel, *Gilead* (2004)—does more than simply explain allusions to biblical texts. He is interested in the ways in which American writers incorporate the stylistic traits of the King James Version for their own purposes, even when they are not themselves rooted in a Christian or

biblical world view. (Barton Swain, New Criterion)

"Alter's book is tightly focused and sweeping in the specificity of its claims. He takes a commonplace of conventional wisdom—the ubiquity the Bible once had in American elite culture—to argue that the Kings James translation created the 'foundational language and symbolic imagery' of the whole American culture, especially its prose fiction. (David E. Anderson Religion and Ethics Newsweekly)[12]

THE KING JAMES BIBLE AND LITERACY

The King James Bible was translated to be read by the average man. The sponsorship of this translation by the King of England made it safe to own in the average home. Other English Bibles had been made available to the English people but there were always local sheriffs, bishops and abbots to persecute Bible owners, even if the national government was not doing so. Now that a Bible, designed for the average man, was sponsored by the King—no sheriff, bishop or abbot was bold enough to persecute private citizens for owning a King James Bible.

It is no accident that literacy flourished as the King James Bible became available. Historian Adam Nicholson writes about the King James Bible: "It is surely no coincidence that its creation coincides with the first great surge in literary levels in England."[13]

Historian John Strype (1643-1737), as quoted by Alexander W. McClure, described the influence of the KJB on literacy in England:

---

12 Customer reviews as posted on Amazon.com.

13 Nicholson, Adam, God's Secretaries, Harper Collins, 2001, p. 236-7.

The Unbroken Bible

It was wonderful to see with what joy this book of God was received, not only among the learned sort, but generally all England over, among all the vulgar and common people; and with what greediness the Word of God was read, and what resort to places where the reading of it was! Everybody that could, bought the book, or busily read it, or got others to read it to them if they could not themselves. Divers more elderly people learned to read on purpose; and even little boys flocked among the rest to hear portions of the Holy Scriptures read.[14]

---

14 McClure, Alexander, Translators Revived, Maranatha Publications, no date given, p. 38.

The Linguistic Legacy of the King James Bible

The Unbroken Bible

12

The Spiritual Legacy of the King James Bible

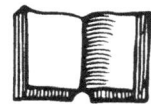

THE SURVIVAL OF THE KING JAMES BIBLE

Over 1,000 English translations of the Bible have been produced since 1611. Hundreds of them are documented in Margaret T. Hills' 1961 book, *A Bibliography of Editions of the Bible or The New Testament*. Many of these translations have been promoted as the translation that will replace the King James Bible. Few of them are still in print.

In 1876 John Read Dore wrote *Old Bibles*. One of the purposes of this book was to prepare the English speaking world for the replacement of the King James Bible by the English Revised Version. He wrote:

> The frequent notices published in the newspapers during the last few years, of the progress being made by the two companies appointed by the Convocation to revise the translation of the Old and New Testament, have

called attention to the fact that before long, the Bible to which English-speaking people have been accustomed for the last 265 years, will cease to be the Authorized version, and a new one will take its place.[1]

He also wrote:

> It is hard to realize the fact that the days of our present version of the Bible are numbered, and in a few years at the most, it will be superseded by a new translation, and be valuable to collectors only, as a copy of one of the disused English versions.[2]

Of course the English Revised Version has long been out of print while millions of copies of the KJB are produced every year.

In 1952, the Rev. Howard Crosby observed that the Revised Standard Version would win universal acceptance within a decade or so after "the old grannies and croakers were dead."[3] He expected the KJB to die with them. The RSV has since been replaced by the New Revised Standard Version. The KJB still outsells the NRSB by a wide margin.

Historian Adam Nicholson writes:

> Of course, alongside this history of dissatisfaction with the inherited text, and of constant attempts to renew it in the light of current fashion, the King James Bible persisted, the touchstone, the national book, the formative mental structure for all English-speaking people. For generation after generation, it gave the

---

1 Dore, John R., Old Bibles, Pickering, 1876, p. 100.

2 Dore, John R., Old Bibles, Pickering, 1876, p. Vii.

3 Thuesen, Peter J., In Discordance with the Scriptures, Oxford Press, 1999, p. 49.

English, and the English in America, a template against which to measure their own utterances.[4]

How do you explain the four-hundred year survival of the King James Bible? Few translations have ever continued in use for one hundred years. There is no purely human explanation for the continued influence of the King James Bible.

THE SPIRITUAL INFLUENCE OF THE KING JAMES BIBLE

The spiritual impact of the King James Bible dwarfs the influence of any other English translation of the Bible. It dwarfs the influence of any other vernacular translation.

When the Bible became a daily part of the common English home, it was the King James Bible that people were reading.

John Richard Green writes:

> No greater moral change ever passed over a nation than passed over England during the years which parted the middle of the reign of Elizabeth from the meeting of the Long Parliament. England became the people of a book, and that book was the Bible. It was as yet the one English book which was familiar to every Englishman, it was read at churches and read at home, and everywhere its words, as they fell on ears which custom had not deadened to their force and beauty, kindled a startling enthusiasm.[5]

Jeremy N. Morris wrote:

---

4 Nicholson, Adam, God's Secretaries, Harper Collins Publishers, 2001, p. 236-237.

5 Green, John Richard, A Short History of the English Speaking People, Chapter 8 as quoted by Ian Paisley, My Plea for the Old Sword.

The Unbroken Bible

Even so, for all the disagreements between different groups of Protestants, something like a common Evangelical culture was coming into being. It had common spiritual resources, for one thing. Chief among these was, of course, the Bible, almost always in the English-speaking world in the King James Version of 1611.[6]

England's common Christian culture was largely shaped by the King James Bible. This culture was later transferred to many of the nations that developed from Great Britain's colonies.

The Great Awakening swept through England and its colonies on the Atlantic seaboard from the 1720s through the 1770s. Millions of people professed faith in Christ. Church attendance in evangelical churches became common; a daily Bible reading became normal. Literacy rates dramatically rose as people longed to read the Bible.

One common denominator in the Great Awakening was that everyone in the English-evangelical world was using the same Bible—the King James Bible.

In 1857, Arthur Cleveland Coxe wrote:

> And now, after two hundred years of the sending forth of colonies, the Anglo-Saxon people dwell in every latitude and longitude; they mingle their blood with other races, and yet remain one with the parent stock. Time, indeed, is working changes; and far-severed branches of the same original family must have their own household feelings, and immediate ties of home. It is not altogether true, alas!, that this mighty people have all 'one LORD, one faith, one baptism.' If it were so, the world would be their easy conquest for the Cross. They

---
6 Morris, Jeremy N., Renewed by the Word, Hendrickson, 2005, p. 69.

do not pray the same prayers, nor with one heart and one mouth, confess the same form of sound words.' But as yet, over and above the common spirit of their laws, they hold fast the great Charter, from which their free laws have proceeded; they possess the same Bible.[7]

Coxe also wrote this about the King James Bible:

> Can it be necessary to argue that no one can inflict a graver wound on the unity of a race, and on all the sacred interests which depend on that unity, under GOD, than by tampering with the English Bible? By the acclamation of the universe, it is the most faultless version of the Scriptures that ever existed in any tongue. To complain of its trifling blemishes, is to complain of the sun for its spots. Whatever may be its faults, they are less evil, and in every way, than would be the evils sure to arise from any attempt to eradicate them; and where there is so much of wheat, the few tares may be allowed to stand till the end of the world. Two centuries, complete, have identified even its slightest peculiarities with the whole literature, poetry, prose, and science, as well as with the entire thought and theology of those ages, and the time, to all appearance, is forever past, when any alteration can be made in it, without a shock to a thousand holy things, and to the pious sensibilities of millions.[8]

The King James Bible was clearly the Bible of the Great Awakening.

In the United States, a Second Great Awakening took place in the 1820s and 1830s. Again, the entire nation was influenced

---

7 Coxe, Arthur Cleveland, An Apology for the Common English Bible, Vance Classic Reprints, No. 48, 1857, p. 7.

8 Coxe, Arthur Cleveland, An Apology for the Common English Bible, Vance Classic Reprints, No. 48, 1857, p. 8.

by evangelical preaching from the King James Bible.

A Third Great Awakening took place from the 1850s through the 1870s. Again, the entire nation felt the influence of evangelical preaching from the King James Bible.

The King James Bible was clearly the Bible of the Great Awakenings. Since a multitude of English Bibles have become common in the English speaking world, nothing similar to the Great Awakenings has taken place.

The aftermath of the first Great Awakening was the modern missions' movement. In the late eighteenth century, pioneers like William Carey and Adoniram Judson called the attention of the English speaking world to the cause of missions. Missionaries would circle the globe preaching the Gospel, translating the Bible and planting churches.

These missionaries were quick to promote the need for vernacular Bible translations. Because of this, some have balked at suggesting that the King James Bible was the Bible of the modern missions' movement. However, the early leaders of this movement were men saved under the preaching of the King James Bible. They were trained under the teaching of the King James Bible. They were called to the mission field under the preaching of the King James Bible. Often, they translated the King James Bible into vernacular languages.

The early English speaking missionaries were joined by a few German, Dutch and Scandinavian missionaries. However, the vast majority of the early missionaries were products of the influence of the KJB. It was truly the Bible of the modern missions' movement.

The King James Bible has impacted many other vernacular Bible translations. As the modern missions' movement sent missionaries around the world, the need for vernacular translations of the Bible was obvious. Very few of the missionaries were Greek and Hebrew scholars. Many of the early translations were done from the King James Bible. A few were done from the Lutheran German Bible or the Italian Diodati Bible.

Sir Winston Churchill wrote:

> In the crowded emigrant ships which sailed to the New World of America, there was little room for baggage. If the adventurers took books with them, they took the Bible, Shakespeare, and later Pilgrim's Progress; and the Bible they mostly took with them was the Authorized Version of King James I. About ninety million copies are thought to have been published in the English language alone. It has been translated into more than seven hundred and sixty tongues. The Authorized Version is still the most popular in England and the United States. This may be deemed James' greatest achievement, for the impulse was largely his. The Scottish pedant built better than he knew. The scholars who produced this masterpiece are mostly unknown and unremembered. But they forged an enduring link, literary and religious, between the English-speaking peoples of the world.[9]

The early translation philosophy of the American Bible Society was to translate from the King James Bible. This policy was later changed to use the Greek and Hebrew Traditional Texts whenever possible. However, all translations were to be judged by the King James Bible. If the vernacular translation disagreed with the King James Bible, it was assumed that the translators had misunderstood the original.

It comes as a surprise to many that the vast majority of

---

9 Churchill, Winston, Churchill's History of the English-Speaking Peoples, Commager, One volume edition, Mead and Co., 1965, p. 160.

The Unbroken Bible

vernacular Bibles used in the world are translated from English Bibles. In recent years, many translations have been done from the American Standard Version, the Revised Standard Version, Today's English Version and the New International Version. However, for the first 150 years of the modern mission movement, the King James Bible was the most common source text for vernacular translation.

Few missionaries have mastered Greek, Hebrew and the vernacular language of their mission field.

Without the preaching of the King James Bible there would have been no modern mission's movement. Without the King James Bible as a source text, the modern missions' movement would have produced very few vernacular Bible translations. Even today, it appears that churches which use the King James Bible often contribute much more per person to missions than churches which do not.

The King James Bible deserves to be called "The Bible of Modern Missions."

Many religious leaders contend that people cannot understand the KJB today. Some church growth "experts" claim that you cannot build a church using the KJB. However, many growing churches—(especially among independent Baptists) are using the KJB. It appears that "bus kids" often have less trouble understanding the KJB than many seminary professors and religious leaders.

Millions around the world still testify to the impact of the King James Bible upon their spiritual life. Two centuries of criticism have not hindered the blessing that the King James Bible is in their life.

How do you explain the four hundred year influence of

the King James Bible? Surely, it is more than a purely human phenomenon!

THE HAND OF GOD UPON THE KING JAMES VERSION

Dr. Dave Sorenson says it well,

> "Now the question must be asked, is the supremacy of the King James Bible a fluke of history or has God had something to do with it? Only a secularist can allege that the flourishing of the KJB over the past 400 years was a coincidence. Who wins the Super Bowl may be a fluke of history. Who is hired as dogcatcher in Dubuque, Iowa, may be a coincidence. Who wins a junior high girls basketball game may be of no concern to God. But to suggest that the preparation, purification, and distribution of the most widely published version of God's Word in history is a coincidence is folly. In the greater perspective of history, it should be apparent that God was involved in every step of the preparation, purifying, and publishing of the King James Bible.
>
> God certainly knew in advance the wide-spread distribution and influence the KJV would have. To the contrary, it would seem that God so-ordained it. Can we assume therefore that He had nothing to do with its historic usage and popularity? There was no such thing as double inspiration or advanced revelation to the KJV translators. However, having said that, it would seem apparent that God has providentially worked behind the scenes in not only purifying and preparing the underlying Hebrew and Greek texts, but also in this dispensation, God has ordained the local church of the New Testament. He has ordained a greater ministry of the Holy Spirit. And, He has exalted His Word. There

can be no other conclusion except that God has had a direct and providential hand in the development and propagation of the most widely used version of His Word in human history.[10]

Historian Gustavus S. Paine draws a similar conclusion:

> Are we to say that God walked with them in their gardens? Insofar as they believed in their own calling and election, they must have believed that they would have God's help in their task. We marvel that they could submerge themselves and assert them, could meekly agree yet firmly declare, and hold to the words they preferred as just and fitting. At the same time they could write and they could listen, speak clearly, and hearken to the sounds they tested, as well as to the voice of what they deemed the divine Author. And that must have been the secret of their grace and their assurance: they agreed, not with other men like themselves, but with God as their guide, and they followed not as thinking them righteous but as led by righteousness beyond them. They knew that human beings are but worms, but that man when he is good and docile may mount up with wings as eagles, to be the child of God.[11]

First of all the translators saw themselves as having the sacred task of reproducing God's original words in English. This task left them in awe of God's Word as they translated every word.

Even skeptic George Bernard Shaw wrote:

> The translation was extraordinarily well done because

---

10 Sorenson, David H., God's Perfect Book, Northstar Ministries, 2009, p. 135-6.

11 Paine, Gustavus, The Men Behind the King James Version, Baker Book House, 1959, p. 169-170.

to the translators what they were translating was not merely a curious collection of ancient books written by different authors in different stages of culture, but the Word of God divinely revealed through His chosen and expressly inspired scribes. In this conviction they carried out their work with boundless reverence and care and achieved a beautifully artistic result. . .they made a translation so magnificent that to this day the common human Britisher or citizen of the United States of North America accepts and worships it as a single book by a single author, the book being the Book of Books and the author being God.[12]

Historian Adam Nicholson describes the attitude of the KJB translators:

> Those who originally wrote the words of the Bible had been God's secretaries, as loyal, as self-suppressing, as utterly disposed to the uses of the divine will as those royal secretaries, the Cecils, had so conspicuously been to Elizabeth and James. Self-abnegation in the service of greatness was the ideal.
>
> Secretary ship is one of the great shaping forces behind the King James Bible. There is no authorship involved here. Authorship is egotistical, an assumption that you might have something new worth saying. You don't. Every iota of the Bible counts but without it you count for nothing. The secretary knows that. Like Robert Cecil, he can be clever, canny, resourceful and energetic but, for all the frustrations, he does not distort the source of his authority. A secretary, whether of God or of king, is in a position of dependent power. He has no authority independent of his master, but he executes

---

12 Paine, Gustavus, The Men Behind the King James Version, Baker Book House, 1959, p. 182-3.

that authority without hesitation or compromise. He is nothing without his master but everything through him. Loyalty is power and submission control. For this reason, biblical translation, like royal service, could only be utterly faithful. Without faithfulness, it became meaningless.[13]

As Nicholson writes: "The English is there to serve the original not to replace it."[14]

Historian Alister McGrath wrote:

> The central objective of the king's translators was scholarly accuracy—the finding of proper English words and phrases to render the original Hebrew, Greek, and Aramaic. Sense and meaning took priority over elegance.[15]

This sense of reverence for the Word of God created an attitude rarely found in Bible translators today. Their sense of awe and responsibility in their roles as Bible translators sets them apart from most Bible translators today. This attitude bonded the translators to the original text.

Secondly, the training and scholarship of the translators of the KJB is without equal.

In the classic book, *Translators Revived*, Alexander W. McClure writes:

> As to the capability of those men, we may say again, that, by the good providence of God, their work was

---

13 Nicholson, Adam, God's Secretaries, Harper Collins, 2003, p. 184.

14 Nicholson, Adam, God's Secretaries, Harper Collins, 2003, p. 210-211.

15 McGrath, Alister, In the Beginning, Doubleday, 2001, p. 254-255.

undertaken in a fortunate time. Not only had the English language, that singular compound, then ripened to its full perfection, but the study of Greek, and of the oriental tongues, and of rabbinical lore, had then been carried to a greater extent in England than ever before or since. This particular field of learning has never been as highly cultivated among English divines as it was at that day. To evince this fact, so far as necessary limits will admit, it will be requisite to sketch the characters and scholarship of those men, who have made all coming ages their debtors. When this pleasing task is done, it is confidently expected that the reader of these pages will yield to the conviction, that all the colleges of Great Britain and America, even in this proud day of boastings, could not bring together the same number of divines equally qualified by learning and piety for the great undertaking. Few indeed are the living names worthy to be enrolled with those mighty men. It would be impossible to convene out of any one Christian denomination, or out of all, a body of translators, on whom the whole Christian community would bestow such confidence as is reposed upon that illustrious company, or who would prove themselves as deserving of such confidence. Very many self-styled 'improved versions' of the Bible, or parts of it, have been paraded before the world, but the religious public has doomed them all, without exception, to utter neglect."[16]

McClure then proceeds to provide the qualifications of the men who produced the King James translation. No other team of translators of any book, of any kind, in the history of the world possessed greater qualifications. The King James translators have many critics. It would be an interesting exercise to compare the qualifications of the critics with the qualifications of those that are being criticized.

---

16 McClure, Alexander W., Translators Revived, Maranatha Publishers, no date given, p. 248-249.

The Unbroken Bible

It is impossible to explain the four hundred years of influence of the King James Bible in purely human terms. Alexander W. McClure states it well in *Translators Revived*:

> Not that the Translators were inspired in the same sense as were the prophets and apostles, and other 'holy men of old.' Who 'were moved by the Holy Ghost' in drawing up the original documents of the Christian faith. Such inspiration is a thing by itself, like any other miracle; and belongs exclusively to those to whom it was given for that high and unequaled end.
>
> But we hold that the Translators enjoyed the highest degree of that special guidance which is ever granted to God's true servants in exigencies of deep concernment to his kingdom on earth. Such special succors and spiritual assistances are always vouchsafed, where there is a like union of piety, of prayers, and of pains, to affect an object of such incalculable importance to the Church of the living God. The necessity of a supernatural revelation to man of the divine will, has often been argued in favor of the extreme probability that such a revelation has been made. A like necessity, and one nearly as pressing, might be argued in favor of the belief, that this most important of all the versions of God's revealed will must have been made under his peculiar guidance, and his provident eye. And the manner in which that version has met the wants of the most free and intelligent nations in the old world and the new, may well confirm us in the persuasion, that the same illuminating Spirit which indited the original Scriptures, was imparted in rich grace to aid and guard the preparation of the English version.[17]

---

17 McClure, Alexander W., Translators Revived, Maranatha Publishers, no date given.

The Spiritual Legacy of the King James Bible

Theologians will debate what terms should be used to define the nature of the divine influence upon the King James Bible. While the theologians are debating, people all over the world will be allowing the King James Bible to speak to their hearts.

While some religious leaders dream of finally producing the English Bible that will finally replace the KJB, little children will be memorizing its rhythmic words.

While university professors in England and the United States complain that the King James Bible cannot be understood, new Christians around the world will be rejoicing in the enlightenment they find in their daily devotions.

The hand of God is the only possible explanation for the majestic four-hundred year legacy of the King James Bible.

The Unbroken Bible

Do We Have a 1611 King James Bible Today?

HOW MANY CHANGES?

"There have been thousands of revisions of the King James Bible!" "There have been four revisions of the King James Bible." "There have been no revisions of the King James Bible!" "There have been 22,000 changes in the King James Bible since 1611." "There have been 75,000 changes in the King James Bible since 1611." "There have been 421 changes in the King James Bible since 1611." "There haven't been any change in the King James Bible since 1611." "I hold in my hands a 1611 King James Bible!". "You couldn't read a 1611 King James Bible if you had one."

All of these statements have been made in connection with the modern debate over the King James Bible. All of them are made by people who recognized as scholars by one group or another. How can such confusion exist about such a simple subject?

The Unbroken Bible

Definitions

Some of the confusion comes because people use the terms "edition", "revisions" and "translation" as if they were interchangeable. They are NOT! There are very real differences in the meanings of these words.

Editions

A new edition refers to a literary work in a new form. The form may be new because of any number of external features. The correction of printing errors, changes in spelling, new footnotes, new marginal references, new parallel verse references, a new type size or font, a new cover or new pictures or maps create a new "edition" of the Bible. They do so without changing the words of the Scripture.

Revisions

A new revision of Scripture occurs when words are changed but only in a specific, limited fashion. Revisions occur when one word is used to replace another in order to make the meaning clearer. This is usually done because the meaning of the translated word has changed. The term revisions is not applicable to a new translation but only when a new word is chosen to convey the same meaning as the original word but in a clearer fashion. Changes can also take place in word order for the same reason.

Translations

A new translation of Scripture takes place when the process of reproducing a word from one language to another takes place. This involves making a decision about what text or texts of Scripture to accept as the original source. It also involves deciding upon a method of translating and rules for translation.

Do We Have A 1611 King James Bible Today?

These definitions of editions, revision, and translation are compatible with the dictionary definitions. These definitions are also similar to the terminology used in discussing the translation of ancient books like the writings of Josephus and the various Greek historians.

EDITIONS OF THE KING JAMES BIBLE

There have been thousands of editions of the King James Bible. There were seventeen in the first three years after it was published. The primary reasons for new early editions were to correct printing errors, change type styles and to standardized the spelling of English words. Later editions have also focused on reference helps, including footnotes, parallel references, chapter headings, maps, and concordances.

Printing errors were numerous in the early editions. The Royal Printer was fined 300 pounds sterling for leaving out the word "not" in Exodus 20:14. It took a long time to weed out all of the printing errors. Occasionally, a typographical error will still be seen in a modern edition of the Scripture.

REVISIONS OF THE KING JAMES BIBLE

It is commonly accepted that there have been four real revisions of the King James text before the modern era. There are about 22,000 differences between the first 1611 King James printing and the fourth revision in 1769. However, almost all of these are the correction of printing errors and changes in spelling. Only 136 changes involve "revising" a word or phrase.

D.A. Waites writes:

> The question is, how great were those revisions? How much has the wording changes? That is why I compared the present day Old Scofield King James Version with

the original 1611. Some say there are 40,000 to 50,000 changes, and if you listened to them, you would think we don't have anything like the original today.

The changes, though are largely related to spelling. For instance, take John 9, the account of the man born blind. Now, the word "blind" in verse 1 is spelled "blinde". It's a change. But is "blind" any different from "blinde"? If there is a change you're talking about, it doesn't affect the ear. Now, in the second verse, "sin" is spelled "sinne". That is a change. Then the word "born" is spelled "borne". But the sound is the same. What I did, was to count only the changes that could be HEARD. And from genesis to Revelation, did i get 30,000? No, did I get 20,000? No. 1,000? No. I got 421 CHANGES TO THE EAR that could be heard, out of the 791,328 words. Just 421. That is actually one change out of 1,880 words. As for those 421 CHANGES to the ear - most of them were minor, just changes in spelling.

There were ONLY 136 SUBSTANTIAL CHANGES that were different words. There were only 285 minor changes of form only. Of these 285 minor changes, there were 214 very minor changes such as "toward" for "towards": "burnt" for "burned"; "amongst" for "among"; "lift" for "lifted"; and "you" for "ye". These kinds of changes represent 214 out of the 285 minor changes of form only.

Thus, you're talking about only 136 real changes out of 791,328 words.

Many people imply that the KING JAMES BIBLE is completely changed from what they had in 1611, that there are THOUSANDS of differences. You tell them about the MERE 136 CHANGES OF SUBSTANCE

Do We Have A 1611 King James Bible Today?
plus 285 MINOR CHANGES OF FORM ONLY.[1]

Most of these changes involve personal pronouns, articles, conjunctions and prepositions. They are a refinement of the wording of the text, and not a substantial word change. A few English words were substituted for words of similar meaning. This was thought to be the best way of presenting the Hebrew and Greek text in English.

Most of the changes are like the following examples: "grinne" to "grin"; "flying" to "fleeing"; "neeged" to "sneezed"; "saveth to" - "and he saveth"; "northwards" to "northward"; and "noondays" to "noonday."

In 1629, a revision was produced by cambridge University. Dr. Samuel Ward and Dean John Bois, from the original 1611 translating committee, were involved in this revision. It is the 1629 revision that dropped the Apocrypha from its position between the testaments of Scripture.

In 1637, a further revision was done by Cambridge University. Over 80% of the changes made in the King James Bible were made by this time.

In 1762, Dr. Thomas Paris, a professor at Trinity College in Oxford, issued a revision of the King James. In 1769, Dr. Benjamin Blayney, a professor at Oxford University, issued a further revision expanding upon Dr. Paris' word. Almost all of the changes consisted in revising the italicized words. These words had been supplied by the King James translators for the purpose of dealing with the difference in the Hebrew and Greek languages and English. These words were necessary for an accurate translation.

---

1 Waite, The Four-fold Superiority of the King James Bible, Bible for Today, 900 Park Ave., Collingswood, NJ 08108

The Unbroken Bible

The 1769 Paris- Blaynew revision of the 1611 King James Bible is what Bible believers normally refer to as the King James Bible today. The number of revisions are so slight that some scholars are not comfortable using the term "revision" to describe it. Instead, they refer to it as an "edition".

A 1769 Paris- Blayney revision of the King James Bible is properly called a 1611 King James Bible because no new translation work has been done and no new textual authority has been introduced. The 1629 and 1638 revisions and the 1762 and 1769 revisions are all properly called the 1611 King James Bible. The 1611 King James Bible was not retranslated for these revisions. This is the way that revisions of translations of all ancient documents are referred.

COULD YOU READ A 1611 KING JAMES BIBLE IF YOU HAD ONE?

Actually, the author has read read two King James Bibles published in 1611. One is in the chapel of Landmark Baptist College in Haines City, Florida. The other is in the chapel of Heritage Baptist University in Greenwood, Indiana. There are also numerous facsimile copies of the King James Bible published in 1611 available. One is in the library at Landmark Baptist College, Haines City, Florida.

These Bibles can be read easily if you remember a few simple rules:

- You will sometimes see an "I" instead of a "J".
- You will sometimes see an "F" instead of an "S".
- An additional "E" will be added to many words.
- You will sometimes see three "S's" instead of just two.
- Vowels are sometimes doubled.
- Consonants are sometimes doubled.

Do We Have A 1611 King James Bible Today?

Those who claim that you couldn't read an original 1611 if you had one, apparently haven't tried.

ARE THE MODERN ENGLISH TRANSLATIONS NEW REVISIONS?

It is common for modern English translations to claim to be another revision of the 1611 King James Bible. The title page of the Revised Standard Version claims that the RSV is simply a 18952 revision of the King James. However, the Revised Standard Version was clearly based on a new textual authority and different methods and rules of translations. Soon friends and foes of the RSV were calling it what it really was, a new translation.

Most English Bibles that followed the RSV admitted to being new translations of the Bible. The New International Version states that it is a "completely new translation of the Bible". However, new translations were often promoted and marketed as a "revision" of the King James, even when they clearly were not. There was something about identifying yourself with the King James Bible that was clearly good for sales.

In 1979, the New King James Bible was released and it clearly claimed to be a fifth revision of the King James Bible. This claim is seen in the article at the end of the translation entitled "The History of the King James Bible". It is also clearly seen in the title!

However, the first four revisions brought lightly over one hundred textual changes. The New King James Version produced over 60,000. In the United States, 60,000 changes is the number necessary to produce a claim for a copyright to a new translation (for a work the size of the Bible). The Thomas Nelson Company was granted a copyright on this basis. In the copyright office, it is presented as a new translation. For marketing purposes, it is presented as a revision.

The New King James translators also used new textual authorities for some of their changes. This is clearly seen in their own article, "The History of the King James Bible". The New King James Bible is clearly a new translation and the claim that it is a "revision" of the King James Bible is deceptive and misleading.

The 21st Century King James Version of the Holy Bible and the Third Millennium Bible both claim to be revisions of the King James Bible. Both are published by the same publishers in Gary, South Dakota. They reject the claim of the New King James Bible to be just a revision. However, neither publication has found any acceptance among Bible believing fundamentalists. The publishers have placed a great emphasis on restoring the Apocrypha to their editions of the King James Bible.

The New Scofield Reference Bible places word change in the text of the Scripture. They are marked by marginal notes which give the King James Bible rendering. It is claimed that this is simply a revision consistent with the works of Paris Blayney. However, the authority for their changes is often a new textual authority and many of their word changes are clearly a new (and different) translation. This is not the kind of revision done previously to the King James Bible.

HAVE THERE BEEN ANY OTHER GENUINE REVISIONS OF THE KING JAMES BIBLE?

A revision was printed by Royal Printers in England in 1806. It is referred to as "The Eyre and Staham" revision. It did not meet a wide reception and was not able to take the place of the 1769 Paris - Blaynew revision.

The King James II was published in the United States in

1971 by Jay P. Green. It seems to be an honest attempt at a real revision (not just a cover for a new translation). However, it never found much of an audience and was soon out of print. There has been talk of reprinting it.

There simply has been no demand for a further revision of the King James Bible. The foes of the King James Bible will not settle for a revision. They want a new translation, with the new textual authority and new translation principles and rules. The friends of the King James Bible have watched it withstand attack after attack. Most of them are in no mood for a discussion of further revision.

DON'T WE NEED A NEW REVISION OF THE KING JAMES?

Fundamentalism have fractured as a movement! Endless debate over the doctrines of inspiration, preservation, and the role of the King James Bible has split fundamentalism into several camps. A revision done by the faculty of any fundamentalist Bible college or Christian University would immediately be rejected by large segments of fundamentalism. There exists no potential of uniting different factions to support a new revision.

Many great soul winning, separated, fundamentalist churches are booming while using the King James Bible. Everyday vibrant, growing ministries are disproving the notion that the King James Bible is a hindrance to the ministry today. People are being led to Christ from the King James Bible. They are growing and maturing in the faith while using the King James Bible in its present form. Despite the stated desire of some for a revision of the King James Bible, there simply is not a serious grass roots demand for one.

The Unbroken Bible

23

The Received Text for the Whole World

I AM NOT ASHAMED OF MY HOPE

Psalm 119:113-120 - I hate vain thoughts: but thy law do I love. Thou art my hiding place and my shield: I hope in thy word. Depart from me, ye evildoers: for I will keep the commandments of my God Uphold me according unto thy word, that I may live: and let me not be ashamed of my hope. Hold thou me up, and I shall be safe: and I will have respect unto thy statutes continually. Thou hast trodden down all them that err from thy statutes: for their deceit is falsehood Thou puttest away all the wicked of the earth like dross: therefore I love thy testimonies. My flesh trembleth for fear of thee; and I am afraid of thy judgments.

In his book, *The Lord God Hath Spoken,* Thomas Strouse writes: "It is the author's opinion that the Masoretic Text, the Received Text and the AV should be used in all missionary translation endeavors" (pg. 24).

The Unbroken Bible

It would seem that this position would be without controversy among those believers who identify themselves as "King James Only" or as "Received Text Bible believers." Yet, many Bible colleges who advertise that they are "King James" do not teach their mission students anything similar to this. Most Independent Baptist missionaries use Bible translations that are very different from the King James text because the translations are based upon the Critical Text.

Many Independent Baptist mission boards take a clear stand on the King James Bible when they are raising money. They require some sort of statement from their missionaries, that they are "King James Only." But the majority of these missionaries use Critical Text Bibles when they are on the mission field. What a strange situation.

A number of major printing ministries aggressively identify themselves as "King James Only" when they are raising money to print Bibles around the world. They identify themselves as "King James" in their presentations in churches. But it is amazing how much of the money that they raise in "King James" churches is used to print Bibles that are based upon the Critical Text. These Bibles are based upon different original languages texts than the ones the King James Bible are based upon. They often contradict the King James Bible in important passages. They are paid for by the sacrificial gifts of King James supporting churches but they undermine the message of the King James Bible. How sad!

In our opening Scripture passage, David is discussing the Scriptures. Under the inspiration of the Holy Spirit he declares that he is not ashamed of his hope. He is not ashamed of the pure Word of God. It would seem that many of our Independent Baptists are ashamed of the hope that they claim to believe in.

If we are going to obey God's command for world evangelism, we need three things. Obviously, we need the Gospel. This has already been provided for us by the Lord Jesus Christ. We can share with anybody from anywhere that the Gospel of the Lord Jesus Christ is for them.

I have had the privilege of pastoring in one of the most multi cultured neighborhoods in the world. The local officials say that we have people born in 160 countries living in Ravenswood (our neighborhood in Chicago).

We have people from 26 countries in our church. It is my great joy to be able to look at anybody from any country, any religious background, any culture, and any background and say to them, "Jesus Christ died for you, paid the penalty for your sins, died for you on the Cross." We already have the gospel. However, in order to be obedient to the Great Commission around the world, we need two other things. We need local churches and we need the Bible. We have to teach people the gospel of Christ, see people, trust Christ and get baptized. Then we have to train them to observe all things in obedience to Him. This training process requires a Bible and a local church. Thankfully, there has been an explosion of local church planting around the world. My heart absolutely rejoices in this.

However, along with the local church, people need a Bible. You cannot teach people "to observe all things whatsoever is commanded of them" if they only have some of the Bible. You cannot teach them everything they need to know if they think they have a whole Bible but they do not. You must put the whole Bible in front of them.

I would like to present a couple of examples to illustrate the problem that we are facing today. Let me be very clear. I am not talking about the modernists. Nobody expects them to be concerned about a good text of the Word of God. I am not talking about the neo-evangelicals! No one expects them to be concerned with the Received Text. I am talking about the problem that Independent Baptists face.

Let me give you a couple of illustrations. The first comes from the book, *Sedition in Missions*, written by Michael D. McCubbins, published in 1996. The author describes the reasons he left one of the well-known Independent Baptist mission boards, AB. W.E. In chapter 6, the debate is all about the text of Scripture.

The AB. W.E. was very concerned about the Bible in the Bengali language. The Baptist churches were using a Bible translation translated by William Carey, the father of modern missions. This translation was from the Received Text. The leaders of AB. W.E. didn't believe that God could use such a Bible.

They made arrangements for a lady Bible translator, Dr. Lynn Silvervale, to translate a new and improved Bible. This Bible would be translated from the Critical Text using dynamic equivalency. This was done in connection with the United Bible Societies. In 1981, the Board of Grand Rapids Baptist College and Seminary granted Dr. Silvervale an honorary doctorate for her translation work.

There was also a problem in the AB. W.E. over the Russian Bible. They abandoned the Received Text Russian Bible for one translated by Pentecostals from the Critical Text. Missionary McCubbins wondered why AB. W.E. couldn't take a clear stand on the traditional text of Scripture and on clear conservative translation methods. He was shocked to find out what was happening in Independent Baptist circles.

The second example hits closer to home for me. For 9 ½ years I had the privilege of being the administrator of the Landmark Baptist College in Haines City, Florida. This was one of the great joys and blessings of my life. While I was there we started a Spanish department in our college. I confess that it was my idea. We hired full-time Spanish speaking staff and arranged for visiting professors from the Spanish speaking world. All the classes were taught in Spanish. We had a good number of students the first year and an even better number of students the second year. It seemed like everything was going great.

However, we kept hearing things from Hispanic preachers that concerned us. They would say things like, "We know Bro. Carter's stand on the King James Bible, and we know your stand on the King James Bible. Why are you using a Spanish Bible that contradicts the one that you are using in English?" We began to ask our Spanish speaking staff about all of this. They kept assuring us everything was all right. The Bible they were using was the Spanish King James Bible. It was exactly the same in Spanish as the King James was in English. The first time that we got that question we simply believed the staff. We did the same the second time. But after awhile, the questions really began to add up.

Finally, Pastor Mickey Carter and I sat down with our Hispanic staff to talk all this out-more about that conversation later. We discovered that, yes indeed; we were using a Bible in Spanish that contradicted the Bible that we were using in English. We were using a Bible which had the Critical Text as its final authority. We were using a Spanish Bible translated under the authority of Eugene Nida and translated based upon translation principles that he taught.

Recently, I have read about Bible believers in Romania who asked why no one seemed concerned that they have a Received Text Bible. They admitted that they were in the minority position. Those who hold to the truth of God's preservation of His inspired words in the Received Text always are. But they wanted to know why no one spoke for them. Not even the organization that supposedly exists for the sole purpose of seeing to it that the whole world has the Received Text.

The Unbroken Bible

Shouldn't someone be speaking for the faithful Bible believers who believe what the Bible says about preservation? I thought that was a pretty good question. How did we get to this place? Why do we have so many people who recommend, use and honor the King James Bible in English but who use translations based on completely different principles around the world?

There are several reasons why we have this problem. The first is simply ignorance. Most of our Bible colleges do not explain this issue at all during their training. I must confess that I went through four years of Bible College without understanding this issue at all. I went to Bible College for four years and graduated with relatively good grades without knowing that there was even an issue or debate about Greek texts. I did not know anything about modernist Bible societies. I had never been taught a word about Bible translation methods. Now to be fair to the college that I graduated from, Indiana Baptist College, it was later turned into a good Received Text school by Dr. Clinton Branine. At the time I attended there, you could graduate from there and not know any of the issues-I did graduate from there and not know any of the issues.

I suspect that this is true with many Bible colleges today. Even many of the schools that promote the King James Bible in English avoid the issue in other languages. They hide behind the cop-out that people that use that particular language must decide. A majority vote will not turn a corrupt base text into a good one. Popular approval won't turn bad translation methods into good ones.

There are other reasons. There are people who support the Critical Text but they hide this when dealing with American churches. Churches that openly use the Critical Text are not where they get their money. In front of an American audience they are King James Bible and Received Text around the world advocates. When they think they can get away with it, they purposely promote the Critical Text! God cannot bless that kind of duplicity.

I discovered this the hard way. When we had our issue over the Spanish Bible at Landmark, we addressed several specific verses. We compared these verses to the Revised Standard Version in English. They matched almost exactly. We could have used the American Standard Version or even the New World Translation of the Jehovah's Witnesses.

One of our visiting professors tried to straighten us out. He photocopied thirty pages from commentaries and mailed them to us. Each of these commentaries explained why the wording of these verses in the King James Bible was wrong. (I still have this mailing.) The King James Bible was based upon inferior manuscripts, according to these quotes. The updated readings that matched his Spanish Bible were based upon older and better manuscripts.

This pastor heads up a prominent printing ministry in Mexico. He preaches all over the U.S. in large Independent Baptist King James only churches. These churches sacrificially send him large amounts of money so that he can print Critical Text Bibles in Spanish (and pay royalties to a modernist Bible Society).

Here is another reason that there is such confusion. The heresy of concept inspiration has infiltrated Independent Baptist circles more than most of us realized. People who believe in concept inspiration believe that it is the meaning (or ideas, or doctrine) that is inspired by God not the words. Now, you have quite a lot of flexibility if you are not bound to the words. For example, Calvin George published a book defending a Critical Text Spanish Bible. It is entitled the *Battle for the Spanish Bible*. This was published right before our debate at Landmark but it addressed many of the same issues. He addressed verses that differed dramatically from the King James Bible. He tried to give all of them a conservative spin. Twenty-seven times he wrote, "The words are different but the meaning is the same." He never pointed out that the words were the same as the Revised Standard Version, but they were.

I would criticize his comments as teaching concept inspiration. His response was that he was a graduate of two well-respected Independent Baptist colleges and that what he wrote was consistent with what he was taught there. He further stated that his book was read and approved before publication by several professors from the college he had just received his master's degree from (one of the largest and most respected in fundamental Baptist circles). To be honest with you, I did not believe him. As time went on, I began to quiz graduates of both schools. Were they taught verbal inspiration or concept inspiration? Some from both schools said they were taught verbal inspiration. Some graduates from both schools claimed that they had been taught concept inspiration. I cannot explain the confusion.

I saw this heretical doctrine in our discussion at Landmark. Pastor Mickey Carter and I sat down with the Hispanic staff (at my request). We had staff devoted to holding services in Spanish on the church staff, we had college staff assigned to our Hispanic department of the college. We met with both.

Pastor Carter spent about an hour explaining the problem that we had. I was quiet. There was no need for me to say anything. Finally, one of our college staff burst out, "Pastor, don't you understand it is not the words that are inspired anyway, it's the meaning." I said, "What did you say?" The leader of the church Spanish program spoke up and said, "That's right. It is not the words that are inspired anyway."

Now the position of our church and college was well known. We were clear on our faith in the King James Bible. We were clear on our position on the Received Text. We were clear on our position on verbal inspiration. Pastor Carter had spoken widely and wisely on all of those issues. I had done what I could in addressing them. How did such people get on our staff?

Everyone had been asked questions about the Bible before they were hired. Today, we know how to better ask those questions. These staff had hidden their positions on the textual issue and on doctrine in order to get the situation they wanted at Landmark. Both of these men would later claim that this was what they were taught at the prominent Baptist colleges that they attended. I would later quiz graduates of these colleges about this and again I got mixed answers.

These men were not neo-evangelicals or modernists. They were prominent Independent Baptists. They realized they had let the "cat out of the bag." They saw our shock at their statements and they knew they were in trouble if their positions became understood in Independent Baptist circles. They immediately invented the story that Pastor Carter and I were expelling all the Hispanic students from the college. They claimed that the Spanish speaking people were being kicked out of the church. They organized meetings with Hispanic members and lied to them. They organized meetings with the Spanish students and told them that they were expelled.

Not a word of that was true. No such thing was ever planned or discussed. They had to create a false issue out of race.

One of the men involved still draws support from Independent Baptist churches as a missionary to Mexico (even though he doesn't minister in Mexico). The other one took most of our Hispanic students and staff and went to another Independent

Baptist college. This college advertises that it is a King James school. However, they continue to give this preacher a base from which to attack the King James Bible (to Spanish audiences), to stand for the Critical Text and to teach concept inspiration.

The same man also holds prominent conferences in the Spanish speaking world. These conferences are largely financed by the sacrificial giving of Independent Baptist King James only churches.

In the same conversation we tried to make an issue out of the modernist Bible translator, Eugene Nida. This same leader told us that the King James translators were "evil and wicked men, unsaved men." He later said that Eugene Nida was a "gracious Christian gentleman and scholar."

We had better get a hold on this. This issue of inspiration and the doctrines that derive from it are huge. Verbal, Plenary Inspiration is a fundamental doctrine. So is a belief in Verbal Plenary Preservation. These doctrines demand a belief in Verbal, Plenary Translation.

Critical Text advocates call everyone who believes in these doctrines a "Ruckmanite." I know that many of you are very concerned about being called a Ruckmanite. I would be too; if that meant that I believed a doctrine invented by Peter Ruckman. However, the definition of a "Ruckmanite" has changed. Today, a "Ruckmanite" is anyone who is winning an argument with a Critical Text supporter. We had better get used to being called some names.

Just for the record's sake, the principle of Verbal Plenary Translation was around long before Peter Ruckman. In 1588 (before the birth of Peter Ruckman and before the translation of the King James Bible) William Whiston wrote this:

"For it behooves a translation of Scripture not merely to take care that you do not corrupt the meaning but also as far as is at all possible not to depart a hand's breadth from the words since many things lie under the cover in the words of the Holy Spirit which are not immediately perceived but yet contains important instruction" (Disputations on the Holy Scripture, p. 165).

You cannot interpret the Bible for everybody, you must translate it. How many times have you taught a passage of Scripture as completely and exhaustively as you can, only to discover blessed truths years later? It is the words that are inspired not just the meaning.

Thomas Armitage would write in the *History of Baptists* about William Carey and his helpers, "From the beginning, Baptist missionaries **were faithful to the principles of translating into the heathen languages every word of the New Testament Greek** for which they could find equivalence. Common honesty required this to say nothing of responsibility to God. And they made no concealment of their action but widely avowed it in their official imprints on letters" (p. 586, 1887 edition). It is not very honest to interpret the Bible for people and tell them you did a translation.

Michael McCubbins wrote this about the battle in the AB. W.E. "Those men who wrote the scriptures were the writers, not the Author. Plenary, verbal inspiration adherents believe God is the author of Scripture. We are asked by Dr. Silvervale to believe that meaning is the important thing to translate, but God said the important thing is words. Not meaning. Illumination is the work of the Holy Spirit, not the translator. God will preserve the words. We do not believe in meaning inspiration as Silvervale prefers, but in verbal inspiration. If we believe in plenary-verbal inspiration and believe in plenary-verbal preservation, then we must believe in plenary, verbal translation" *(Sedition in Missions,* p.84).

The Unbroken Bible

The book, *God's Secretaries,* is a very secular book written on the history of the King James Bible. The King James Bible has great historical and literary influence. It means much more to many of us but you cannot deny its historical influence, you cannot deny its literary influence. Adam Nicholson (not to my knowledge a believer) wrote this: "The King James translators do exactly what Luther had described as absurd. They **mimic precisely the form of the original.** No searching for the language of mothers or of the man at the market stall. **They acted in other words as God's Secretaries**" (p. 195).

That indeed should be the goal of all Bible translators- to act as God's secretaries. We should reproduce the words that God gave. These are pure words. My dear friend, Dr. Williams, who I admire so much, and I are having a little debate over whether or not we should use the word pure for accurate translated words. It is a gentleman's debate. He is a gentleman by nature and I am working on being one.

I believe that accurately translated words are pure words. It is the responsibility of the Holy Spirit to work in the hearts of the readers and help them to understand the meaning.

Another reason we have such an issue is pride. The world admires the Critical Text. The non-Christian world does. Our brother spoke a few years ago and mentioned it again today, about how much the Moslem world admires the Critical Text. Madam Blavatsky, who founded Theosophy, admired the Critical Text. Charles Taze Russell, who founded the Jehovah's Witness, admired it. If you want to be considered "scholarly" by unsaved religious leaders you had better admire it too.

Lost religious leaders admire dynamic equivalency. They have had to change the name for it several times, but they admire the idea of making the translator the final authority instead of recognizing the words that God gave as the final authority. If you want to be considered scholarly by the unsaved religious world, you had better admire dynamic equivalency too.

Bible college leaders and professors are especially vulnerable to this temptation. Who wants to be mocked by those that the world considers your peers? Faith and sound doctrine will never be considered "scholarly" by unsaved people.

Let me make this clear - **A bad translation from a good text shows more genuine scholarship than a good translation from a bad text.** At least the translator knew enough doctrine and history to understand where he should start.

Let me tell you what has happened to many of the Hispanic preachers in the Independent Baptist sphere. Many of these people were very influenced by the ministry of Dr. Jack Hyles. He used a number of cliches to describe his loyalty to the King James Bible. By the grace of God, these cliches represented sound doctrine. Many people repeated them. I'm not sure that many of the people who repeated them understood why they were true but they were true.

Many of the Spanish brethren simply repeated these same cliches about their Critical Text based Spanish Bible. They had no idea what they were saying, but it sounded good. As one of them admitted to me, "If I admit our Bible is not the infallible, inerrant Word of God (he was talking about the Critical Text Spanish Bible), I have to apologize for my last, thirty-six years of preaching." But his preaching had been wrong.

Pride makes people hold to positions that they know are wrong. Pride makes people demonize anyone who tries to discuss the truth.

The issue is the truth-not our pride. Another issue is cowardice. Many people start to stand for the truth but when they realize how much criticism they will take-they back up. When they realize that those who are embarrassed by the truth will publicly attack them, demonize them, and try to destroy them, they change their position. They become neutral or change sides. **But, how can someone be a man of God and afraid of men at the same time?**

When we were first dealing with this issue at Landmark Baptist College, Dr. Carter asked me to call a well-known leader in Independent Baptist circles. This man was considered a King James Bible defender and was well known for promoting the printing of the Received Text around the world. We wanted his perspective on our situation.

I called him and got him a plane ticket to fly to Central Florida. I picked him up in Orlando and drove him for an hour to our campus in Haines City. I talked to him about the issue during the whole trip. Dr. Carter and I talked to him for five hours. The next morning I drove him back to the airport and talked to him for another hour. We were not discussing what to do but when and how to do it. Doctrine was not debatable, but we were discussing timing and strategy.

This leader insisted that we must make our move now. He hammered that at us-that we must move now! He promised to support us. We moved right away!

A few weeks later he met with several Hispanic Independent Baptist leaders in Mexico. These leaders can be particularly aggressive and vicious in trying to destroy anyone who disagrees with them. We soon received a letter from this leader saying that he had switched sides. He had to abandon the issue of the purity of text for the sake of world evangelism (I still have a copy of the letter).

Now, the same man, in connection with a large, prominent Independent Baptist college, is trying to establish a committee to instruct the Independent Baptist world on Bible translation.

He once stood for Received Text Bibles around the world. Now he stands for Received Text Bibles in some languages and Critical Text Bibles in other languages. He wants to lecture the Independent Baptist World on Bible translation. God spare us from such leadership as this.

One of the statements that I have heard Mickey Carter say several times is this, **"It's not just what a preacher says that tells you what kind of man he is, it's what he is afraid to say."**

By the grace of God, as many of you here know, God has raised up Dr. Humberto Gomez to provide a Received Text Bible in Spanish. Many people have worked with him. I admire them all. Without apology, the King James Bible is one of the sources for the Reina Valera Gomez along with older Spanish Bibles and the Hebrew Masoretic text and the Greek Textus Receptus.

In October of 2006, Dr. H. D. Williams, Dr. Rex Cobb, Dr. D. A. Waite, Dr. Steve Zeinner, Dr. Humberto Gomez and I spent eight hours with a Bible printing ministry. This is probably the most influential printing ministry in Independent Baptist circles. This meeting resulted in a decision to print the Reina Valera Gomez. Around the Hispanic world, Bible believers are begging for the Reina Valera Gomez. It is impossible to keep up with the demand, so this was a great step forward.

After printing one edition, this publisher quickly

abandoned the RVG. They were under great criticism. Men like Calvin George, Jeff McCardle and Victor Paez criticized the RVG for being similar to the King James Bible. I wonder if the financial supporters of this ministry know that it is frightened to print a Bible that is the same as the King James Bible. The critics of the RVG are not ashamed of using Spanish Bibles that read exactly like the Jehovah's Witness, New World Translation. However, the King James Bible infuriates them. I wonder why?

My successor at Landmark Baptist College, Dr. Charles Brown wrote an article about the psychological effect that the King James Bible has on some people. They are not afraid of any English Bible, but the King James Bible. He wrote, "I would pose a possible answer. Maybe the King James Bible reminds people of the 'old time religion.' It presents a holy God, sinful man, salvation by grace, through faith, not of works and results in the commanded holy life of the believer. None of these concepts are particularly popular today. Many modern day Christians like their theology buffet-style where they can pick and choose what they believe" (Landmark Anchor, September 2004). Amen.

Thankfully, there are printers more loyal to the Received Text than the one I referred to before. Thankfully, there are printers who are not ashamed of the King James Bible. Thankfully, there are braver printers. The RVG continues to be printed in response to the great demand.

Money is a huge issue in all this discussion. People ask, "Will standing for the truth cost me support?" "Will it result in criticism?" "Will it cause people to misunderstand what I am doing?" Let me say clearly that the answer to all these questions is, yes. If you take a clear stand for a Received Text Bible in any language of the world, you will face vicious criticism and slanderous, dishonest personal attacks. **The truth always demands such a price tag.**

I want to talk about the solution to this problem.

First, we have to aggressively teach Verbal, Plenary Inspiration to our young people. Some would say that it is a shame that Bible colleges don't get this right and that they deceive our young people. But we should teach this so clearly that our young people can tell when they are being misled. I think it is a terrible shame when young people grow up under our ministries and go off to Bible college and do not recognize it when they are taught wrong. We must teach Verbal, Plenary Inspiration at every level of our ministry. We must teach that Verbal Plenary Inspiration demands Verbal, Plenary Preservation. We must teach that Verbal, Plenary Preservation demands Verbal Plenary Translation.

Verbal, Plenary Translation is a greatly neglected doctrine. But it is vital. It is a common figure of speech to refer to an expert as "Someone, who wrote the book on the subject." Well, my friend Dr. H. D. Williams really did. The only good book on the subject that I am aware of is, *Word for Word Translating of the Received Text, Verbal Plenary Translating* by Dr. H. D. Williams. All of our Bible college professors should read this. All of our Bible college presidents should read it. It should be in all of our Bible college libraries. This is a huge issue. We can no longer relax and trust modernist, Bible societies to tell our missionaries what Bible to use.

The principle is clear! We would not let a modernist preach in our pulpits. We would not let a modernist teach in our colleges. Why should we let a modernist translate the Bible for us? For me, this is a no-brainer.

Secondly, we must start demanding something from our Bible colleges. We had better start asking our Bible colleges specific questions about what they teach on these issues. We had better ask more than just what Bible they use in English. What do they teach about the Bible in other languages?

There are more Independent Baptist Colleges than we can possibly support. Maybe we should support the schools that teach the same things about the Bible that we do. Schools that teach the King James Bible is God's preserved Word in English, schools that teach that the Received Text should be the base text for Bible translations around the world.

Thirdly, we should start asking questions of our missionary candidates. There are more missionary candidates then we can support. I get several calls each week. I have to turn most of these people down. I have to turn down good people. The hardest thing I ever do as a pastor is turn a Landmark Baptist College graduate looking for support down. There are more missionaries than we can support.

Do you think it is about time we start asking missionaries what they believe about the Bible? If they are going to minister in Japanese, or Swahili or Romanian or Russian, let's quit asking them what they believe about the King James Bible. Let's start asking them what they believe about the Bible in the language they will minister in.

I am aware that many of these languages don't have a good Bible available. But it certainly ought to be the burden of their heart to get one. Maybe God did not call them to be a translator. That is not the ministry for everyone. But certainly they should support those who are trying to provide a good Received Text Bible in their language. Maybe we need to send this message, "If you want our mission dollars, we had better be able to trust you on the subject of the Bible."

Fourthly, we need to start challenging printing ministries! We receive wonderful letters pleading for money to print Bibles.

They are needed so desperately. We all know that people need the Bible desperately. We should start asking some questions! Where did their Bible translation come from? Can we trust your ministry to print only Received Text Bibles?

The modernist Bible societies will print all the Critical Text Bibles anyone can use. They will do it cheaper than Baptist printing ministries can. We should print the ones we can trust.

We are very burdened as a church about this. We invest several thousand dollars a year in foreign Bibles. But I have not spent one penny on a Bible that I did not know where it came from. I no longer will send any money to a printing ministry that is not committed to printing only Received Text Bibles.

You see, the other crowd is very aggressive. They are always calling Received Text Bible believers "divisive." When anyone threatens the "status quo" they go on the attack. All the pressure is being put on by their side. Maybe it is time for our side to put some pressure on. We are Independent Baptists. We don't have to support any particular college. Let's support the ones we agree with the most! Let's find out what the colleges teach. Let's know more than what they say in their ads. Let's be brave enough to ask questions. Maybe we should quit paying for the things that we don't believe in.

Our cause has paid too big a price for not addressing these issues. It is time for all of us to stand for Received Text Bibles around the world, in every language, for every group of people.

The Unbroken Bible

The Unbroken Bible

The Unbroken Bible

ABOUT THE AUTHOR

Dr. Phil Stringer

Dr. Phil Stringer is the Vice President for Church Relations at the Dayspring Bible College (Quentin Road Baptist Church). He was formerly the pastor of Ravenswood Baptist Church of Chicago.

He has been in full-time ministry for 44 years and has served as youth pastor, evangelist, college professor and administrator, and pastor. He was ordained by the Lifegate Baptist Church in 1975.

Pulpit Ministry
He has spoken at over 430 churches, schools and colleges. He has spoken in 49 states, as well as Washington D.C. and Puerto Rico and several foreign countries including Canada, Mexico, Vietnam, Syria, The Philippines, The Bahamas, Barbados, Trinidad, Suriname, Guatemala, South Korea, Grenada, Singapore, India, Columbia, St. Lucia, Ghana, Togo, Ethiopia, St Vincent, England, Wales and Japan.

Teaching Ministry
Every year Dr. Stringer teaches as a visiting professor at several colleges. He has taught full courses at 23 colleges, 11 in the United States, and 12 in other countries. He has spoken at nine other colleges.

Boards
He serves on the Advisory Councils for First Light Baptist Mission, the Graceway Bible Society (Canada), the Bible Nation Society and the Shalom Native Mission. He is the Vice Presi-

dent of the King James Bible Research Council. He serves on the Board of Directors for the Center for the Study and Preservation of the Majority Text. He is on the Board of Trustees for the Dayspring Bible College.

Author

He is the author of several books and booklets including: The Unbroken Bible, Evangelism Made Simple, The Faithful Baptist Witness, The Transformation, Fifty Demonstrations of America's Christian Heritage, The Bible and Government, Biblical English, The Real Story of King James, The Means of Inspiration, A History of the English Bible, In Defense of 1 John 5:7, Misidentified Identity, Many Infallible Proofs, The Westcott and Hort Only Controversy, The Scripture Cannot Be Broken, Ready Answers, The Da Vinci Code Controversy, The Messianic Claims of Gail Riplinger, the Received Text for the Whole World, Majestic Legacy, The Occult Connection of Gail Riplinger, The Foundations of Our World Vol. 1 and Vol. 2, The Heaven Rescued Land Vol. 1 and Vol. 2.

Education

He graduated with a Bachelor of Science in Bible degree from Indiana Baptist College in 1975. He received a Masters degree in Christian Education from Freedom University in 1980. He received a Doctor of Philosophy degree in English Bible from Landmark Baptist College in 1997. He received a Doctor of Religious Education degree from the American Bible College in 2004.

Awards

Dr. Stringer was awarded the honorary degree of Doctor of Divinity by the Asia Baptist Bible College in 2002. He was awarded the honorary degree of Doctor of Literature by the American Bible College in 2002. In 2007, he was awarded the Heritage Baptist University alumni educator of the year. In 2008, he received the Hoosier Hill Baptist Camp pastor of the year award.

The Unbroken Bible

He can be contacted at:

Dayspring Bible College & Seminary
27875 N. Fairfield Road
Mundelein, IL 60060
773-816-1240
Email: philstringer@att.net

 **More Resources From BNS Press**

Surviving This Babylon
Dr. Douglas Levesque

Ancient secrets for Modern Survival. America has become a modern Babylon and the secrets for survival can be found in the Word of God and the example of Daniel's Excellent Spirit. **$14.95**

Transformation
Dr. Phil Stringer
Dr. Douglas Levesque

America's Journey to Darkness. The culture war in America has transformed this nation's morality and conscience on marriage, life, morality, science, technology, and many other fronts. **$19.95**

Available on Amazon.com or Biblenation.org
Call 989-720-2267 for bulk ordering

The Trail of Blood
J.M. Carroll

This reprint of J.M. Carroll's classic work *the Trail of Blood* tells the story of the church, following the trail of the true Christians down through the centuries. A trail often marked by martyrs and persecution. **$5.95**

Desiderius Erasmus
Dr. David L. Brown
Dr. Rebecca J. Howell

The Man, His Important Work, and Its Consequent Influence. Erasmus is the great influencer of the Received Text and consequently, the English Bible and King James Version **$9.95**

More Resources From BNS Press

The Courageous Church
Dr. Douglas Levesque

Proper local church doctrine and practice produces courageous churches. This book is a call for renewed commitment and faithfulness to the Word of God in the area of local church doctrine and church membership. **$14.95**

The Confident Shepherd
Dr. Douglas Levesque

Leaders are shepherds. All shepherds have a flock that must be led with the confidence of our chief shepherd, Jesus Christ. Gain that confidence to lead from this treatise on Philippians 1:6. **$9.95**

Available on Amazon.com or Biblenation.org
Call 989-720-2267 for bulk ordering

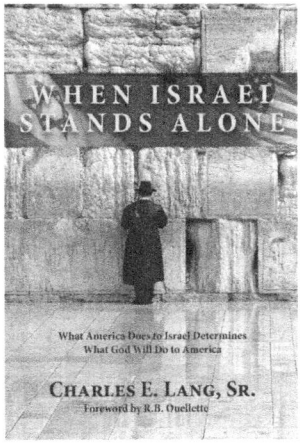

When Israel Stands Alone
Charles E. Lang Sr.

Why does Israel matter? How does God's covenant with one man and his family, thousands of years ago affect the modern political landscape so dramatically? How should Christians respond? **$14.95**

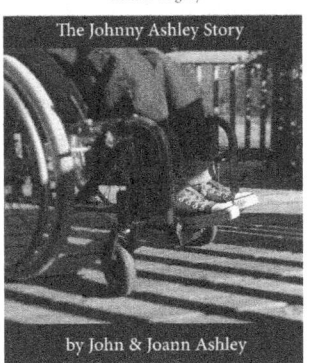

In Spite Of
John & Joann Ashley

The Johnny Ashley Story. Discover the inspirational story of Johnny, who in spite of severe birth defects and dozens of surgeries, lived his life to the glory of God and the inspiration of others. **$9.95**

The Unbroken Bible

Made in the USA
Monee, IL
04 December 2021